Yvon

newmerology

newme

From Sex to Stocks,

rology

It's All in the Numbers

Nick Newmont

JODERE
GROUP
san diego, california

JODERE

GROUP

Jodere Group, Inc.
P.O. Box 910147
San Diego, CA 92191-0147
(800) 569-1002
www.jodere.com

LIBRARY OF CONGRESS CATALOGING-IN-PUBLICATION DATA

Newmont, Nick
    Newmerology : from sex to stocks : it's all in the numbers / by Nick Newmont.
        p. cm.
            ISBN 1-58872-037-3
        1.Numerology I. Title.

BF1623 .P9 N4 2003
133.3'35—dc21

2002024529

ISBN 1-58872-037-3
06 05 04 03   4 3 2 1
First printing, January 2003
PRINTED IN THE UNITED STATES OF AMERICA

Editorial supervision by Chad Edwards

Book design by Charles McStravick

contents

Acknowledgments

I have had many numerological discussions with colleagues that stimulated the initial thoughts that went into the creation of this book. Those people were an inspiration to me to pursue the meta-physical arts as a way of life. But one friend, Melodie Tollefson, urged me years ago to study. Since I have always loved numbers, especially being an avid fan of sports statistics, I shifted my focus away from palmistry and astrology to numerology. Every client became a working case study. Without my clients, this book would not be possible. I thank every one of you who have sought my advice, even the ones who have lovingly and humorously tried to prove me wrong—you know who you are.

As for the content of this book, much of it came through the channels, either during a client session or vividly in my dreams. Since we cannot trace the source of numerology we can only say it comes from God. Therefore, as a conduit I am thrilled and eternally grateful to God, the angels, and my own spirit guides for allowing me to share this information.

The steps to getting a book published are numerous and precise. As of 1999 this was a process of which I knew nothing. At that time my friend and Vedic astrologer Carol Allen introduced me to her sister, Linda Sivertsen, already a published author and book proposal writer. Linda took an

newmerology

immediate interest in the concept and not only guided me through the process, but wrote most of the proposal based on taped interviews with me. We worked long hours and along the way had some great laughs. Her experience and knowledge made the proposal happen, and ultimately, the book. I thank Linda for making the book a reality and for listening to my jokes and imitations.

Linda spread her enthusiasm to Arielle Ford, another inspirational and spiritual force who represents me. I am appreciative of her friendship, support, and interest in Newmerology. A special thanks goes to Debbie Luican of the Jodere Group for publishing my book, especially after initially saying she wouldn't take a numerology book. It is an honor to be included in Jodere's group of authors representative of the highest integrity. Debbie's advice and words of confidence, while writing the book itself, meant a lot to me. She became an avid fan of the material and actually named the subtitle. I thank Chad Edwards for making the editing process a breeze and everyone at Jodere for being continually helpful.

And finally, thanks and love to my wife, Audrey, for her support throughout this process and for asking quite frequently, "what are my numbers today?"

Introduction

W hat's so "new" about Newmerology? After all, the practice of reading numbers for their predictive and revelatory qualities dates back at least 5,000 years to ancient Egyptian, Indian, Chinese, Greek, Chaldean, and Hebrew cultures, and continues more or less in traditional form into present day.

Newmerology is a breakthrough from the interpretations and usage that most contemporary numerologists work with today.

Newmerology is a different system, with new discoveries and tools culled from my years of practice as a psychic, certified hypnotherapist, and healer in Los Angeles. The addition is different than what you may be accustomed to, the conclusions are different, and the interpretations are more expansive and specific. Much of what this system reveals about your life, relationships, career, finances, children, destiny, and year ahead has literally never been set to print before.

Newmerology tells you when to buy and sell specific stocks, what companies have the greatest chance for success, and what numerological factors to consider when investing. It shows how to name your child to encourage a smooth path for them in life, how to choose your business name and address for optimum success, and how to plot your life decisions, whether it be buying a house, getting married, picking a lover, traveling, studying, or taking on new ventures.

Newmerology is designed to help you take the best advantage of the universal energy that radiates around you and through you.

The knowledge in this book results from tracking thousands of case studies from my clients' lives and businesses, business cycles, my own life, and those close to me. For more than a decade, I have used numerology as a financial consultant, guiding people in their business and investment decisions. I have employed numerology in conjunction with hypnotherapy, helping people through life problems and decisions. So prevalent and consistent were the numerical patterns I observed that they became, in effect, a set of new numerological tools and techniques. They were "newances" on the established system.

I discovered Rebirth Cycles, when we have a one-year opportunity to start our lives anew and return to our life's path, in case we have strayed. I found times I call Intersecting Numbers, one-year-long periods that provide the optimum circumstances for advancing our reputation, making a dream come true, or playing into our personal strengths.

Some of the biggest breakthroughs have occurred in the area of relationships. Techniques such as Crossed Paths, Mirroring, and Bonding can tell why people are magnetically attracted or repulsed by each other, why communication may be inherently difficult between two individuals, what a marital partner, friend, child, or business associate is really about, how the issues between two people are likely to play out, and what that relationship might teach both parties. These techniques also indicate how the dynamics in a relationship—even a long-term relationship—might change in the coming year and how to best adjust to them.

These analytical approaches proved so trustworthy that I have applied them with high degrees of success to businesses, personal finances, and the world at large, allowing me to predict the exact day the Dow Jones broke 8,000 (July 16, 1997), the Nasdaq 2000 crash, the Presidential election snafu of 2000, and important periods for world leaders, cultural figures, and the U.S. Many of these predictions were made publicly at conferences, on radio, or on my public access television show, which has been airing in Los Angeles since 1995.

Mostly, I have used the tools of Newmerology to help my clients see their way through difficult periods in their lives, to help them realize that if something isn't working, it just might not be the right time. I also guide them in determining what areas of their life they should concentrate on during any specific time for the most opportune results.

But often, I simply lead them onto a better path, one that matches who they truly are, using the Compound Number calculations and interpretations, perhaps the most significant innovation of Newmerology. The Compound Number—rising as high as 99, the number of completion in classic numerology—creates a depth of meaning that can lead to practical insight into character, career, aspirations, motivation, weaknesses, strengths, and personal and interpersonal destiny. In this system, you are a not just a 6, but a 24/6, a 33/6, a 42/6, yielding depth and distinction to the numerological characterizations. The Compound Number gives our lives and the specific years of our lives a theme that many other forms of numerology do not address. This book gives you the precise definitions for the Compound Numbers derived from the Birth Date and name. You will not come away wondering what your Compound Number really means.

The Personal Year Cycle, which begins on your birthday and lasts until your next birthday, also takes the form of a Compound Number. The Compound Personal Year provides the basis for discovering the highest and best use of your energy at varying years, months, and even specific days in your life, enabling you to align with the natural currents of your life.

Taken together, I have found that the techniques in Newmerology have proven more than 90 percent accurate at determining what is likely to happen, why, and especially when.

For this reason, this book has been designed as a personal resource that you can use repeatedly and apply to many aspects of your life. The emphasis here is on *you*. Not an outside spiritual counselor or consultant. This is the other distinctive aspect of Newmerology.

Unlike predictive sciences that require years of study and experience, Newmerology is devised so you can use it without the help of an expert. Newmerology takes this ancient science, modernizes it, makes it user-friendly, and puts the empowerment tools into your hands.

The beauty of Newmerology is that it is simple, but not simplistic. All you need to know is your Birth Date and name as they appear on your birth certificate. That's it. This book reveals how to use these early imprints to lead fulfilling lives. And you don't need to know what time you were born and you don't need to understand every bump and line on your hand.

Professional predictive readers have long used numerology when they counsel their clients. *So, why should a reader know more about your life than you?*

Newmerology hands you back your life. It helps people make choices. It serves not as a crutch, but as a resource for realizing your highest destiny and who you truly are.

This system is the next wave in the lost art of numerology. Newmerology is accurate, in-depth, and far-reaching. It is also actually easy to do, so you can spend more time living your life and less time trying to figure it out.

chapter 1

What Newmerology Can Do for You

Numbers are everywhere, in virtually everything we do. When is your birthday? Your anniversary? What's your address, phone number, zip code, bank account, or credit card number? How many years have you been married? How many times have you married? How many children do you have? What are the winning lottery numbers? Where did your stocks close today? How many calories did you eat, sit-ups did you do?

It may be virtually impossible to live in the world, whether in the city or country, rural or urban lifestyle, without using numbers. Numbers are part of the natural land scape of our existence. Numbers define our lives.

When someone is born, a business incorporates, or an important event occurs, a number is immediately attached. Numbers bookmark and identify the important, life-defining moments of our existence, literally from cradle to grave.

Numbers serve as a form of access and direction. What is one of the first things parents teach their children as they venture into the world? Their address, so they can always find their way home.

newmerology

6

Radio stations identify themselves by their location on the dial, 93.1, 106.8, etc. How do you find a book in the library? Through the Dewey Decimal System, a system of numbers.

The worlds of business and sports are fueled by numbers: profit and loss statements, stock quotes, balance sheets, scores, performance statistics, and on and on. Neither business nor sports as we know them could exist without numbers.

Numbers frame our pop culture so ubiquitously that we barely notice anymore. The biggest band in the world was known as "The Fab Four," The Beatles, whose main competition at the time were The Dave Clark Five. We listen to string quartets, and measure the cost of everything—time or currency—in numbers. Numbers define our sense of space: the number of rooms in a home, the square feet, the four-sided square, three-sided triangle, five-sided star. It goes on, seemingly, infinitum.

We use numbers consciously and unconsciously, every day, in every aspect of our lives. And yet, we resist numbers, even fear them. When we feel overwhelmed by vastness, under appreciated amid a large organization, or tethered by bureaucracy, what's our reaction? "I feel like I'm just a number." When a seemingly inevitable incident occurs to someone, what's a common response? "His number was up."

Numbers can strike quiet terror in our hearts. Who will ever forget September 11, 2001? The numbers *911* were already ones that meant emergency. We sense that numbers can obscure our identities, abscond with our sense of self and individuality, rob us of the attention we deserve, and deprive us of a semblance of control in our lives. We resist numbers because unconsciously we know they are important, and yet, we seem to exercise little power over them. How many people refuse to balance their checkbook? They don't want to know how much money they have—or not. Numbers appear limiting

The irony here is that a number may be limiting, but numbers infinite. Add zeros and they continue to grow. The truth is that the nature and role of numbers in our lives depends mostly on our perspective. If you complain that you're "just a number," Newmerology's response is: "Well, yes, you are. But in a positive way."

you are your numbers

Newmerology's goal is to help you know yourself better and gain a stronger sense of identity. It aims to ground you in who you really are: your character, gifts, strengths, weakness, motivation, and desires. Then, your true self is ever foremost in your mind and heart, and effortlessly guides and infuses your life. Newmerology reflects upon our lives in a way we normally wouldn't think to do so. It gives us the opportunity to view the numbers of our lives as symbols of the meaning of our lives.

Our numbers—derived primarily from the Birth Date and the name as it appears on the birth certificate—are a language, a system of symbols that communicate who we are and where we are going. Like all languages, they have a vibration, one that reverberates through the digits themselves, their sums, and combinations.

Each letter of the alphabet also has a numerical value. Therefore your name, your child's name, or a business name takes on numerological vibration. It radiates meaning in a Meta language, the language of numbers. And like all languages, the numbers are sending messages. Newmerology unlocks the secret code of numbers as they communicate who we are, what we want, why we want it, and when it will happen.

The main numbers of our lives consist of:

➤ *The Birth Path Number* derived from the Birth Date.

➤ *The Environmental Influence Number* derived from the full name as found on the birth certificate.

➤ *The Conscious Desire Number* derived from the vowels of the full name.

➤ *The Subconscious Motivation Number* derived from the consonants of the full name.

➤ *The Dharma Number* derived from the sum of a Birth Date and full name.

newmerology 8

These numbers compose our *Newmerological Realm.* Keep in mind that these numbers do not dictate, but reflect who we are, where we are in life, and what we can be.

timing in life is everything: your cosmic clock

In a perfect world we would not need Newmerology. The truth is that in our hearts, we know, feel, and inherently understand why we are on this planet. But the external noise of everyday life, the blitz of modern existence, and our microwave-timed world scrambles our inner antenna so we can no longer "read" our own energy. Everybody wants immediate results. We want things done in five minutes. No, make that five seconds.

Our sports teams no longer hire a new coach with a five-year plan. The team must turn around in a year or two, or else the coach is fired.

Finances? The standard wisdom used to be buy and hold. Now we day trade, which caused a lot of people to lose their shirts.

As we engage in a world of immediate gratification, we have come to expect the same of our lives. We are not gearing ourselves for the long-term. Amid this climate of instant outcomes, we lose our sense of self. Our inner knowing drifts. Our need for immediate gratification overwhelms our higher intelligence. We forget the inherent pace and continuity of our existence.

Numerology helps us view our lives from a greater temporal perspective. It serves as a metaphysical clock that indicates what time it is in our life, when our energy supports certain activities and when it does not. If we go against the grain of that energy, we're literally going against ourselves, because the numbers are just representations and reflections of aspects of ourselves.

Numerology identifies fortunate and less fortunate periods in our lives so we can literally get out of our own way and follow our inner flow, especially for the timing of events and focus of our lives. When we know how to identify and interpret our numbers, we know how to gain greater hold over our lives. More success. More joy. Less fear. Numerology lets us optimize our efforts and reach for our highest potential.

As Numerology calculates the individual metaphysical clock, it does the same for the world at large. The same principles that apply to private lives also apply to businesses, organizations, entities, and influential leaders.

When we look to invest in the stock market, we look at the chart of the stock (usually the initial public offering date), and the charts of the stock exchanges (depending on which one it's in). We take into account the numerological chart of the president, the chart of the country, and the chart of Alan Greenspan. As with an individual, Newmerology examines the numerological currents in effect and makes predictions for growth and contraction accordingly.

Yet, despite its ability to time the future, numerology does not presume that life is predetermined. People are afraid of the predictive sciences because they're concerned that they are giving away their power. And sometimes they are, if that is their choice.

Numerology wants you to embrace your life, not surrender it.

Numerology simply reaffirms what we already know intuitively, on a gut level. We have a purpose in this life, a path studded with meaning that we have picked before we were ever born. When we stay on the path, our lives may be filled with ups and downs, joys and pain, easy and difficult decisions. But we know we are tending to the business of life according to its true course, not a distorted one.

9

chapter 2

Adding it Up, Newmerology Style

ave you calculated your numbers before? Used other books? From a formula provided in a magazine? Just casually on your own? If you have, pretend you know nothing about numerology. The process of finding your numbers in Newmerology is based on the Kabbalah, not Western numerology. It is unique from many other systems commonly in use today. Don't worry. A penchant for advanced calculus is not required. All it takes is second grade math.

Newmerology arrives at its number based on plain ol' addition. But *how* you add up the numbers, *which* numbers, and *in what order* is at the basis of Newmerology's expansive approach. By adding the numbers according to Newmerology's specific formulas, you will discover that your Birth Date and name reveal volumes about your life, personality, relationships, and destiny.

Each of the following chapters provides step-by-step instructions for arriving at the correct numbers. Each of these numbers is part of your *Numerological Realm.*

Follow all the instructions *exactly*. And, like a magic formula, they will unlock new doors of insight and opportunity for you.

newmerology

how to find the base number

In numerology, the Base Numbers are: 1, 2, 3, 4, 5, 6, 7, 8, 9, 11, and 22. Your Base Number, derived from your date of birth, will *always* be among these numbers.

All forms of numerology use the numbers 1 through 9. An element that distinguishes Newmerology is the correct use of the Master Challenge Numbers, 11 and 22. In some systems, the 11 would never reduce to a 2, and the 22 would not be accounted for at all. In Newmerology, a 2 and 11, and a 4 and 22 have different meanings. If your Base Number calculations initially result in a 2 or a 4, you will need to perform an extra step to see if it is really an 11 or 22 instead. Whenever you see a multiple of the number 11, (22, 33, 44, 55), you know that the pressure is on. These numbers are called Master Challenges because the characteristics of the number are coming from both sides, the conscious and subconscious mind. Factors of 11 create anxiety. They also create very successful people.

Below are several examples for finding the Base Number in Newmerology. Each example accounts for a different rule. But truthfully, the process is simple. Just follow the steps exactly.

Example #1

Birth Date: December 17, 1956
Equals ⇨ 12 / 17 / 1956

step one: add the year across to reach a double-digit number.

$$1 + 9 + 5 + 6 = 21$$

Rule to Remember: When adding the year's digits across, the sum should always consist of two digits. If your year begins in 2000 or after, make sure your sum begins with a 0. Example: The sum of the year 2002 added across would be 04.

step two: add the double-digit year number with the month and day.

$$12 \text{ (month in two digit form)} \quad 05$$
$$17 \text{ (day in two digit form)} \quad 10$$
$$+ \; 21 \text{ (year reduced to two digits)} \quad 66$$
$$= 50 \quad\quad\quad\quad\quad\quad\quad\quad \overline{} 81 = 9$$

Rule to Remember: Keep your month and day as double-digits. Do not reduce them to single-digits.

step three: add the sum across to get the Base Number.

$$5 + 0 = 5$$

The Base Number is **5**

Example #2

Birth Date: July **3, 1968**
Equals ⇨ **7 / 3 / 1968**

step one: add the year across to reach a double-digit number.

$$1 + 9 + 6 + 8 = 24$$

adding it up, newmerology style

step two: **add the double-digit year number with the month and day**

$$07 \text{ (the month)}$$
$$03 \text{ (the day)}$$
$$+ \ 24 \text{ (the year reduced to a two digit number)}$$
$$= 34$$

Rule to Remember: Since the day and month are single-digits, put zeros in front of them to make them into two digit numbers. Therefore, July would be represented as a 07.

step three: **add the sum across to get the Base Number**

$$3 + 4 = 7$$

The Base Number is 7

Example #3

differentiating between a 2 and 11, and 4 and 22 Base Number

Birth Date: September $28, 1981$

Equals ⇨ $09 / 28 / 1981$

Rule to Remember: There is a vast difference between a 2 and an 11, or a 4 and 22 personality type, as we explain in the next chapter. *If your Base Number comes out to a 2 or 4, you must check to see if it is really a 2 or 4 or an 11 or 22 instead. Check by adding the full year, month, and day using simple addition, the kind you learned in second grade.* See the following examples.

step one: add the year across to reach a double-digit number

$$1 + 9 + 8 + 1 = 19$$

step two: add your double-digit year with the month and day

$$\begin{array}{r} 09 \text{ (month)} \\ 28 \text{ (day)} \\ + 19 \text{ (year)} \\ \hline = 56 \end{array}$$

step three: add the sum across to get the Base Number

$$5 + 6 = 11$$
$$1 + 1 = 2$$

The 56 reduces to both an 11 and a 2. Which is it? We add another step to find out.

step four: add the full year, month, and day using simple addition

$$\begin{array}{r} 1981 \text{ (the full year)} \\ 28 \text{ (day)} \\ + \quad 09 \text{ (month)} \\ \hline = 2018 \end{array}$$

step five: add the numbers of the sum across

$$2 + 0 + 1 + 8 = 11$$

The Base Number is 11

E x a m p l e   # 4
Differentiating between a 4 and 22 Base Number

Birth Date: June 27, 1960

Equals ⇨ 6 / 27 / 1960

step one: add the year across until you reach a two-digit number

$$1 + 9 + 6 + 0 = 16$$

step two: add the two-digit year with the month and day

$$
\begin{array}{r}
06 \text{ (month)} \\
27 \text{ (day)} \\
+\ 16 \text{ (two digit year)} \\
\hline
=\ 49
\end{array}
$$

step three: reduce the sum to get the Base Number

$$4 + 9 = 13$$
$$1 + 3 = 4$$

The **49** reduces to a **4**. So now we must add another step to see if it is really a **22**.

step four: **add the year, month, and day using simple addition**

$$
\begin{array}{r}
1960 \text{ (full year)} \\
27 \text{ (day)} \\
+ \quad 06 \text{ (month)} \\
\hline
= 1993
\end{array}
$$

step five: add the numbers of the sum across

$$1 + 9 + 9 + 3 = 22$$

The Base Number is a **22**

Now that you know how to arrive at the correct Base Birth Path Number according to Newmerology, the next chapter explains their significance and what they mean. The fun is just beginning.

chapter 3

The Birth Path Number

the person you choose to be

There's a reason why we bring out the cake, ice cream, and gifts on birthdays. In numerology, the day that marks our arrival onto this planet defines who we are, according to our character and personality.

It sounds far-fetched at first. What about upbringing? Incidents that shape the psyche? Don't they make us who we are as well? Of course. But we all have a reason for being here. In numerology, that reason is represented in the date of birth.

The birthday, and its corresponding Birth Path Number, is who we chose to be. It indicates the basic course of life; what we are here to live, to learn, to be. The Birth Path Number reflects our consciousness, the *"Who"* we are going to be for all of our life. Our Birth Date provides the blueprint for our destiny. It throws light on the life path that enables us to fulfill the soul's journey, one that numerology believes we chose long before we were born.

Our destiny is created with our consent. *We* pick our Birth Date and the course of our lives, not an outside force. We know this because our lives are filled with constant choice. We can go left or right. Have chocolate or vanilla. Be a lawyer or a teacher. Live in the East or the West. Get married or stay single. Raise children or not.

If a God or a larger force determined our destiny, we would not need choice. We would have a life groomed to perfection from the onset, with none of the inner and outer conflicts or sense of opportunity or loss that comes with making decisions. There would be no margin for error and life truly would be fated.

To be alive is to choose. One of our first choices is our date of birth and how we are brought into this world. Difficult or easy, natural or cesarean, six weeks early or three weeks late, our arrival into life initiates the perfect set of circumstances for our soul to fulfill its chosen goal.

If we keep true to our Birth Path Number, then we keep true to whom we really are, even though that can be one of the hardest things to do over the course of life. From the moment we are born, to the moment we die, that's a path. But there are curves on that path. Life throws us curves that are challenges that in turn, make us stronger.

We get pulled astray from who we are because of the myriad of distractions within everyday life; we tend to trust what other people think and say rather than trusting ourselves; we focus on what we don't have rather than what we do; and we want to prove someone else's belief about us is wrong.

But the one universal commandment is: Honor thyself. When you keep true to whom you really are, you honor yourself. Then, you come from a place of love, truth, and integrity that radiates out to people around you. You feel at ease in your own skin and you get what is yours, when you are supposed to get it.

Often we give into instant gratification. We want that BMW now. We allow ourselves to get caught up in transitory relationships that have no future. Yet, things can only happen in their right time. When we let go of the timing of events, we stop choking them to death and give them the opportunity to happen.

The patterns of life work off the Birth Path Number because the Birth Path Number is your character. And, as they say in the theater, *Character is destiny.*

21

the meanings of the base birth path numbers

My clients often ask, "Are some numbers better or worse than others?" There's no such thing as good or bad numbers, it's what you do with the energy. The Birth Path Number and its meaning resonate with your inner core, since it is, in effect, your soul's number. You will find that you identify with your Birth Path Number in ways that may or may not be immediately apparent to others.

One special note: The Birth Path Number does not necessarily correlate with or indicate what you do for a living or a career. The Birth Path Number is who you are, which may or may not be reflected in your occupation.

You learned how to find your Base Birth Path Number in the previous chapter. Here are basic definitions of the Base Birth Path Numbers 1–9, 11, and 22.

1

You are truly individualistic and independent. The number 1 represents the father, the male or yang energy. The first number and the number of the self is 1. Therefore, you feel and see to it that you come first. You have a tendency to want everything yesterday due to your high level of energy and drive. You believe in being forceful to get what you want. Taking orders and getting "no" for an answer sends you into orbit. Thus, as a 1 personality, you are better off working for yourself. Since Universal Creation began on the first day, the 1 signifies pure or raw creativity. You are unique and believe in the concept of spontaneous generation, which means creating from scratch. If there is no recipe, you'll create it. Ones are not necessarily artistic, but are creative in business. You possess more of an abstract mind, allowing you to solve problems by "coming in the back door." This nonlinear approach to answers gets independent thinkers into trouble as you can beat your superiors to a solution, unintentionally causing the boss to look badly or foolish. In this situation, the 1 is asked,

the birth path number

"How did you come up with that solution?" and the response is usually, "I don't know, I just did." The artistic side of the 1 personality is as a writer, either as a hobby or as a profession. The 1 personality would make a good attorney. The saving grace of a 1 is sense of humor, which is normally dry, sarcastic, cynical, and most often, misunderstood. The downfall of the 1 is too much ego, becoming selfish and boastful. Due to your will and pride, you can believe you are impervious to the pitfalls that challenge mankind and can approach these situations with the reckless abandon of "Damn the torpedoes, full speed ahead." Remember all of you 1s out there, Rick Nelson sang "Fools rush in, where angels fear to tread." (Just in case you are curious, Rick's Birth Path Number was a 9, at the other end of the numerological spectrum.)

2

The 2 is the number of partnership and emotions. It represents the mother energy, the female, or yin. Since the number 2 is passive, you are shy, reserved, and prefer to stay in the background. You prefer to cooperate and go along with little resistance. You are interdependent if not codependent. You are good at assisting mainly because you like to help others, making 2s the perfect "Girl Friday" or "right-hand man." You must use caution, however, not to let people walk all over you. On the other hand, your diplomacy may aggravate people. They may see you as trying to break up their confrontations or as someone who is just plain weak, afraid to take a stand, or voice an opinion. You may get caught in the crossfire of other peoples' arguments and end up looking like the bad guy. Because the number 2 indicates "we," you may spend too much time looking for Mr. or Ms. Right. Spend more time pleasing yourself instead of others and you'll find that you are happier. Also, be willing to ask for help. It's a sign of strength. The 2s have a musical rhythmic side that keeps them balanced. Even under your desk at work, you may find your toes tapping.

3 ✓

The 3 represents communication and, therefore, indicates dealing with people. As a rule, a 3 Birth Path is a social, friendly, and outgoing person. The voice rules everything a 3 does. If you are this path, you must take full responsibility for everything you say, because you will have something to say about everything. Your opinion counts to everyone around you. You are a natural leader, but avoid leadership and try to remain in the rank and file because you prefer to be one of the "guys." Ultimately, those around you will elevate you into leadership roles because you are a problem solver. Friends and coworkers will hang on your every word. To paraphrase the old E.F. Hutton commercial, "When a 3 talks, people listen." This makes 3s natural sales people no matter what the occupation is. People are your natural resource, so you must remain positive, optimistic, and honest toward them. If you ever engage in lies, gossip, or spreading false rumors, people will turn their backs on you. You are not the kind of personality that can become reclusive for an extended period of time. You need people and people need you. The 3s are expressively creative and can do anything involving the voice whether singing, acting, or speaking. A 3 definitely has a flair for the dramatic, but you should keep the drama on the stage and out of your personal life.

4

When we talk about the 4 path, we are talking about someone who really stays on a path. If you are a 4, you look for safety and security in everything you do. The number 4 represents foundation, the formation of the Earth. The 4 is the four-sided figure, or the box. As a 4, you seek the safety and security of the box, thus you are cautious and conservative. Your approach to life is practical, logical, analytical, and systematic. The more organized you are, the more comfortable you are. You need solid footing and certainty. The 4s are the builders, engineers, accountants, and architects. They build from the ground up. Instead of getting in the middle of a project that someone else has started, you will tear it down and start over due to your need for solid foundation. You are detail oriented and are concerned with "the bottom line." You are not a gambler and should not engage in any risky endeavors. You prefer to earn everything you get, but this attitude may escalate into workaholism. Be careful that you don't make things harder than they need to be. Find ways to offset a tendency to be narrow-minded and critical.

5

A 5 takes many paths. The 5 is represented by the five-sided figure, the pentagram or star. Because of your charisma, people like you and you like people. You like to come and go as you please. You don't like confinement in any way, shape, or form. The 5s are like cats. You don't put a leash on a cat. A cat knows where home is. A 5 tends to be restless and impatient. You need a lot of stimulation. You can handle little routine because you get bored easily. You may sabotage a good job because of your struggle with confinement. A prime example of a 5 is Captain Kirk in the movie *Star Trek II: The Wrath of Khan*. Captain Kirk was the only cadet to pass a "no way out" training test because he didn't believe in the "no-win" scenario. He accomplished this feat by reprogramming the computer. A 5 will make up the rules as you go along. At the same time, you are a catalyst, intentionally stirring up things to satisfy your need for excitement. As a 5, you are a born traveler, wanting to explore new places, new things, and new ideas, another Trekkian example. Also, because you do not subscribe to traditional rules and systems, you are prone to the "messy desk syndrome." You have a random way of organizing that is hard for fellow workers to understand. However, complete disorganization drives you crazy. You are extremely talented in many ways. Focusing on one issue at a time and finishing the task at hand is your challenge. If you are not careful, you will scatter your energies, and like a star, eventually burn out.

6

The 6 path is full of responsibility. You present yourself as honest and trustworthy and tend to take on more than your share. Issues of love, home, and family influence you. The 6 home needs to be beautiful, serene, and melodic. As beautiful as your home may be and as domestic as you may be, your home is your sanctuary, not a party house. You like nature and need balance with plants and animals, as well as a periodic trip to the mountains or the woods to unplug from man-made clutter. Your standards are high in everything you do and have, until it comes to relationships. Your humanitarian side, which makes you a natural therapist or healer, inadvertently interferes in your dealings with people. Because you are sympathetic, you tend to turn the other cheek too often. This causes you to pick romantic interests that you try to fix. It is better that a 6 marry later in life, after learning from experience that you cannot fix people. Remember, most people don't feel that they have a problem, or if they do, they don't want you to fix it. The 6s also are talented in occupations dealing with the home, such as real estate, interior design, or architecture. Your flair for design includes fashion, painting, or sculpture. You also are adept in the healing and beauty arts, which could include massage, facials, and alternative healing. You must be careful that you are not so stubborn that you wait around to see how bad things can get before you vacate a losing situation.

7

The 7 is the spiritual path. You may be religious, philosophical, metaphysical, or wise. You wish to know anything and everything about anything and everything. The mysteries of life lure you to ask questions to which the answers are highly debatable. While you are interested in the occult, you are a skeptic. I think skeptics are believers turned inside out. If you didn't care or weren't interested, you wouldn't ask the questions. A 7 is open-minded and observant so you can analyze the facts. You will not accept anything as gospel until you have worked it out for yourself, which usually takes a while. A 7 often says, "Let me get back to you on that" or simply asks, "Why?" A 7 thinks a lot. I call them "grinders," which means they work or chew on one thought for a long time, especially before they go to bed. This late night mental activity causes 7s to dream a lot or be prone to insomnia. You may be a somnambulist, which means you walk and talk in your sleep. Thus, you must be careful of what you read and watch on television before bed. As a deep thinker, you do not like physical work but love high philosophical conversations and can be an intellectual snob. You avoid mundane small talk like it's the plague because you are a perfectionist and have high expectations of those around you. This creates much disappointment in your relationships, making you ultimately a loner. You retreat into yourself so far that people may perceive you as strangely mysterious and criticize you for your reclusive behavior. A 7 must meditate, if not for the spiritual connection, at least to unplug their brains. The 7s are neither leaders nor followers, but eventually find a spiritual path that leads to happiness. They may find themselves tormented until they do so. Sharing knowledge makes you happy, thus you are the student and the teacher. Be careful with mind-altering substances.

8

The 8 path is the hardest. It is the path chosen for material success. An 8's success results from thought and hard work. If you are an 8, you will achieve by finding a balance between your material and spiritual sides, without sacrificing one for the other. Some of you may have been taught that religion or spirituality required relinquishing earthly desires. This is not true. We can have it all. We are here to be happy on all levels. The 8 personality must learn to work for the good of humankind and not be greedy. If you continuously chase money you will never catch it. You may wake up one day and realize if you turn around and look behind you, the money is trying to catch up to you. As an 8, you must learn to respect and manage money. You are attracted to big business and big money and may find that you may manage large corporate dollars better than your own finances.

This definitely gives you the ability to be a leader or an executive. You can be attracted to politics or big government. Ethics and morals are a must for an eight, due to the allure of power. You are prone to notoriety or achievement in your field of work, therefore, it is wise to be friends with people in the media.

9

This is the path of service to humankind. You are compassionate and tolerant. Because of your sensitivity and empathy, people will seek your help and you are glad. The 9 is all about helping people. The 9 sits at the other end of the karmic spectrum from the 1. The 1 self-initiates and the 9 must subscribe to "what comes around goes around." A 9 cannot tug on the Universe for power, money, or love. You must do for others and wait for the rewards, trusting they will come. The 9s must be careful of friends and family members that become "psychic vampires." These are people close to you that test your love and compassion the most. It is intriguing that strangers will appreciate you more. You have a strong appreciation for the talents of those around you. You are not artistic yourself, but you are an aficionado of the arts and may be a collector of creative work or may attend a lot of performances and movies. You are good at any institutional or charity work. Vacillation is the undoing of a 9. Be direct, decisive, and complete projects before starting anything new.

11

The 11 path is the master challenge of two. As an 11, people will look to you for inspiration and guidance. The 2 side of your nature will make you shy, but you belong in the spotlight. You find yourself interested in and working in the media. You have natural psychic abilities and would be wise to use them as your own guide. How you live your own life is an example for others. Your downfall could be in telling others "Do as I say not as I do." If you are an 11 path, your challenge is to self-empower, and turn love inwardly to find balance within instead of seeking balance with a partner. An 11 must especially learn to love yourself before you can love another. Your psychic side integrates the left and right brain, which will sometimes create mental pressures or anxiety. To release this pressure, go within and quiet your mind through meditation. Staying self-centered is your key to survival. Maintaining relationships can be challenging. Balancing the commitment to you and others is like walking on the fine edge of a razor blade.

22

The 22 is the master challenge of the 4 path. As the 4 is the builder of the four-sided figure, the 22 is the master builder. A 22 builds pyramids. The pyramids are four- sided but they culminate at the apex. The 22 path has Universal goals and sees things on a grand scale. Like a 4, you believe everything must be earned, but you do everything bigger and better. You also have a charitable, even philanthropic side that wants to help others based on your own successes. You have the ability to build large foundations that attract many followers and can become international. The 22 also represents issues or conflicts with the mother. You must work out conflicts with your mother so she is not an obstacle in your path. Being a 22 is harder on a woman than a man because she goes through periods of having to choose between family life and career. Good, bad, or indifferent, a 22 will see the mother's life as an inspiration that causes the person to be success oriented. If you shy away from the 22 challenge to do big things, you may feel a lot of "what ifs" later in life.

is that all there is? absolutely not

The Base Birth Path Number is only the beginning. If you are a 7 Birth Path Number and know other 7s that seem substantially different than you, that's not a surprise. Your full Birth Path consists of a triad of numbers. These three numbers fill in the detail of your character, path, and the destiny you chose for yourself.

29

chapter 4

Compound Numbers

the big three:
defining the main and minor influences on the base number

Ellen and Charles share the same Birth Path Number—**6**. Like all **6**s, they are both responsible and trustworthy. They love home and family and put a lot of energy into making their house beautiful. Ellen, however, loves to change the look of the house as often as possible. Her design sense is offbeat and she has moved many times in her life.

Charles, on the other hand, detests moving. He likes a structured household. He tends to be a stickler about rules in the house and tries to exercise control over this domain.

If numerology works, how can these **6**s be so different? Charles is a **42/6** and Ellen is a **51/6**.

The two numbers sitting atop of the **6** comprise the Compound Number, perhaps the most important element in Newmerology. The Compound Number adds depth of meaning and "newances," addressing the variety and differences among people with the same Base Number. The Compound Number represents the defining qualities that influence the basis for who we are and what we do.

As I tell people in my sessions with them, "Not everyone is a six is a six is a six." There are, after all, different ways of getting to a Base Number. In the case of **6**, they are: **15/6, 24/6, 33/6, 42/6,**

newmerology

51/6, 60/6, 69/6, 78/6, 87/6, and a 96/6. That's ten different kinds of 6 personalities, ten ways of defining the 6.

Although they look like a fraction, the Compound Number and Base Number really operate as a triad. This triad of numbers is used to characterize each element in the Newmerological Realm.

how the triad of numbers operates

The Compound Number influences and shapes the character of the Base Number.

The Base is the foundation. The Compound's two top numbers act as modifiers to the Base, the way adjectives modify a noun. To use astrology as a comparison, think of the Base Number as the Sun Sign, the first digit of the Compound Number as the Rising Sign, and the second digit of the Compound Number as the Moon Sign.

The Compound Number has a Main and Minor Influence on the Base Number and, at least, some influence on each other. The Compound Number may stimulate or repress the Base Number meaning. As an example of how the Main and Minor Influences function, let's use Charles's and Ellen's Compound Birth Path Numbers.

the main influence number

The first digit in the Compound Number is the Main Influence. The Main Influence represents who or what consciously affects the individual. It dictates, impacts, or has a level of control over the other two numbers. It is active; so much so that it sometimes exerts as much effect on the character and personality as the Base Number. The Main Influence also impacts the Minor Influence Number.

As a 42/6, Charles's Main Influence is the number 4, the digit to the top left. This means he is supportive, sometimes controlling. He probably is a fair, but strict parent. The 4 influence the 2, representing a partner or the emotional life. This tells me Charles is either supportive or controlling of

his spouse. He also combines logic and emotions, thus he may be somewhat stoic. Or he may analyze his emotions.

As a $51/6$, Ellen's Main Influence is the number 5, the digit to the top left. She is unstructured and changeable. Since the 5 influences the 6, this accounts for her eclectic decorating style. She herself may be changeable. As the 5 influences the 1, she may have had many relationships or may have been married before.

The Main Influence Numbers in this situation differ greatly. Charles's 4 is structured and Ellen's 5 is unconfined. Although they both want the same thing, they may drive each other crazy in their approach.

the minor influence number

The second digit in the Compound Number is the Minor Influence. The Minor Influence impacts only the Base Number. Its sway is passive and subconscious. As mentioned above, the Main Influence colors the Minor Influence. It is on the receiving end of the Main Influence's energy.

As a $42/6$, Charles's Minor Influence is the number 2, the top digit on the right. The 2 influences the 6 as emotions or a partner affect the house or family responsibilities. Because the Minor Influence indicates what is in the back of his mind, Charles has deep emotional connections to his family that he may not demonstrate due to his stoicism. He also allows his spouse to run the house more than he may realize.

As a $51/6$, Ellen's Minor Influence is a 1, the top digit on the right. This means that she is the influence on family matters. Thus, we have more of a matriarchal household because 1 is a take-charge number. Since the 1 is the Minor Influence, Ellen has more control of these situations than even she may acknowledge. To sum up this couple, he has more influence over her, but he defers the influence over the house and children to her. Both of them are similar and yet so different. Ultimately, they are good for each other as they balance each other.

Rule to Remember: The Main Influence affects both the Minor Influence and the Base Number while the Minor Influence only affects the Base Number. The energy flow among the triad of numbers works as follows:

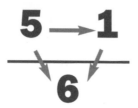

celebrity example

Let's take a look at the triad of numbers for someone with whom most of us are familiar: Gwen Stefani of the band, No Doubt. She has an excellent Compound Birth Path Number for the music business—a **38/2**.

Like Madonna, she is a **2**, which is naturally musical and rhythmic. Madonna is a **47/2**. Being ruled by the number **4** makes her a no-nonsense good businessperson. The number **3**, on the other hand, rules Gwen. She is more naturally outgoing to counteract the passive and shy side of the **2** personality. The **38** combination means that people will help her be successful and, of course, she uses her voice and creativity. She must remember that the down side of **38** is people with their hands in her pockets, the Main Influence Number **3** (meaning people) impacting the Minor Influence **8** (meaning money). She must protect her assets and realize that not everyone is her friend, especially a friend in need. Her triad of numbers points to a long successful career. In **2002–2003**, her Personal Year Cycle is $10 + 3 + 4 = 17/8$ (the number of the star). She hits her peak in **2003**. The only thing that could derail her over the next **3** years would be a failed romance.

finding your compound birth path number

Each element in the Newmerological Realm—Birth Path, Conscious Desire, Subconscious Motivation, Environmental Influence, and Dharma Number—has a specific formula for finding its Compound Number, which is located in their respective chapters.

To find your Compound Birth Path Number, add the double-digit year, month, and day together, the sum of those numbers creates the Compound Number.

Example #1

Birth Date: October 18, 1937
Equals ⇨ 10 / 18 / 1937

9/29/1954

step one: add the year across to reach a double-digit number

$$1 + 9 + 3 + 7 = 20$$

1+9+5+4 = 19

step two: add the double-digit year number with the month and day

20 (two digit year)	
10 (month)	
+ 18 (day)	
= 48	

19
9
29
57

Rule to Remember: The Top Number is always exactly the sum. Do not reduce it to a lower double-digit number (e.g., The sum of 48 is the Compound Number. Do not reduce it to 12).

35

newmerology

step three: **add the sum across to get the Base Number**

$$4 + 8 = 12$$
$$1 + 2 = 3$$

The triad of Numbers is 48/3

(handwritten) 5 + 7 = 12
1 + 2 = 3
57/3

Example #2
Gwen Stefani

Birth Date: October 3, 1969

Equals ⇨ 10 / 03 / 1969

step one: **add the year across to reach a double-digit number**

$$1 + 9 + 6 + 9 = 25$$

step two: **add the double-digit year number with the month and day**

$$
\begin{aligned}
& 25 \\
& 10 \\
+\, & 03 \\
\hline
=\, & 38
\end{aligned}
$$

The sum of 38 is the Compound Number.

step three: **add the sum across to get the Base Number**

$$3 + 8 = 11$$

step four: we must check to see if the Base Number is really an 11 or a 2 so you add an extra step and do the simple math

$$
\begin{array}{r}
1969 \\
10 \\
+ \quad 03 \\
\hline
= 1982
\end{array}
$$

Add across $1 + 9 + 8 + 2 = 20$

$2 + 0 = 2$

Gwen Stefani's Compound Birth Path Number is **38/2**

Example #3
New York Stock Exchange (NYSE)

Birth Date: May 17, 1792

Equals ⇨ 05 / 17 / 1792

step one: add the year across to reach a double-digit number

$1 + 7 + 9 + 2 = 19$

newmerology

step two: add the double-digit year number with the month and day

$$
\begin{array}{r}
05 \\
17 \\
+\ 19 \\
\hline
=\ 41
\end{array}
$$

The sum of 41 is the Compound Number.

step three: add the sum across to get the Base Number

$$4 + 1 = 5$$
$$41/5$$

The NYSE's Compound Birth Path Number is a 41/5

additional "newances" to remember about the compound and base number

➤ When the Main Influence Number duplicates the Base Number (e.g., 39/3, 19/1, etc.), the Base Number is intensified and that person or entity has a more pronounced Base Number personality.

➤ When the Minor Influence is 0, as in 60/6 or 50/5, it magnifies the Base Number ten fold. God's number is 0. It means all or nothing. Extreme circumstances occur when 0 is present.

➤ While the Main and Minor influence the Base, they will never overshadow it. A 41/5 will have security issues, but it will still need freedom and change.

> When the Compound Number is a double, such as 33, 44, 55, it takes on both the positive and negative side of the number (positive and negative of 3, positive and negative of 4, etc.). The positive or negative aspect that the number may increase depends on the person directing the energy. The double Compound Number also exaggerates the Base Number characteristics. As mentioned before, 11 and 22 are pure master challenges, and are not reduced to lower numbers.

Now that you understand how to arrive at the Compound Number and that the Base and Compound work as a triad, we will breakout the definitions for all the Compound Numbers in the Numerological Realm.

compound numbers in relation to birth path

The Birth Path 10s

The Main Influence Number dictates the theme of the Compound Number and strongly color the entire triad of numbers, meaning the entire identity and character.

When the Main Influence Number is a 1, this puts emphasis on the self. This gives the person more control in situations. For individuals with a number 1 as the Main Influence, it is often better for them to own their own business. They tend take a direct approach and their opinion is important to them. They make good attorneys and good writers.

10/1

You have personal power and a need for attention. You have difficulty taking orders. You are in command of yourself and your direction in life, especially in relation to occupation. You should work for your self. You are an extremely independent, nonlinear thinker. You can be stubborn and rely on yourself to succeed. Because the **0** reference is God's number, you can be power crazy, creative, and original in your approach to life. You are willful and must keep your ego in check as you could be a fanatical leader or paternal or strict. The self is your main influence.

11/2

Your issues center on self-empowerment vs. codependency, being high strung and nervous. You need to self-empower and understand self-love before one can love another. Until the psychic senses are developed, you may be too sensitive to the needs of others and at times may feel like your head is in a vice. You are very inspirational to the masses.

12/3

You are social, friendly, and direct. You put yourself before your partner. You are supportive of a partner or you may try to control your partner. Any emotional relationship must evolve from friendship. If you are a man you must be careful of trying to overpower women. You normally have a good balance between your male and female energies. You are purely creative and abstract. You are a natural leader of people, but you must be careful of not overpowering your friends. You are an idea person. You will have an equal amount of male and female friends. You may also have a strong lyrical side.

13/4

You work well in structure and like the feel of security, law, and order. You are a leader of people, giving you the ability to be a boss or a manager in a company. This number represents the ability to communicate oneself. You like your friendships to be meaningful and reciprocal. You may be popular but you only socialize with a few good friends. You express yourself in a creative way and you have the ability to use your artistic talents as your work, not just a hobby. You have the ability to get people to do things for you. Be careful that you do not become too bossy. Even though you are a linear thinker, your abstract side influences your decisions.

14/5

You are a calculated risk taker. Freedom is important to you. But as a 14/5, you like to create the structure and foundation on your terms so you can control all situations. This feeling of control gives you the freedom that you want and need. This number has athletic connotations. You have the dexterity of the 4 and the versatility of the 5. You have the ability to organize and be patient when the situation calls for it. But you must have balance in all situations. You have the ability to work at several jobs at the same time, or own several different kinds of businesses.

15/6

You are warm and fuzzy with people until they get too close. You are changeable which can be source of any dysfunction. You'll go through many personal changes before you can settle down into a marriage. You will marry later in life or perhaps not all because you have a fear that whomever you get involved with will be a karmic situation that you may not be able to get out of. Thus, you may change relationships as often as you change your underwear. You understand what it takes to be in a relationship but don't always listen to your own advice. The relationship with your family may be distant or you may have been adopted. You use your home as a place of sanctuary, a place that you can escape to. Still, you may move many times until you find the right home. Your need to "get away from it all" causes you to get back to nature. Your connection with plants and animals may be stronger than with people. At the same time, your humanitarian nature and instincts about people are strong. Be careful when you are in a relationship that you don't try to change that person too much. You are the one who must change. You are a natural therapist, but a bit of a loose cannon in that you may experiment in areas of expertise where you are not properly educated or accredited.

16/7

You are a loner, spiritual, wise, and philosophical. You desire to know anything and everything about anything and everything. Your opinion and feelings mainly influence your mind and your belief system. This makes you opinionated about philosophy, spirituality, and religion. You have a great influence over the people around you, including your family or people like your family. As the 6 influences the 7, the opinions and feelings of those around you have an influence on your mind. But because the 1 influences both the 6 and the 7 in this case, you are at the least dogmatic and expressive about your beliefs.

You may have philosophical differences with family members or work associates and you do not back down from your belief systems. You will carry out your beliefs to the point of breaking away from the traditional religion that you've grown up with, and explore more of a spiritual path. Although you come off as dogmatic, your job is not to come into this world and argue with people, and it is

not to impose your ego on people. It is to help people, grow, and understand that there is more to life than they may think. Your ability to work and get along with people is an integral part of the 16/7. With the 1 as Main Influence, you are individualistic and independent. You don't like to take orders. As a 7, you are a loner and would prefer on most days not to interact with people. As the 6 influences the 7, you have the ability to heal people on a very deep level physically, emotionally, or spiritually. You could be an alternative therapist or perhaps a teacher. Because of your dogmatic style, you are better off as a teacher, as opposed to a therapist because you don't leave a lot of margin for error.

Your expectation of perfectionism is up front and overt, so you make no bones about what you expect from people. You must learn to understand people and practice what you preach, and know that some people have different levels of potential and abilities. Some people are not going to cow tow to you or give in to your levels of perfectionism. Allow people around you to learn or accept what you have to say gradually. If you try to institute what you want or what you believe too rapidly or too harshly, the energy becomes destructive. You also must learn to keep your temper out of what you do.

You have the ability to swing from being quiet and mild mannered to a bombastic style. Try not to be belligerent when you feel people are not listening to you, or not agreeing with you. You don't like when somebody tries to shove information down your throat, so you must give that same regard to others. Learn to see both sides of an issue. Remember, information is something to be shared and studied. You need a lot of stimulation, especially in conversation. If it isn't philosophical or deep, it bores you to tears. You can achieve greatness in what you do as long as you keep your ego out of it. If you focus on helping people heal, you will get the appreciation that you feel you deserve. But do not go looking for that recognition. Do not go asking for it. That's when the ego gets in the way.

17/8

You are a thinker and a planner and you put those plans into action. Your individuality and personality goes into what you are creating. Whatever you create sets an example that others may wish to follow. In the Tarot, the 17/8 card is the star, making the 17/8 the most creative of all the 8s. We usually think of 8 as being successful in business. You are successful in an individualistic way. Through the ages, the 17 has been known as the number of royalty. The plural of royal is royalties. If you are in a creative field, or the entertainment business, which you may be with this number, you know what royalties are. It's reoccurring money that comes from an original accomplished performance. The 17 means the individual is creating from the soul, the deep part of the mind, and from the heart. This, in turn, flows down and influences the number 8, the endless loop, and in this case, the endless loop of money through royalties.

If you are a 17, you are inventive. You could invent a product or a method of doing something that you patent or trademark, so the money continues to come in. As a 17 you must be aware of your own intentions, and keep your ego out of what you do. This is tough, because your independence and individuality affects your mind. Everything you do means a lot to you. It is heartfelt. You do have a drive for success and do desire to make money, but you know how to balance your spirituality and your material side so that it works for you. You have some strong gifts that you must use wisely. The 1 indicates the Main Influence in your life. You are a leader in all senses of the word, but must be careful that you do not become too dictatorial. You have the ability to shine in all circumstances. It's important that what you create truly has a positive effect on people. As the number 7 influences the 8, there are times that you could be unaware, or become ungrounded or simply just not care about money. You may not have a problem making money, but you must manage it wisely. By the same token, you must be careful that you do not sell yourself or your creations short for money.

Your creations are unique. Others may wish to copy your style, but just like a signature, which is not really forgeable, your style cannot be perfectly copied. You also have the talent for getting deep within your mind. You have a way of digging in so that your conscious and your subconscious

flow with each other. Your aim is to own your own business, but it will be big. The more you try to pull away or try to retreat, the more things seem to grow. But when you do disappear for a while, people will not worry about you. They will be curious about what you are up to and what you're going to come back with. What is your latest creation? It will be hard for you to escape notoriety, even when you want to be left alone. You truly are the star, and you'll always have a good moral influence on society no matter what you create. You don't like to come across as cheap in terms of money, nor do you like what you create to be cheapened or tainted.

In everything that you do, there seems to be, at the least, an underlying message. You have the ability to run for political office and work in high government, but you don't want to get involved in anything that is tainted. You do a lot by feel. If it doesn't feel right, you don't do it. If it feels good, then you'll do it. You're very much into your senses. Overall you're probably ahead of your time in everything that you do. This is part of what makes you a trendsetter. As you go through your life, you must remember to stay grounded and interact with people. If you don't, you could go up into your mind so much that you become, even at middle age, somewhat eccentric, such as what happened to Howard Hughes. So you must retain control of your faculties.

18/9

The number 9 is associated with compassion and being of service to people. It is also associated with completion and bringing things to fruition. This concept is accentuated on an individual level more than any other number because the 1 represents the individual. The number 8 means success, big business. In the simplicity of the number 8, we know that money is important. But with the 9, we also know that any money that's earned must be accompanied by a willingness to give back, to be of service. As the 18 influences the 9, your individual accomplishments, especially monetarily, must be shared so that they benefit those around you. It's up to you to be compassionate, and to use your attainments toward helping people. You could reach a level of success that helps you to form, or helps you to feel complete on whatever level you choose. You develop a value system, in which you come to terms with the concept of money and learning how to manage money in every way, shape, and form.

Because the number 9 also represents a form of counseling or teaching, your successes are best shared in showing others how to do what you've done, or by simply giving some form of motivational seminars. You can be a leader sharing your knowledge and success with others to help perpetuate what you've done. So you can help others achieve a level of success. The 18 represents leadership, but it also can be dictatorial. Remember to be fair, and know that the people underneath you helped you get to where you are. Otherwise, you have a tendency to be bossy and full of your ego. Remember, you carry a lot of strength and a lot of clout and you have the ability to help a lot of people find their way. On a teaching level, you literally have the ability to attain a level of a professorship teaching in a large university or college. You share your experiences with students.

19/1

You are individualistic, but also compassionate toward yourself. This number is much different than a 10/1. The 10/1 is the all or nothing, where the possibility of an ego can be out of hand. The 19/1 has the ego in check. The 19/1 is the individual feeling complete in him or herself. You may feel compelled to do compassionate things, which in turn benefit you. So, you must check your intentions. What are you doing and why are you doing it? You're a good therapist. But as a 19/1, the therapy that you perform for other people resonates back to you. You have a lot of lessons to learn, and by helping others you do help yourself. If you allow yourself to become greedy and selfish, then nothing is going to work for you. But as you allow yourself to contribute to the betterment of others, to be compassionate, and understanding, your life will go smoothly. You do have the ability to be independent in terms of owning your own business. You don't like the feeling of being confined in any way, shape or form. And when you are successful, you feel as if you have completed yourself.

The Birth Path 20s

When the number 2 is in the Main Influence position, emotions, a partnership, or some issue or theme of the mother rules the number. Remember that before we have an intimate relationship or marriage, our emotional partner is our mother or representing the feminine energy. Partnership can also represent business. When you have a 2 as the Main Influence, you must take great care in dealing with business and money. Emotions can get involved where emotions shouldn't be.

20/2

Your nature is to be somewhat shy or withdrawn. But you embody the concept of still waters run deep. All of a sudden you may go from being shy, to forthcoming. You show a lot of depth of emotion and demonstrate it physically. You are passionate about whatever you do and have strong emotional likes and dislikes. You experience a lot of ups and downs in relationships and a lot of ups and downs emotionally. Be careful that you do not allow yourself to be susceptible to extreme highs and lows, creating manic mood swings. You have a tendency to react to emotional situations strongly. And yet, you do a lot for people. You have a lot of give, and not a lot of take. Because the 0 indicates the all or nothing, you may give until you feel drained to the point where there's nothing left.

You may come across as, or try to present yourself as, the ultimate partner. You may search for "Mr. or Ms. Right" throughout your entire life. You really need to focus on yourself more. You have a strong feminine energy, whether you are a man or a woman. The need for balance of the male/female is necessary. You have strong musical inclinations and the concept of music and rhythm means a lot to you. On a professional level, you can make the ideal second lieutenant or administrative assistant. Whether a man or woman, you will go to great lengths to help and please, and not really expect anything in return. You must learn to ask for help when you really need it. It is not a sign of weakness. It is a sign of strength.

21/3

You are somewhat of a social person, but because you're ruled by the 2, you are somewhat shy and into giving. You may wish to please everyone. You find yourself somewhat in conflict, because the number 2 does represent staying in the background, while the number 3 means using your voice. With the number 1 in the minor influence, you allow a partner to support you and take charge in most of your endeavors. You are also friends with that partner. You and your partner, especially a marital spouse, share the same friends and your relationship probably evolved from friendship into romance. As a 21/3, you have the talent to help people achieve success. If you use your vocal talents, it would be in the area of music, but you would shun the starring role. This configuration actually makes a really good background singer or studio musician.

You have the ability to influence people. But there is always someone behind you supporting you. You come into this world as having a pretty good relationship with your mother and father. You are both intuitive and sensitive, but have a tendency to doubt and second-guess yourself to death. You must learn to use the power of the 1 in the Minor Influence to create confidence. You as an individual must speak your mind as opposed to being passive-aggressive.

22/22 or 22/4

It is possible when we have done the math to have a Birth Path Number that is 22/22 or 22/4. You are global. You have come into the world to do big things. The 22 is the master builder, the master architect. You are analytical and pragmatic, and would rather tear something down and start all over as opposed to getting in the middle of someone else's project. You do not like feeling unsure or on unsafe footing. You are accountable for everything that you do, and although you are somewhat

conservative, you are a calculated risk taker because you know in order to do big things, you must sometimes go beyond the norm.

You may have some issues or conflicts with your mother that need to be resolved. Your mother may be a heavy influence on your life—good, bad, or indifferent—that inspires you to break the patterns or cut the apron strings from her so you can go on and do big things. If you are a **22/4**, as opposed to a **22/22**, this becomes difficult because you are pulled in both directions of having a great career versus being a dependable family person. You may struggle between greatness and the day-to-day of life. If you are a **22/22**, you must make sure that you see the forest for the trees. In all your grand accomplishments you may miss out on the fine details. Even in a contractual situation, you might miss something in the fine print. With a **22/22**, you can find yourself falling into delusions of grandeur, or wanting to do everything in a big way.

23/5

You must make sure that you do not lose focus on how you handle people. Do not take your friends or people close to you lightly. You may easily choose a partner who influences your friends, or a partner that creates too much change in your life. As the number **2** influences the **5**, the concept of marriage will work with someone who allows you to come and go as you please. Your approach to marriage may be an open marriage, combining the emotional intimacy of the **2** with the social side of the number **3**. Or you simply may not take other people's feelings seriously. Although you may not intentionally hurt people, you must pay attention to your intentions. Your aim is to please everyone, your intimate partner and your friends, and your challenge is to find balance in all these social situations.

Professionally you can handle people well. You will see talents in other people more than they see in themselves. With this number, you could be a good talent agent or personal manager and help people find work. You must make sure that you continue to subscribe to ethics in business, even though there may not be formal laws that apply to what you do.

24/6

Having a partnership, love, home, family, and marriage is important to you. You have a tendency to allow emotions to overrule your logic, especially when it comes to affairs of the heart. The possibility of disappointment with marriage can come early enough that it may set you off from relationships until late in life. As the number 2 influences the number 6, peace of mind and also peace and harmony in the home are important to you. You are shy and withdrawn and seldom entertain in your home.

Because of the emotional value of the number 2, your house may be like a museum. But no one will ever see it because you hold dearly the intrinsic value of what you have. And what you have may have great monetary value, but you do not acquire things for money or about money. It is simply because you like them. As the number 4 influences the 6, your home will be architecturally sound, with a defined style. What you have in your home will be decorated precisely, with an overall theme. On an emotional level, you are prone to guilt trips, and it is difficult for you to look at the faults for those close to you without initially turning the other cheek. You may turn a blind eye to their faults. You are prone to choosing emotional partners who have issues instead of choosing someone that has the same standards that you do. Your high standards of taste seem to go out the window of a beautiful home when it comes to choosing a romantic partner. Romantically, you choose fixer-uppers.

25/7

You are prone to mood swings. Your emotions dictate the changes that you go through, which can cause you to be distant or critical, at times, in your search for perfection. As a 25/7, your emotions may cloud perception, causing you to be somewhat of a hypocrite. If you're not careful, you may not see your own faults even though you're quick to point out the faults of others. You are an extremely shy person, which at times can be misunderstood. You are also emotionally deep, but find it difficult to convey or communicate your feelings. Your belief system is broad but you are private about it. You most likely believe in many forms of philosophy and spirituality, but most people would never know it unless you choose to talk about it. Your need for emotional freedom will allow you the freedom to travel the world to places of mystery, spirituality, and mysticism. You may come off as not caring about what makes people tick, but, in fact, you're deeply interested.

26/8

You have the ability to be successful and make money with a partner in a family owned business. This is the sharing of a partner's abundance. If you have this number, abundance also means fertility, perhaps to have a family, certainly to be abundant in love.

On a material level you have expensive taste, as both your emotions and your possessions have an influence on your money. However, instead of wasting money, what you buy is an investment, which becomes a family heirloom. Whenever the number **2** closely interacts with the number **8**, emotional attachments to money are indicated, making you either obsessive-compulsive about spending or miserly. Your ability to share or inclination to be greedy dictates how you manage your money, so it's up to you to find a happy medium with your expenditures. You have executive and leadership qualities, but your feelings for the people you work with or those that work for you may get in the way of effectively doing your job. On the other hand, you will be seen as a humanitarian and someone who is sensitive.

compound numbers

27/9

You are emotional about your belief systems, and sensitive to your inner-most thoughts, creating a lot of compassion. You can be too soft for your own good. It is essential that you have a partner who is spiritual and shares the same belief system as you. As you may have emotional attachments to your spirituality, you must keep in balance strong feelings, and stay away from any hint of fanaticism such as using your belief system or religion as a form of power. You have a lot of insight and strength as a teacher or a counselor. You can help those around you get to the next step. Your quest for knowledge is infinite.

28/1

You are independent and unique in the way you do things. You have a lot of will and like to control situations that you are involved in. You have strong emotional attachments to money and what it can obtain, and must be careful that you do not become obsessed with power. You have a side to you that fools people. While you can be aggressive, you also have the ability to passively and slowly plan your methods of attack.

You have the ability to be successful behind the scenes, such as a writer or composer who writes for other people. You are emotionally strong and may allow your pride to get in the way of asking for help when you really need it.

29/11 or 29/2

Partnerships and intimate relationships are troublesome. Relationships may last for a number of years and yet they still come to an end. You must learn to love yourself and self-empower before the right partner comes into your life, especially if you are a true 11 personality. If you are a 29/2, you must come to grips with compassion on a humanitarian level. You must love the world and the universe before trying to channel or focus that love into one individual. The 29/11/2 configuration can experience extreme circumstances in relationships. Sometimes, they just do not work until you let go and really allow love to come to you. In this way, you embody the true concept of the number 9. You do not tug on the universe for power, possessions, or love. As opposed to the 20/2, you are not searching the world for "Mr. or Ms. Right." You may just want a relationship badly and allow yourself to get into situations that just take up too much time and space. Instead, you should let go and apply the patience of the number 9, so that the situation can come to you.

The Birth Path 30s

When the number 3 is in the Main Influence position, communication and dealing with people is key. No matter what the Base Number is, we must remember that when we are ruled by the 3, we must be optimistic and positive, and never involve ourselves in any negative communication, such as gossip or lies. People are your natural resource, and if you mistreat it, that resource can run out. People and communication are synonymous with each other. Because people do talk, your reputation is always at stake.

Due to the mathematics, it is rare to have a Conscious Desire and Subconscious Motivation in these numbers. They are not listed. It would take a multi-name corporation to cause the math to add up to a number that is in the 30s or higher. If these numbers show up, especially in a company name, you know that the entity is trying to project itself as attractive, or attempting to draw people.

30/3

Communication is the key to your life. With the **0**, your situations with people will be extreme. You are expressive, especially with the voice, and may realize after it's too late that words may have slipped out that you may not have wanted to.

You are a natural leader, but you find because you want to get along with people, you push away leadership. You're extremely intuitive. You have an extremely abstract mind. The combination of intuition and abstract thinking ability gives you a inventive, innovative approach to problem solving. It even gives you the ability to look at items or things that already exist and allows you to reinvent them, or just simply take a new approach to an old idea. There are times that you must trust your hunches, no matter how crazy the ideas seem, and see them through.

Your words have a great effect on people, and you must take good care with what you say because of the extreme nature of how the **0** affects your relationships with people.

You try to be friends with everybody. At some point, you must realize that it does not work. You are a salesman at heart, but must be careful that you do not come off as schmoozing people, for then they will lose trust in you. You've come into the world to be popular, but do not take advantage of people. You are normally exuberant and your laughing, fun personality is contagious. Your approach to business is also abstract. Your approach is based more on feeling than thought.

31/22 or 31/4

People influence you or push you into a leadership role. You speak what's on your mind without creating great upset. The **31/22** or **31/4** are good numbers for management. You have the ability to lead people, and the ability to get people to work for you. You express yourself as a problem solver, and you fit well as a team player into the company environment. You may be a boss, but you lead by example.

You like people and may know a lot of them, but your friendships are select. You're not judgmental of people; you simply choose to have a few people as close friends, where those relationships are reciprocal.

You are organized, not only physically but also in thoughts, so you choose your words carefully. However, if you are not careful, those around you have the ability to influence you too much, offsetting the foundation that you greatly need or upsetting your inner security.

Any work that you do that's creative is actually technically creative or in some form of design.

32/5

You are a people pleaser. You communicate your emotions. You like a good blend of friends. Whatever the state of your romantic life, you like the feeling of being somewhat footloose and fancy-free. You must be careful that you do not become fickle in your relationships with people. You must learn to take your friendships seriously as friends may come and go in your life. Your ability to deal with the public is incredible. Your viewpoint is from various angles, but you must be careful that you don't agree with people just to make them happy.

On the negative side, you can lose your patience with people, which can cause you to walk away from friendships without really saying what's on your mind. You are not just popular, you are charismatic and you may have a lot of good friends without ever claiming that one person is your best friend. You do not try to possess people, and also you do not allow people to possess you. Oddly enough, you can come off at times as communicative and still shy.

33/6

The 33/6 is known as the Christ number. As we have studied in theology, Christ lived supposedly to be 33-years-old. And, of course, 33 is a multiple of 11, so here we have the master challenge of communication and dealing with people. Because the 3 is set over 6, which is the number of humanitarianism in healing, the challenge comes in taking responsibility in helping people. While one half of the world will thank you and love you, the other half may resent you and hate you. But as a 33/6 Birth Path, you are loyal, honest, and sincere, and aim to make a difference in people's lives.

The notoriety and recognition that can come to you is boundless and you have the ability to overcome all obstacles and problems. At times, just as you come up with a solution, somebody comes up with a problem right behind that. You must do what you do without looking for approval, notoriety, or recognition. It will come to you when it's time. When you go into a mood, a feeling that you're not recognized or appreciated for what you do, all the good work that you do seems to go out the window.

You have all the dynamics of a performer, especially in the acting field. For the most part, you are a crowd pleaser. But people do have a big effect on you. You must be careful in trying to help people. Be careful in playing therapist to your friends. You may tell them things that they don't especially want to hear or are not ready to hear. You can end up feeling victimized or crucified yourself.

Your ability to be creative and artistic is strong. Your abilities in terms of interior or clothing design are inventive and original.

The love that you have for people is not always translated in return as pure romantic love. So you could find yourself looking for love and marrying late in life, or even not at all.

34/7

You are wise, philosophical, and somewhat of a natural teacher. You find yourself lost deep in thought, and wanting to know what makes the world tick. You are both creative and logical. You have an advantage in the way you think. You are able to see both sides of things or approach issues from the left and right brain.

You do need your space to regenerate yourself. The more you retreat, the more people are drawn to you. Your mysterious side makes people curious about you. The more you try to withdraw into your home and into your space, the more people come toward you. Even though you prefer to be a loner, you must deal with people. People have a lot to share with you. People may feel that you are above dealing with them on a mundane level, such as returning timely phone calls or just being kind. Do not allow yourself to be judgmental of them. Listen to what people tell you. At that point, simply say thank you for the information, then retreat, and examine it for yourself. You don't have to accept what people say as gospel.

Your logical side sometimes gets in the way of your spirituality as you try to make sense of the mysteries of life. And that definitely can get in the way.

35/8

You have the ability to make money and make a lot of it. The only problem is, because there's so much energy around the number 8 with the 5, there is the ability for that money to go out just as fast as it comes in. As a 35/8 you must manage money. Your social side tends to scatter it. Now, in a positive way, the 35 means your communication in dealing with people will help you grow.

While the 3 usually represents sales, the number 8 is a manager, an executive. So this is a great number for a sales manager. If a company that you're interested in investing in is a 35/8, this is a company that is going to have its ups and downs, but overall it is strong. With the 3 and 8 together, we see the extremes of people helping you to be successful, but at the same time getting their hands into your pockets. We always want to watch how people operate when it comes to money. You are a leader by example. Maybe you were in sales for a while but got promoted through your efforts. Your qualifications as a leader put you there. You really earned it.

As a 35/8 you may be generous with your money, so if people come to you in need you may be prone to lend it to them. You also have the ability to earn money in an off the beaten path means, or nontraditional way that has to do with dealing with people. This could be somebody who is in an unsavory business such as prostitution or a pimp, or an unsavory entertainer, say as an exotic dancer, porn star, or something of that nature. It could also indicate dealing drugs on the streets.

The ways money can be earned is wide open for the 35/8, but because the number 5 is so spontaneous, the ability to lose this money is also there. Especially if money has been gotten in an unsavory way. It's cash. It's unaccounted for, and when money is unaccounted for in anybody's life, that's how we end up losing it. When people deal in a lot of cash, it has a tendency to disappear. There's a lot of magic in money, especially cash.

36/9

You have a strong humanitarian side and a strong compassionate side. You also, however, have a strong need for recognition. Now as a rule, 36/9 does not indicate someone who wants to be an actor or performer. In fact, this number is especially good for therapists. The 6 indicates helping people to heal or gain appreciation. But because the 3 gives a drive for appreciation or recognition of your accomplishments, you have the ability to be an expert in the field of therapy, or in some form of humanitarian endeavors. In either case, you will want to be front and center, speaking or lecturing about what they do. You could also write a book.

Your first job, however, is to be of service to people. You must speak humanitarianism, speak compassionately, and act in accordance with that. At times you may feel frustrated that things are not moving as fast as you would like. With the Base Number of 9, however, you cannot tug on the universe. You must wait until the power, the light, and the money you want comes to you. You may simply have to do your work, and out of nowhere, recognition and media attention come to you.

You may feel a certain amount of antagonism with friends, causing friendships not to last long. You may have them for a number of years, and through communication, which includes arguments, or not seeing the person, or simply not seeing eye-to-eye, those friendships fall away. As a 36/9 you may have an early exit of a family member, possibly through divorce of parents, or an early transformation.

You are interested in the best of everything. The 3 is the artistic eye, the 6 is the designing side, and the 9 is the appreciation of the arts, giving you high standards. You want the best, but you have to be willing to get it for yourself.

37/1

As a 1 personality, you are naturally forceful and aggressive. You always want to get your way, and you will not like being told that you can't have your way. As the number 3 influences the 1, people do try to influence you, and you will speak back, creating in you the possibility of a headstrong, if not argumentative personality. As the 7 influences the 1, your mind is always going to be working, or a lot will be on your mind.

The 37 represents people influencing your mind or wanting to get into your head, and also you wanting to communicate what's on your mind, including your belief systems. The 37/1 is communicative and philosophic. Your challenge is to say what's on your mind without blowing people away. You veer from speaking a lot of philosophy or hypothesis that goes in no direction, to all of a sudden being brutally honest. You have the ability to speak about deep things. By the same token, you speak in a dogmatic way, as if there is no other solution. You must be fair as to how you share information. You must be willing to listen as you communicate what you know about the mysteries of life, metaphysics, and spirituality. You must speak with compassion so you do not come off as a know-it-all or full of yourself, or full of your ego.

38/11 or 38/2

The 38 represents people helping to make you successful, people bringing you money, or your voice creating success. The 38 is the power of the natural leader moving up the corporate ladder. It is the artistic or expressed communication bringing success. How this will play out will depend on whether the person can live up to the 11 energy, which is being center stage and an inspiration, or just being a 2 and being very shy.

The negative side of 38 is people getting their hands in your pockets. If you are a 38 Birth Path, *do not ever lend money or you will not get it back.* As a 38, people will see the money or the strength and feel that you have enough. So if you give them money they will see it as a gift, not a loan. Anything that you do with money has got to be done contractually and agreed upon on paper and made legal. If you are an actor, performer, or a singer as a 38, you must make sure that someone besides yourself looks at your contracts, such as an accountant or a lawyer.

As a 38/2 you will find yourself wanting to talk and be social and outgoing, and at the same time, you are very shy. So you struggle in dealing with people while at the same time you look for partnership. You must make sure that your need for partnership does not put you into codependent situations that make you a doormat. Because you like to do so much for them, people may take advantage of your good nature.

Behind closed doors you are very emotional and sensitive. You can be a downright sexual dynamo. Just as you are willing to help people, you must be willing to accept help.

39/3

The **39/3** represents the endings of friendships and social situations. The **3/9** represents friendships coming to an end. And since you are a **3** personality, everything you do is highly influenced by communication and the people in your life. As I said, **3/9** represents people coming to an end. But just as we have endings, we have beginnings.

So I call the **39/3** personality the social recycler. Case studies have shown that a **39/3** may end up with people from earlier times back in their life. People come and go literally. People will last in your life for a number of years. As they exit, new people come in. It is very important that you end friendships with intention and closure. It is up to you as a **39/3** to properly handle all your social situations.

Ruled by the **3** and having **3** as the Base Number, you are expressive, artistic and creative. The key to what you accomplish, whether personally or professionally, comes from the number **9**, the compassionate, tolerant side of you. The **39** represents speaking with compassion. This will also draw people into your life that are compassionate. Your dealings with people must have a lot of patience. You must be willing to teach and learn from the people in your life. And because the number **3** represents a natural intuition that you must learn to trust, you are also empathetic. You are going to be very sensitive to people, and must allow those sensitivities to work for you. If you are hard on people, and do not allow compassion to rule your relationships, you will draw people to you that literally give you a hard time, or just simply drain you.

As a **39/3**, friends come to completion. It's up to you to help people while you are in a relationship with them, and get them to move on to where they need to be. You are most likely energetically charismatic and attractive, even if you don't think so. You will attract people to your physical self, and as you are trying to heal people or work with people, you may find that you have the ability to draw to you physical situations that you did not intentionally look for. You may have to reject people or turn them away because you may have created an energy that causes people to want to cross physical boundaries.

You must maintain a very, very distinct separation between your friendships and your business life, or you could cause yourself great problems and embarrassing situations for you and those around you.

As a 3 and a 39/3, you are very prone to the comments and criticisms of people around you, so this number can cause you to be the target of criticism, gossip, or rumors. You must be very careful what you do with your public life.

You also are an excellent teacher. You communicate well and you understand people. You also are a fine teacher of the arts because you are also a student of the arts. The level of appreciation that you have of artistic creations is very high and very astute.

The Birth Path 40s

When the number 4 is in the Main Influence position, you are ruled by the concept of the box, a four-sided figure. A part of you, for better or worse, is contained. You prefer law and order. You are a linear or left-brain thinker. You have a strong need for the feeling of foundation and security, professionally, personally, and emotionally. You are ruled by rationalization, pragmatism, and have a conservative, traditional approach to life.

The number 4 in the Main Influence position controls, influences, or even manipulates the number that's in the Minor Influence. The number 4 represents the controlling factor in your life.

40/22 or 40/4

Think of the 40/4 as a little stick man in a box, with another box ten times bigger sitting on top. The little stick man has his arms up trying to keep the ceiling from caving in.

That's the reason I refer to this Compound Number as the pressure cooker. Your belief in security causes you to be a workaholic. As a **40/22** and possibly **40/4**, you either put yourself in a position of being consumed by pressure or finding a way by work and by work only, not luck, to be on top of the box, or the pyramid, the image for the number **22**.

As a **40/22** (with the **0** representing all or nothing), your work either makes you very successful or very trapped. A **40/4** seems to stay the same level, never really rising above, just simply keeping your nose to the grindstone. Your feelings of hard work, ethics, and morals keep you somewhat restricted to a simple, mundane way of life that never really allows you to color outside the lines.

Your style of doing things is usually "play not to lose." But eventually you feel trapped by your conservative approach. Through work and patience you have the ability to get through anything. You're physically strong, but should not take your health for granted. Your analytical ability is second to none, but you must also allow for play and emotions to surface in your life. If you are a **40/22**, you may have extreme issues or hardships that were placed upon you by your mother. Make sure that you work out these issues to your satisfaction.

41/5

The 41/5 lives the Perils of Pauline. As a rule, the 5 is someone who likes their freedom and the ability to come and go as they please. But in this number, the 1 is in the Minor Influence and subject to the 4 as the Main Influence Number. So, what we have is the boxing of self. You have a need for structure, security, and organization and, yet you get yourself into predicaments or situations that cause you to compromise your much-desired freedom, causing some very hard lessons. You try to think things through (the 4 logic) while the number 1 dictates more of an abstract, individualistic approach to life. Meanwhile, the 5 wants freedom. You can end up compromising your need for freedom and individuality based on a false sense or need for security. To avoid this situation, don't make rash decisions, quick judgments, or dive into things based on need. Rather, make sure you go after something you really *want*. If you get yourself into the downward spiral of making decisions based on need, you will get yourself into a predicament. You have a tendency to go from the frying pan into the fire, both in relationships and in work.

The solution is to create a solid structure or rules for yourself that actually allow you to come and go as you please. Eventually, you may want to work for yourself. Most people with this number work for a company for a while, then realize that they just can't handle the structure even though they like the security.

When it comes to your personal life, make sure you set up boundaries for yourself that other people have to respect. The 5s easy going, freedom-loving behavior can cause people to disrespect them. Respect the boundaries that you set up for yourself, and people will respect you in turn. When you say that you are going to do something, especially as a 41/5 parent, you must do it. Action must follow your words.

Your key to success is to take action in a very structured way, so that you have guidelines that you can follow. Follow the guidelines you set up for yourself, and you will feel very free within that structure. The more you structure yourself, the more effective you become and the more of a catalyst for change you become in the situations around you. You also have the ability to take unstable situations and make them stable. This is a part of your strength.

42/6

You are responsible, loyal, honest, and trustworthy. With the number 4 in the Main Influence position, your family environment is going to have a lot of rules. You may be a very strict parent, or someone who simply has a lot of guidelines for what goes on in the home. On a personal level, your level of responsibility is ruled by hard work. You're not the kind of person that says one thing and does another. You definitely have the ability to put your money where your mouth is. You don't expect people to do something that you wouldn't do yourself. You are somewhat the cornerstone of the family, with the ability to support your partner and support the family. However, if you are not careful, the vibration of the 4 can degenerate from support to control and manipulation. There's a fine line between being supportive and in control.

Allow family members, especially your spouse, to have a certain amount of autonomy. You must trust that as your children grow up they have the ability to do things for themselves. If not, you could become the manufacturer of codependency. Remember, part of the vibration of the 6 is being the fixer, and the 2 vibration may simply be your need to be needed, or a need to feel important. In business arrangements, you must be certain that partnerships are equal and that you're supportive of that business partner, but not carrying the load.

In marriages, the number 6 can represent failed marriage in early life, and a suggestion of waiting until maturity to marry. The 42 may hold a partner at arms length creating hardships around the partner that results in a split or a divorce. It's very important for you to maintain a sense of balance between your work, your romantic partner, and the amount of responsibility that you take on. You simply may be the breadwinner of the family.

As a 42/6, the architecture or interior design of your home may have rigid aspects to it. You're not the kind of person who drifts very far from the norm in decorating. Whether in terms of design or emotional application, your family values are very traditional. One last thought about the 42/6: Your need to control a partner may come from a mother who may have been passively influential, but was the main disciplinarian of the family. Whether you are a man or a woman, you may fear that you could end up marrying your mother or find those same qualities in a spouse. The 42 also

represents control of the emotions. So, as much of a family-oriented person as you may be, there is going to be a certain amount of stoicism that comes into play. Even so, you are the caretaker.

43/7

As a 7 you are wise, intellectual, and very interested in exploring the depths of knowledge. And as the 4 and 3 influence you as a 7, you're able to see both sides of things. You are influenced by the concept of logic and reason (4), but at the same time you have a right brain, creative, more abstract side (3). Now as a 43, your ability to channel and, yet intellectualize and understand what you are channeling, is very strong. However, you must be careful not to edit what comes in. The 4 and 3 create the intuitive seam of the logical and creative brain.

Your interest in learning about everything will be very balanced. On one hand, you will be very studious and know that you have to do things "by the book." On the other hand, you will naturally perceive things and take them in without studying. You have the ability to be logical, business oriented, and creative and artistic at the same time. You will work for what you learn by studying and reading, yet, by the same token, you allow yourself to learn through entertainment, such as television and going to movies. Everything for you is a learning experience.

As the number 3 influences the 7, people will want to get into your mind and influence how you think. As the number 4 influences the 3, you may try to control people or keep people at an arm's length so they don't influence you too much.

The prototypical body posture for 43/7 is the arm out, straight out with the palm of the hand facing toward the person, kind of dismissing them, the way football players stiff-arm a defensive player. I have actually witnessed this in 43/7s. This is symptomatic of the 7, wanting to learn, but not wanting concepts to be shoved down their throat as gospel truth, until they have read and studied it, and come up with their own solutions or hypotheses. Because you are ruled by logic, anything that you do creatively will be something that you study, so that you can learn

the technique. This is where the 4 really comes into influence, because it overwhelms the 3. You come away feeling more satisfied with the fact that you have studied whatever the topic is, and are knowledgeable about it. You like the fact that you have credentials.

Even though you may be more of a loner and like your space, because of the number 3, you must have people in your life. You must allow communication to take place. You can be judgmental or a little bit of a perfectionist. You may categorize people. At the very least—or I should say the very worst—you could be a little bit bigoted if you're not careful. So, be careful about how you segregate your feelings about people, including those in your immediate social structure. You may have quite a few friends, people you party with, go to concerts with, and get intellectual stimulation from. But you will learn as a 43 to simply have fewer good friends in your life, where you have good reciprocal relationships with them.

As the 4 influences the 7, you may be more comfortable with having a formal or structured spirituality, such as a religion or organization that you can go to and interact with people. Eventually you may find yourself in a teaching or a leadership role in a spiritual organization.

Sometimes, 7s are perfectionists and hard on people because they expect a certain level of performance. As a 43, you will be able to analyze people and see how they can perform. You will get the best out of people by simply putting them into the position they belong, expecting no more and no less of what people can do.

44/8

The number 8 by itself is the toughest path number, because it represents the path or the road to success. There are varying kinds of 8s, especially in how people view, handle, or manage money. But 44/8 is a multiple of 11, representing master challenge issues. This makes 44/8 the toughest of all the 8s.

The illustration for the 44/8 is the little stick man holding up two big cement blocks in each hand, meaning that he has got to stay balanced or else he will fall over. The 4s represent structure

and foundation, and when we think of structure and foundation, we usually think of it as being on the ground. Here the stick man is trying to hold up these big foundations in the air, making the 44/8 very prone to pressure. People with a 44/8 take life very seriously. So, the pressure is not so much about physical pressure or health matters, although health matters come into play if the stress becomes too much. The 44/8 experiences pressure to perform. That can mean working on two things at once that make money, which is a good thing. It can also mean working two jobs just to make ends meet.

As a 44/8, it's up to you to definitely manage money. The 4 represents conservatism so you can save money and use it wisely. As a 44/8, it's better to use conservative investments. Volatile stocks are not wise for you, since the 4 denotes the need for accounting, security, and conservatism.

Some people have cracked under the pressure of the 44/8, especially when there have been multiple Rebirth cycles involved. Some of these people did not live out all the Rebirths and make it through a Rebirth Year. The 44/8 also has a tendency to simply be hard on themselves, with expectations too high and impossible to reach.

However, the 44/8 existence is not a hopeless one. When you exceed the master challenge presented to you, it actually makes your life better. You're climbing a bigger mountain than everybody else, but once you climb that bigger mountain, the level of achievement and recognition is higher than people climbing really small mountains or none at all. And this is where the hope comes in. *When people achieve Master Challenge Numbers, it brings them to a level that a lot of people will never reach because they weren't challenged enough to achieve that high of a pinnacle.* The bigger the challenge, the bigger the level of attainment.

The 44/8 should not run away from challenge. But you should use a lot of common sense, especially in your approach to money. The 44/8 must perform a balancing act between a very structured or stressful job where you may have to work very hard, and issues in your personal or family life that take up just as much time and effort. As the number 8 represents leadership and management, the 44/8 will have a lot put on your shoulders. You've come into this life to take on a lot. So, if that's what you've come into this lifetime to do, why run away from it? Just simply do it.

Do your best to stay away from legal entanglements because the number 4 represents the system, law, and order. Try to keep your life very clean of unnecessary lawsuits.

Your ability to earn money is great, and I emphasize in bold hyphenated letters, *e-a-r-n*, earn. If there is a stock that you're interested in that has a 44/8 Birth Path Number, it's designated for long-term growth. Remember we're talking about a business and money. So a business with this number is not going to crack under the pressure. The 4 and 8 are really about work, business, and money. This stock is good to buy for the long haul.

The 44/8 makes a good leader in the military or in law enforcement.

45/9

The 9 represents completion and compassion, being of service to people. It represents the ability to understand how people feel. As the 4 influences the 9, you may be a sensitive businessperson, no matter how structured you are or how analytical or logical you may be. This sensitivity carries over in your business. You have the ability to understand what people want, whether they be your employees, or clients. You are adaptable.

As a 45/9, there is vacillation between structure and no structure. You must be very careful that you are not too adaptable, pliable, or too malleable. If you are, you will find it difficult to make decisions. The 45/9 personality has a tendency to be nice, but the niceness does not always get you very far.

The 45/9 also has a tendency to be very accommodating, but not overly demonstrative or overly creative. Just as you are very hardworking, you can also be that lazy. You are very prone to inconsistencies in the energy output, both in your work or how you handle your life. The 4 is all about work, get up and go, get the job done. The 5 is the energy that is scattered. The 45/9 needs to balance or prorate your energy, because you may be up out of bed quickly on Monday and be so tired Tuesday that you can't get out of bed. Then, Wednesday, you're up again. Thursday you can't get out of bed. Friday you're full of energy, and then by the time Saturday comes, you're glad it's the weekend.

You sit in the middle of the conflict between 4 and 5. The 4 and 5 really don't like each other. They are diametrically opposed in how they are defined. But by the same token, you can have the best of both worlds. You can be very businesslike, but you can be involved in a business that is a little nontraditional or somewhat off the beaten path.

The 45/9 is a good number for an architect; however, it's not good for an engineer. While the architect is angular, and somewhat finite, the 5 allows for a little more creativity or free-flowing form.

As a 45/9, you are better off working for a company as opposed to being self employed, because you are ruled by structure. And if the Minor Influence of the number 5 comes into play, you can be very prone to laziness. Any changes you look to make may require some kind of legal approval or committee approval. If you allow this to carry on into your everyday life, you may always be looking for approval in everything you do.

Another way that the 4 influences 5 is that the system causes change. So if you do work for a company or an organization, you may find yourself being controlled by them. Or they may move you a lot, or you could be on the low end of the totem pole when it comes to anything that they're doing. As a 9, you have to wait for things to come to you. Sometimes, you're very impatient and at other times, too patient.

Many people born with this number have a tendency to be unpredictable as they do go to extremes. Travel, especially business related travel, will be a big part of your life.

If you're looking at a stock that is a 45/9, especially in the Birth Path Number, it may drive you crazy, because it will have a lot of ups and downs.

46/1

By choice, you take on a lot. As 4 influences 6, you become the cornerstone of the family. Perhaps from a young age, you sat in some kind of support of the family, or maybe you are the sibling who was always very supportive of other family members.

Maybe you were somewhat of a caretaker for people in your family, young or old. As a $46/1$, whether you're male or female, you are the person that your family turns to. If you are a man, then you look at things as if you are the patriarch of the family, and if you're a woman, you are the matriarch. When applied to a woman, I call this number the Rose Kennedy syndrome, because she was such a strong matriarch to her family.

The 46 represents the ability to support the family with strength and fervor. It is very common for a $46/1$ to be a single parent. The $46/1$ also represents legalities with a family. The 1 is a great number for an attorney. The $46/1$ makes a good family or divorce attorney. A $46/1$ is also someone who is able to work out of the home, or create or become the foundation for a homegrown business.

While a lot of 1 personalities don't look before they leap, you as a $46/1$ have a tendency to take more calculated risks because you have a lot of responsibility resting on your shoulders. You have learned what it's like to be responsible for people around you, and the people you care about. Whether they work for you, or whether they are family members, you know that you have other people's interests at risk and at heart.

The $46/1$ personality also has the ability to do design work, such as interior design, architecture, or technical design on the computer. You could be a very good real estate agent, especially a commercial real estate agent.

47/11 or 47/2

Because the number 2 represents partnership, wanting to be with someone, and being very highly emotional, the 47 affects the 2 much differently than any of the other 2s. The number 4, which is logic, affects it and as we know, logic doesn't always coincide with emotions. It is also affected by the number 7, which is on one hand spirituality, but on the other hand being alone. Anyone who is a 2 does not like being alone. The number 4 influences the 7 by imposing a logic on spirituality or a formed belief system. Now, the way this comes together in a $47/2$ is that you want a structured belief with a partner. This structured belief can also impact the kind of partner you think you should have. Or the kind of partner you think is good for you. As a $47/2$, you have engulfed yourself in heavy karmic lessons regarding partnership. This is based on your own stubbornness and not wanting to break old habits and patterns. You have a tendency to really get clobbered in relationships time and time again.

You need to look at the kind of partners you've been with, examine why those situations didn't work, and then move on. Get out of the rut. Your belief system is creating the rut. The $4/2$ is boxed emotions. You have to get out of that box. The $7/2$ is also the mind of the partner. So you spend more time trying to figure out what's going on with your partner than figuring out your own issues. Part of the weakness of the 2 is not to ask for help, so the solution to a $47/2$ dilemma is literally to get formal therapy, and work through the emotional issues, so that you can be a good partner.

On your own, you do have very structured belief systems. Once you've figured out your own head, your life goes better. As you go through your life with a partner, you may recognize at some point that you really don't need one.

You're basically a very shy type. You like to hide literally behind four walls. If you could live in a castle with a moat and very high walls, that would suit you just fine. You have an interest in formal forms of a spiritual belief system. You have the ability to lay the groundwork, no matter what field you're in, for other people to follow your example.

The more you learn to support yourself, instead of supporting the belief systems of a partner, the better off you are. You have a very basic structured rhythmic side to you, and have the ability to lay down the basis for rhythm or musical studies that people may follow or study for a long time. You also have the ability as a $47/11$ to be a good marriage counselor or a therapist.

48/3

You have the ability to turn expression, creative art, or use of the voice into your form of work, which influences how you make money. A $48/3$ is someone who is creative but not necessarily considered an artist, such as a hair stylist. This doesn't mean that you can't be purely artistic and have this number. It's just that since the number 4 influences it, there is a lot of left-brain logic influence going on. And since the 4 influences the 8, the intention here is to do this form of work as a means to earn your money. So the more creative you are, the more you open up and deal with people, then the more stability you will have in your life and your job, and the more money you will make. The $48/3$ is good for someone who makes their living using their voice, such as someone who is in sales. Because of the creative and artistic side, this is also very good for someone who works in the fashion industry. This is also a very good number for someone who would want to be in radio.

Part of the reason that this number doesn't equivocate directly into a performing artist is that most artists really do it because they like the work. It's not about money, although we know that there are a lot of actors and singers and pure artists that do make a lot of money at what they do. For you, money is part of the deal.

Now the other part of a $48/3$ is a gold digger, or a namedropper, or someone who is very intense about their money. If you do not like what's happening with the people around you, especially when it comes to social structure, you go into the reverse of the social and friendly 3, and become very snobby.

As a $48/3$, you have a tendency to be the most materialistic of all the 3s. Status comes into play in regards to your friends.

You could be an investment counselor stockbroker with this number, because your intuitions would blend in with the logic that you know about your studies with charts and money. You could be very good at advising people on when to buy and sell. A company whose Birth Path Number is $48/3$ is a good investment on the stock market.

If you are a $48/3$ you must be very careful that you do not indulge in expensive habits. This could drain your money. There is a side of you that does like to party and have a good time.

compound numbers

49/22 or 49/4

The difference here between the 22 and the 4 is actually doing something very big, or something that ends up solid but mundane. So, the basis here is really the size of the outcome of the situation. Our focus is on the influence of the 49. The 49 means the work or the foundation, either coming to an end or coming to fruition. This configuration is best explained as steps. Whenever the job that you're on or the project that you're involved in comes to fruition, you take a step and then you plateau again. Even if you're on a job in the same company, you will be involved in projects that are a step at a time, a step at a time. Often, you hold a job for a period of time and then move on to the next thing and then to the next, and then to the next.

Now in the past we've said that the 22 on the bottom represents conflict with the mother. The 49 comes into play here as the foundation that comes to an end. This means that the situation on the home front in relation to the mother was always on shaky ground or just kind of waiting for the other shoe to drop. Maybe the mother wasn't quite stable. She could literally suffer from some kind of nervous disorder. The people who are 49s look for stability with the knowingness that it doesn't stay that way.

On a philanthropic level, a 49/22 is someone who creates a foundation, an institution of compassion or service to mankind that grows in time and becomes something big. The 49/22 can be a very, very selfless number. When you are immersed in the concept of a 49/22, the ego is completely out of the way.

The Birth Path 50s

When the number **5** sits in the Main Influence position, you are ruled by change. You are illustrated by the pentagram,

which means you can go five different directions at once. You will have a natural feeling of adaptability and may have an energy that keeps you on edge or even on the move. You may have to learn patience or to stand pat and simply leave things alone long enough to see what can happen without you constantly fueling the fire. You are like to be a catalyst.

50/5

Because the **0** represents all or nothing, the **50/5** represents change to the nth degree. This is the number of the catalyst, the master magician, and the manifester. If Merlin the Magician had a Birth Path Number, this would be it.

The symbol for the **5** is the pentagram. The energy that moves in this pentagram is very big, very strong. You are not only a catalyst, but also very charismatic. People are very drawn to you. At times, just mystified by you. You have the ability to be a jack-of-all-trades. The question that lies within: what will you master? This does not imply that you are a master of none. This is a matter of how much you will focus on and master over time. Because with this number, you have the ability to master all. It is simply a matter of how you apply yourself. If this number is carried into the negative, you could be the laziest person on earth.

newmerology

With the **50/5**, your changes have changes. This number is like the Tasmanian Devil in the Bugs Bunny Cartoons before he comes to a halt. You live in the eye of the hurricane. You are in constant movement. You take very little time to rest because you are continually thinking about moving on to the next thing. Because you are the manifester, you have to think positively at all times, for your thoughts become physically evident very quickly. If you think positively, your life will be positive. If you think negatively, well, let's not imagine that. On a personal level, you're quick-minded and mercurial. You have the ability to get yourself in and out of any situation. You are definitely a chameleon. The power of the energy that you have is constructive. It's also destructive. You have the ability to affect everything around you like no other Birth Path Number. But should you choose to become impatient, you can become self-destructive, and sabotage every good thing that you have. Not everything moves as fast as you do. Give every seed you sow a chance to grow.

In personal relationships and romance, commitment is a challenge for you. You must allow yourself to settle down at some point. But you must sample many things before you buy. You are not the kind of person that likes to sit in wonderment of the past and think "what if." If you find a situation that's hard for you to commit to, you will try to change that situation so it suits you. You must be careful of tricking yourself into situations that you do not want to be a part of.

You are as nontraditional as they come. You literally can be involved in any occupation as long as you have the ability to come and go as you please. The esoteric arts fascinate you. If you do anything in the realm of spirituality and metaphysics, you must become a participant, instead of a spectator. It's very important that you keep your body fit, for your ability to move is important physically, as well as mentally. Overall, you're multitalented, but you must cultivate all those talents and resources so they can work for you. As you go through your life and mature, find a way to focus and tailor down your involvements so that you do not burn out. If your energy is not maintained properly, you can become a loose cannon, therefore becoming unproductive to yourself, and everyone and everything around you.

51/6

You will change and modify yourself to adapt to the responsibilities and rigors of family life. This is the number of a prototypical late bloomer because changes keep occurring that keep you from committing, or keep you from being responsible, at least until you are done rebirthing. As a 6, you truly want love, home, and family and the peace of mind that the sanctuary of your own home brings. Still, the 51/6 has seen a lot of dysfunction in the home. You chose to be born into changes in the house, so you may move many times in your life. You may have dysfunction where one of the parents, especially the father, may not have been present. Either he worked a lot or he exited the family when you were in need of having a father. By the same token, 51 is the changing and adaptable self. You grow in maturity so that you can accept responsibility on all levels. If you are an individual that has Rebirthed only once, the level of your responsibilities as a child from 9-years-old on would be tremendous.

The 51 means that there's a noncommittal side to you. You may want to settle into a relationship, but a part of you may sabotage relationships along the way. Once you do grow up and learn responsibility, you become very much an authoritarian kind of parent. It doesn't matter if you're a man or a woman, you carry a lot of male energy and become the head of the household.

Occupationally, you are very talented in the healing arts, whether medicine, r psychology, or alternative healing. You are better off as an independent therapist or healer as opposed to working in an institution such as a hospital. You are a little independent and a bit of a loose cannon.

You are better suited to the alternative methods of healing, however. In your house, the need for change and alternative methods will show up in the way you decorate, or redecorate in the same location several times. Your style may be very different. You may employ or combine methods of design or architecture that most people wouldn't even think about doing. For you, it works.

Your style in your home or your dress may make a lot of noise, but you actually like things fairly quiet. It is very wise for you to marry later in life or possibly not at all. Definitely do not have children until you have grown up yourself.

52/7

A 7 is a loner, the person who goes up into the mind. The 7 is the wise or studied or spiritual one. But of all the 7s, the 52/7 the moodiest because 52/7 represents changing emotions, changing moods. It seems the more you try to understand yourself, the more confused you become. As the 5, 2, and 7 work together, you have the ability to focus on teaching whatever it is that you choose to learn. But, by the same token, if it's something that doesn't interest you, you become as scattered as desert tumbleweeds in the wind. When you have a 5 over a 7 (5/7), this is the changing of the mind. With a 5 over a 2 (5/2), we also have the change of partner. Therefore, you can be very fickle when it comes to intimate relationships. Because you are born with this, the mood changes start from a young age, and you must take great care of how you deal with emotions, whether yours or the people around you. You may be an emotional loner and push people away. In maturity, you may have many relationships, or simply change partners out of boredom. The 5/7 is manifested spirituality. Your belief system will grow as you grow. You have a tendency to intellectualize in nonconventional ways. But the intellectualization is affected by your emotions. So if you're angry or upset, your rationale becomes very tainted. You can be very difficult to deal with, not just with other people, but also very hard to live with within yourself.

Part of your challenge is to see things as they really are, not your perception and how you rationalize it. You become bored very easily with anything or anyone that loses stimulation for you. When you are no longer stimulated, you simply move on. You have very deep spiritual beliefs, but prefer not to participate in any traditional communal worship or religion. Because you are affected by your moods, when you feel like doing something you're very productive. When you're not in the mood, you let everything slide. Again, on a personal level, you may be wise beyond your years, your challenge is in how you apply this wisdom in your everyday life. Combining a 5 with the 7 does not allow for the most grounded and centered of behavior. However, anything that you do in the field of research and studies that have to do with change and betterment suits you just fine. Turn your wisdom into knowledge without becoming a know-it-all. Allow your desire for perfection to inspire you and motivate you without turning that into high expectations of everyone around you.

If you're looking at a stock that has a Birth Path Number of 52/7, be very careful because it is predictably unpredictable. Do not start a business on a 52/7 day because its Birth Path Number will render it invisible or at least not visible enough for people to want to do business with it.

53/8

The number 8 always reflects a person who has chosen a tough path; a path to material and monetary success. With the 8, money management is always a must. Any time 5 and 3 get near the 8, money management becomes even more important. Here we have growth in money, change in money, money coming and going as it pleases, and taking it further into the negative, the scattering of money. As the number 3 influences the 8, people either help you to be successful, turning to you for your leadership, or they look to see what they can get from you. Be careful in how you handle money publicly. You could become very flashy, one of those people that carries a big wad of bills in their pocket. You also can become a real "good time Charlie," going out to a bar or a club, and buying drinks for everyone, or simply feeling that you have enough money or at least ready cash so you will give people money without fully knowing what your real financial circumstances are.

You have the ability to make a lot of money in sales, communication, expression, and anything that has to do directly with people. But your motto with money is, easy come, easy go. You like the nontraditional way of doing business. When it comes to investments, you're more prone to go after the quick buck or volatile stocks, as opposed to blue chips or slow continued steady growth. When it comes to running the business, you are a risk taker, and you're willing to do things that many people won't. You know that many times long shots do pay off. You are somewhat of a gambler. You may find yourself prone to going to the horse races, playing the lottery, or going to Las Vegas or Atlantic City. You are a natural motivational speaker and a natural leader within your business. You may do things differently, but you are result-oriented where many people are just plain goal-oriented. As the 3 influences the 8, you will put your money where your mouth is. You're not afraid of a challenge. You're not afraid of a dare. You're the kind of person that won't back down in a fight. You feel that there are not many obstacles in life, if any at all.

Because you're more abstract in the way that you deal with numbers, you don't always look at one and one equaling two. You're much better at calculating percentages and the potential of where business can go. You're a natural in statistics and probabilities, so you could be a natural analyst. But you are not an accountant, nor projecting the flow of business. Your motto is to let other people account for it. You simply would rather go out and perform or just do it. You're a good leader, but not the person to lead people into battle. You may win the battle but you may incur too many casualties along the way.

54/9

You may deliberately change the structure in your life or change jobs many times. It is not haphazard change, but it still is change in the structure. Because a 9 personality has to wait for things to come to them, you have the ability to wreak havoc in your life. The worst problem that you can cause yourself is vacillation. Although you favor change, you still want security. You may initiate certain changes and then forestall them, or second-guess them. You must stay away from second-guessing. At times, you're extremely impatient. Other times, you have more tolerance than anyone on the face of the planet. You're both scattered and organized. Overall, you are a stickler about law and order. You may find yourself being involved in more than one form of work. One may pay you money; the other may be involved in charities and organizations. Be careful that you do not allow yourself to be drained by charity or organizational work. Be sure that it does not become a form of distraction or a diversion that takes you away from the path that you're supposed to be on.

The 5 and 9 both make references to movement and travel. But the 4 is all about structure, and the 9 is patience. So, this number doesn't seem to make a lot of sense. It somewhat contradicts

itself. You must be very clear on who you are and make changes in a very gradual way. You are a good therapist, especially a physical therapist or a massage therapist.

If you're looking at buying a stock whose path number is 54/9, this is a stock that may, as a company, make a lot of changes, but there's definitely long-term growth potential as well. This is not something that is going to return instant dividends.

55/1

You are the more talented of all the 1s and the most multidirectional. The challenge of the 55 is to multitask and recognize and take advantage of opportunities as they come without spreading yourself too thin or scattering yourself across too many projects or over too wide an area. Because you are independent and want to do things yourself, you must be careful that the concept of wanting to do everything for yourself, or take all the credit in certain situations does not haunt you. Since 55 is a variable of 11 or master challenge that sits over 1, you are the one who creates the most challenges in your life.

Sometimes you see the big picture without seeing all the details. You must take time to examine and look at each situation before you throw yourself into something that gets you in too deep. You have the ability to do a lot of different things in a lot of different ways, but at the same time biting off more than you can chew. You definitely overcommit, since you are ruled by change in the Minor Influence. You really have more energy than you know what to do with. You're constantly on the move, very impatient, always wanting things yesterday, and not always willing to go through the process of attaining what you want. You are as changeable as the weather in March. You must allow yourself to finish tasks, and recognize the feeling of completion and satisfaction that something actually is accomplished. You could start a million things and not finish one. You are very prone to anxiety and nervous tension, which when it's converted to an adrenaline rush, gives you the energy that you need to work long consecutive hours.

You definitely should be self-employed. Even in being self-employed, you should have a job where you are able to get out and really do your own thing. If you do work for a company, you're better off doing something that involves travel, such as a flight attendant, working on a cruise ship, or even working in the travel industry where you have the opportunity to travel. The ability to come and go as you please is very important to you. Settling down into a committed relationship absolutely scares you. Before you commit to someone else, you must learn to commit to yourself. You love to do things your way, and at times, since you don't always know what your way is, confusion reigns. You're not just a risk taker; you're a daredevil. You can find that you throw yourself into risky situations, even on a physical level. You could try stunts and experiment just for the thrill of it. You definitely have a fearless approach to life.

Since you're so talented and have the ability to do anything, you may also have found that you skipped chunks of school or not completed college because you were ready to get on with life, and feel at times that certain organized situations, including studies, only hold you back. You are definitely one who attended the "school of hard knocks." You're a gutsy individual. Even if you are small of stature, you get into athletics and sports. When you take time to focus and apply your energies, you can be as productive as anyone. You're a good problem solver, and therefore, if you can focus on one business, you make a great business consultant.

56/11 or 56/2

You have changed homes or made a lot of moves. You may have even run away from home. With the **56**, there is change in the home that many times leads to dysfunction. The **56** can also mean growth in the family. You may come from a broken family or have parents that divorced and remarried. You may have stepbrothers and sisters, or even, if there's new children, half brothers or sisters. Growth in the family can come in a multitude of ways. Because of the change factor with your home and family, you will feel some emotional reluctance or hesitancy to get into committed relationships.

This means you are emotional. Your heart goes out to family members, especially the mother. You may have insights or a mature approach to a family situation that turns you into somewhat of a parent, even if you are still relatively young. In playing out the vibration of the 11, and a 2, you may have a shy side, where you really want to stay away from notoriety or public involvement, especially in relation to your job. But that may not work for you if you are an 11. For you are naturally not just charismatic, but also electric. Your way of influencing people is not only dynamic, but also inspirational. You gained this inspiration from what you learned from your family's situation.

You would be very wise to marry later in life and learn from your experiences. If you feel truly that your family environment is disruptive, then follow what the 56 says and move away from home, allowing yourself at some point in time to settle down.

You are very sensitive to the home environment in terms of decor. Certain colors will create reactions in you. Some are stimulating, some create anxiety, and some make you feel very peaceful. You must honor what you feel. It's not your mind playing tricks on you. Your style of decorating will be somewhat different. It will be very personalized. You really know what you like and what you want. Especially as an 11, you may literally have psychic abilities when it comes to healing. Your sense of touch will be incredible, so if you wish to do some form of hands on therapy, you'll know exactly what is going on with your client or your patients and know how to help them.

Your sensitivity level is off the charts, so you must trust your instincts. If you feel you have precognitive abilities, you must use them and not suppress them. If that energy is internalized too much you'll become very high strung and nervous. You may change partners often until your emotional needs are met. You have a high standard in emotional situations, especially marriage. Do not drop your guard, do not drop your standards. Hold out for what you want and what you feel you deserve. You will have it.

57/3

You are a different kind of communicator. You use your voice and express yourself just like all the other 3s, but you are the most different or the quirkiest of all the 3s. You've heard the phrase "Bad news so shoot the messenger." This is who you are. You have come into this world to present information to people that you don't necessarily want to say or information that maybe people don't necessarily want to hear. You prefer to be happy and friendly and energetic, but your mind works differently.

The 57 is about changing the mind. It represents alternative forms of belief, of spirituality, and on a bad day, the scattered mind. So you would be very wise to formulate your thoughts clearly before speaking. You're prone to sudden changes in the way you think. You make snap judgments, and these belief systems come out of your mouth ultimately creating confusion for the people around you. Just as people have gotten used to you thinking and believing one way, you come forward presenting information that is different from what you have previously said. You have the right to change your mind, that's true, but always remember that because you are a 3, people put a lot of emphasis on what you have to say. They're always listening to you, so you definitely can cause confusion, even without meaning to.

As a 3, you are optimistic and positive. So, even if it is bad news, you have the ability to present it as constructive criticism. You can find hope in the bleakest of situations. It's very important to you to speak the truth. And when you receive new information, you get very excited about it and like to talk about it.

Compared to the other kinds of 3s, you are not artistically creative, but you're intellectually creative. So no matter how tough the situation may be, you are always seeking a solution. You look for a way to help people out. You are very open-minded. You like to think and ponder different forms of belief systems. Even though you are a communicator, there are a lot of things that go on in your mind that even you don't understand, and those are the things that you don't talk about. You have a strong desire to travel to remote places of the world that you would like to study. You get your pleasure out of deep, deep conversations, talking about situations that really don't have a resolution, but you like to hypothesize. You make a great teacher of the abstract mathematics, such as geometry,

trigonometry, and anything that is not basic. You are very interested in cosmology, the formation of the universe, and anything that takes your mind beyond this plane and the earth that we live on. You may get bored with people at times, but you yourself are not boring. You are the happiest when you are saying what's on your mind. Just make sure you are taking responsibility for what you say.

58/22 or 58/4

You may feel a little bit of a conflict. You will want to stay very safe and secure in your basic approach to life, but at the same time, you need to grow and move. If you try to restrict growth with this number you're really working against yourself. You may be stubborn enough to resist change, but you move forward nonetheless. The best choice for you is to simply go with the flow, and let change take you to the level of success that you really want. As a 4, you're not going to do anything foolish, so any risk that you're going to take is calculated. The moves that you make in business are thought out and planned out in your head and on paper, so they will work. You have the ability to be successful in different kinds of businesses and at different levels.

Because the number 8 also represents politics and large-scale government, you have the ability to affect the law making bodies. These abilities are magnified and enhanced because you become a master in all these aspects. One of the most famous examples of a 58/22 is Bill Gates. Everything is done big. You are less conservative, more concerned with rising to the top. As with a 4, you do reap rewards from hard work. It's not luck. And as a 22, the structure that you form is very big, so when we talk about the ability to affect government bodies, this becomes very enhanced.

The problem that can come for you as a 58/22 personality is simply becoming power crazy. Once you get on a roll with the money, and it really grows, it becomes very easy to get caught up in the money side of your life. You could become a very goal-oriented workaholic. As a 22, the concept of being charitable, creating foundations that benefit mankind, or being philanthropic comes into play. So, if you are very wealthy, part of your Birth Path Number is to give back and be of service

compound numbers

to mankind. Because in the concept of the **22**, which we refer to as a pyramid, there are people underneath you who have helped you get to the top. It's up to you to lend a helping hand, reach down and pull people up to the top with you. If you're looking to buy a stock, that is a **58/22** or **58/4**, this is a good stock to buy and own. There will be a volatile side to it. It will incur ups and downs, but over the long haul it's a good investment.

As a **58/22** or a **58/4**, you are a good solid businessperson no matter what business you're involved in. You are very good at working with money, whether as an accountant or a CFO in a corporation. You are very good at working with investments and stocks. You're also very capable of being in political office or in a government position. You may also be inclined to be around architecture or some form of engineering on a large scale, such as a developer.

59/5

You experience a lot of change, but you like those changes to come to an end. You may be restless or impatient, yet you are looking for things to stabilize. You may be naturally noncommittal. Even in a marital situation, you may find yourself continually on edge, not wanting to be confined or corralled. You may live in more than one location simultaneously, or simply own property in a location other than where you normally live. As a **59**, change is a part of your life. The **9** represents compassion. So the changes that you cause must be of service to people. They must be compassionate changes. Unlike other **5**s, you can finish tasks that you start.

Your style or manner of doing things is somewhat unorthodox or off the beaten path. But it is with good intention. You definitely resist anything that is confining, whether a situation, ideas, or even confining thoughts. Even with you being very changeable, you are a stickler about law and order. You need to do things your way.

You're very prone to exhaustion. You must plan your day and your time very carefully, or you will find yourself throwing your sleep patterns off. You may find yourself working on projects into

the wee hours and end up sleeping during the day. This comes from not always planning the day correctly, or not always taking advantage of available time when you have it. There is a side to you that sometimes says "the hell with it. I'll do it when I feel like doing it." This is where you can sabotage good situations. You like working with people who are different. You choose situations in your life that are different from the norm.

Your choice of being different is a preference for yourself. It's not aimed at causing disruption in other people's lives. You will have to watch your diet, as you can be very prone to fluctuations in your weight. Occupationally, you are better off at working with people and helping people achieve the power they need to attain, which comes back to you in many unforeseen ways. Your notoriety and reputation is based on how you help other people. So, you are a very good independent consultant, counselor, or teacher. Although you are somewhat therapeutic, you don't really have the patience to help and work through very deep problems.

The Birth Path 60s

When the number 6 is the main influence, the issues encompass health, healing, humanitarianism, family, things in the house, dealings with nature, and high standards. A sense of design is strong. The occupation of architect, as well as real estate and escrow, are either a 4 or a 6. Nurturing and being parental, whether maternal or paternal, is part of the 6 as a Main Influence. If the number 6 influences you, you are going to have a load on your shoulders—mostly family responsibilities.

60/6

You have a very dynamic home life involving major responsibilities and big family issues. The 6 represents responsibility. You could have very strict parents, a highly dysfunctional family, or you could be an orphan. If adopted, you could have a struggle finding the birth parents. Most likely, you have multiple siblings. A **60/6** usually ends up as executor of the family estate. However, you will bear the family responsibilities that go along with it. Because of the **0**, the home life tends to be an all or nothing scene.

61/7

This is the guilt number—big guilt, especially as it relates to family. The family influences you, or family responsibilities fall onto you. Sometimes, this number indicates philosophical differences with the family, or the family influencing you philosophically. You could suffer religious persecution from your own family, if your belief system differs from theirs. It could involve a situation where the family is deeply religious or devout in their beliefs. Religion plays a strong role in your family and the way you were raised. Guilt is going to come into play and can create family dysfunction.

62/8

A family owned business would be good for you. You and money make good partners, although emotions and spontaneity can be involved. Your family has emotional attachments to money. The **62/8** represents someone or an entity that has done their homework in terms of estate planning, savings, and insurance. It indicates a lot of family responsibility, loyalty, and trust with money. Your family has put money away for younger members in the family, so it is not spent frivolously.

63/9

The 63 is very similar to 36. However, a 36 is usually a person that's in some kind of healing realm and wants a lot of attention. You are focused on healing work with less need for attention. You are a compassionate individual. But there are dangers here, because things you do come to an end in this number. People with the 63 and the 36 usually have problems in their intimate relationships with people. They may be good in the kind of work that you do. The 63 is a humanitarianism being, someone who is very good at communicating humanitarianism or being humanitarian to people in the form of healing people. This is a good number for a therapist. But, with the 6 and 9 together, problems may exist in the personal life and in personal dealings with people. The 63/9 is often not a real happy person. There is usually some kind of drama or issues going on surrounding relationships. Personal relationships don't last with this number. You may need therapy, or you may be a therapist or act like a therapist for friends. With the 3 on the back end, it's all about the people. The 63 can put undue responsibility on other people. And that may be one of the reasons that relationships come to an end.

64/1

You may work out of your home, have your own business, or a home start-up business. But you need support and you get it from your family or from outside sources. With the 6 (trust and responsibility) and 4 (work) together, you take responsibility for a lot of work. You are a very honest, hardworking, roll up your sleeves kind of person. You can be trusted to get things done. You are, after all, a 1, a self-starter. Sometimes with this number, the family ends up encroaching on your space later in life. You could take care of the parents when they are older, which may or may not be easy. You could work in the family business, or work for your family, a situation that may put restrictions on you.

65/11

Your family moves. It also causes change, disruption, and often dysfunction. Like the 56, you may feel like running away from home. But as a 65, no matter how far you run, the family comes with you, literally or figuratively. You may have been an army brat, because the family moved so much. As a 65/11, you may be anxious and high-strung.

66/3

You face challenges. The 66 is a factor of the emotional, anxious 11. You may harbor extreme anger. If the 33/6 is the crucified, the 66/3 is the crucifier. This is the number of morbidity. You benefit by learning how to deal with people. At your most positive, you can be a healing force. At the negative, you can be destructive. You can utter damaging words. You're either going to fix it or break it with this number. You may have been abused as a child, especially verbally, as much or even more than physically. You may have found it very difficult to please people. Because of this, you may lash out in frustration. You can experience extreme pressure from the family.

You may be very stubborn, but you will definitely go into battle for your family. You may have a very fierce personality, but you can also be fiercely protective.

67/22 or 67/4

This is a good number. With the 6, 7, and 4 together, you are someone who takes responsibility, works hard, and is spiritually motivated. You could work as some kind of therapist with spiritual influences, such as bodywork: a massage therapist, hypnotherapist, or a hands-on healer. The family will influence the way you think, creating structure. The reason that's positive is because your family really supports you. For instance, your father could be a doctor and really support your education in the same field. Your family is supportive of your education since the 7 refers to school and education.

68/5

You are a very inventive number. You are powerful and yet you are a healer and a humanitarian. You could be a doctor, physician, healer, or someone who is very advanced in their field. Your family could make a lot of money by growing a lot of businesses.

69/6

Responsibilities come to an end. Any time you see the 9 on the back end, it's always something that's coming to completion. This is a very good number for someone involved in a charity or in the medical field, like a doctor who works in ER. You have deep feelings, yet you are unaffected by the concept of death. You could be involved in a hospice or with something that pertains to mortality. You have the 9 in this configuration. You feel compassion and empathy and, on some level, pain. The 6 represents money that is unearned.

The Birth Path 70s

The 7s are the higher mind, a situation where you are both the student and teacher. The highest Birth Path Number we had in the twentieth century was 71/8. (As you practice with the math, you will see that the Birth Path Numbers of this century are much lower. The highest Birth Path

Number of **2003** is **48/3** (12-31-2003). The numbers from this point are too high to apply to the aspects of the name.)

70/7

In terms of spirituality, your attitude is all or nothing. In the negative, this number can indicate religious fanaticism. In spiritual beliefs, the world is black and white. There are the believers and the nonbelievers, the all or the nothing. This number represents a very strong belief system for good, bad, or indifferent. You are way up inside your own head—way up there. In the positive, this could make you a deeply spiritual person, possessing wisdom. In the negative, you could be a member of a cult or even lead a cult. Remember, the cult leader is someone who talks about God, but really the person worshipped is in his or her own mind.

71/8

Spirituality influences you and in turn influences your money. This is actually a good combination, because it represents a balance between the spirit (the **7**) and the material world (the **8**). The more spiritual you become, the more you channel whatever you need in terms of yourself, your power, and your creativity. This has all the elements of the **17/8**, but without the ego involvement. The **71** is more about God and spirit. You are very much a leader, someone who can show others how it's done. You could be high up in a corporation that has made money and then come back and show others how they can get there too.

Note: From 72/99 to 99/9, the explanations apply to Dharma only.

chapter 5

The Environmental Influence Number

will the real you please stand up?

> *"You want to go where everybody knows your name."*
> Newmerology puts a twist on the *Cheers* theme song:
> *"You want to go where everybody knows your number."*

Really. In Newmerology, the name can create complications in life. Your name serves the seemingly obvious and simple function of providing a handle, a way of identifying yourself to the world. Your name, however, also expresses a numerological identity. Each of the letters of the alphabet possesses a numerological vibration. Therefore, words carry a numerological current. When those words are your name, they, like your Birth Date, communicate messages about you. The Environmental Influence is how people see you.

The complications arise because your name is usually not of your own making. While your soul was choosing your date of birth and, therefore, your Birth Path Number (your character, identity), your parents were on this planet racking their brains trying to figure out what to name you. Based on what? Well, there's Aunt Katherine, who is lobbying for a family name, preferably hers or her

husband's. There was your father's favorite baseball player that year or your mother's favorite actor. Most of the time, your name is your parents' subconscious opinion, projection, or fantasy of whom you would, could, or should turn out to be. Your parents create the label that begins at infancy and continues through the rest of your life.

People around you feel the numerological vibration emanated by your name and from that they assume things about you, develop expectations of you, and form opinions about you. To varying degrees at different times in life, the opinions of others matter. That's why we call the name the Environmental Influence Number.

The rub here is that **99** out of **100** times, the Environmental Influence Number is different than the Birth Path Number. Remember: Who you really are—forever, as long as you are incarnated in this lifetime—is denoted by your Birth Path Number (your Birth Date.) People are reading you as the numerological vibration of your name. Meanwhile, *your* experience of yourself and your life, how *you* identify internally, takes the form of your Birth Path Number. So what people see is not what people get. And what you project is not necessarily who you are.

Celebrity Example
Madonna

Madonna's full name is Madonna Louise Veronica Ciccone. Her Environmental Influence Number is a **39/3**, meaning that people see her as someone who is outgoing, with something to say. But her Birth Path is a **47/2**, which means she is reserved, shy, emotional, caring, soft, and guarded. Her Birth Path Number has come out as she has gotten older, started her family, married, and moved to the U.K., outside of the U.S. media spotlight. Madonna once said that part of her ambition was to live up to her name. She did it. Now she can be who she is. By the way, the name Madonna alone is a **17/8**—raw creativity and spiritual depth creating an endless loop of money. Royalties.

One more interesting note here: Madonna is a big fan of Britney Spears. Britney's Environmental Influence Number is **39/3**, the same as Madonna's.

how the environmental influence number can impact you

Madonna may have lived up to her name, but many people have difficulty reconciling their image (Environmental Influence Number) and identity (Birth Path Number). The disparity is just too great. The image/identity paradox can create an identity crisis, cause people to deny major aspects of themselves, thwart self-acceptance, and produce crushing pressure due to unrealistic expectations.

Example

Debbie is a Birth Path Number 57/3. Her Environmental Influence Number, however, is a 22. Being a 57/3, she is social and conversational. She is free and easy with a bit of mystery to her. But because of her 22 Environmental Influence Number, people read her as someone who can do big things. They want to put her in a position that is high profile and high pressure. And that is not what she is about. People have big expectations of her. And, because she is a 3, she has a need for attention. But Debbie does not want to be bossed around, nor does she want to take on the kind of challenges implied in her 22 Environmental Influence Number.

the environmental influence number and career choice

Very often, the Environmental Influence can lead to confusing, inappropriate, or just plain wrong career choices. Everyone has been the recipient of comments like, "You should be a ____." "You would be a good ____." Such well-meaning advice is usually the world reacting to the numerological message of your name. And because people have a tendency to believe others rather than themselves, they can get on the wrong path. That's why so many people wake up one day and realize, even if they have a good job, that they really dislike what they are doing.

Example

Sam's full name was an **8**, which means that people saw him as successful and corner office corporate material. He was groomed for management, put on the management track, and given the perks and preferences accorded management. But Sam was a **5** Birth Path. He liked the freedom to come and go as he pleased. He was given a lot of responsibility at work but all he wanted to do was go home. Eventually, the job proved just too ill a fit and he left. The world acted on its impression of him, which was flattering, but unsuitable for his freedom-loving nature.

You need, in fact, to follow who you are, as signified in your Birth Path Number.

the name's value

Is the name just a false mask? Yes and no.

Sometimes the misidentity that accompanies the name becomes an asset. A fun **3** may have a name that conveys a **4** and enjoy the rewards accorded a hard worker, whether it is true or not. Or the shy **2** could have an **8** Environmental Influence Number and walk into levels of success that would generally require a more aggressive nature. The Environmental Influence Number has its advantages.

The trick is to recognize whether it is your Environmental Influence Number or your Birth Path Number that is operating in your life at any given time. If you are conscious of the difference between your image and your true identity, you can plug into your Environmental Influence Number when it suits you, or not.

If your Environmental Influence Number stands in too sharp a conflict with the Birth Path Number, you will need to make hard choices between perception and reality at different points in your life. Just remember, it is the Birth Path Number that points the way to overall happiness, fulfillment, and a life of no regrets.

Ideally, the Environmental Influence Number would match the Birth Path Number. Then what people see is what people get. Image and reality align. If you have the opportunity to name a child, it is wise to plan ahead and prepare a few names that will match the child's potential Birth Path Numbers. (More about that in a later chapter.)

the power of name changes

Many people sense that their name really doesn't fit them and change it as soon as they muster the courage. Some people change their names for professional reasons, some for show business reasons, and some, in fact, most times, for marital reasons. Whatever the cause, name changes have tremendous consequences on how you are perceived and how the world treats you. *A name change can alter your life dramatically, for good or ill.*

Celebrity Example #1

MC Hammer
real name: Stanley Kirk Burrell

Birth Date: March 30, 1962
Birth Path: 51/6

MC Hammer enjoyed a wildly successful pop music career under this stage name. As MC Hammer, his Environmental Influence Number was a 20/2. People saw him as rhythmic and musical. At one point, however, he shortened his name to simply, Hammer and his career began a downward spiral. As Hammer, his Environmental Influence Number became a 13/4, which is rigid and abrupt. And that's why it didn't work.

Random Note: Name changes only affect people who never knew you as your old name.

Celebrity Example #2

Anna Nicole Smith
real name: Vicky Lynn Hogan

Birth Date: November 28, 1967
Birth Path Number: 62/8

As Anna Nicole Smith, this model's name has an Environmental Influence Number of 31/4. The number indicates that people would criticize the way she ran her life, which is just what happened when she married a very wealthy, but very elderly man, decades her senior.

However, her birth name, Vicky Lynn Hogan, has an Environmental Influence Number of 36/9. If she went by her real name, people would have felt sympathetic towards her. Of course, her Birth Path Number, 62/8, shows that she really is all about money. The 6 represents inheritance or ways of getting money that is not earned. Does she have a mercenary side? Yes, but part of her actually did care for her now wealthy, deceased husband.

business name: ka-ching

One name you have control over is the name of your own business. When you pick the right name or change the name according to numerology, the effect can be magical and business can go through the ceiling. If the name has a difficult numerological vibration, the business will have an uphill struggle.

Example #1
Amazon.com

Environmental Influence: 29/11

Anytime the 11 is in the Environmental Influence, it creates a sense of awe. The 11 is a magnet. It's like a big neon light. People are drawn to it.

Example #2
Webvan

Environmental Influence: 22

Don't create a start up where the name comes out to a 22. The 22 creates great expectations. Everyone around you will expect the business to conquer the world. For a startup, like the fledgling online grocery delivery service, it was too much pressure. Expectations were unrealistic, leading to its demise.

Example #3
New York Yankees

Environmental Influence: 38/11

Again, we get the 11, and again, people are in awe of this team and support it. We'll discuss how to pick the best name for a business in Chapter 17.

newmerology

finding your environmental influence number

(handwritten, top-left margin, diagonal):
HERNAN CORTES GONZALEZ
95-95/5 369251 76581358
=33=6 =26=8 =43=50
7 =8 = 7
=16 123 =6

Calculating the Environmental Influence Number in Newmerology requires, as always, that you follow the steps *exactly*. Special rules apply for names that contain 11 and 22.

The Numerical Values of the Alphabet are:

1	2	3	4	5	6	7	8	9
A	B	C	D	E	F	G	H	I
J	K	L	M	N	O	P	Q	R
S	T	U	V	W	X	Y	Z	

(handwritten):
CORTES   GONZALEZ
369251=26=7   76581351 =36=9   = 13+16+26+36+28 = 119 =(11)

(handwritten, left):
JOSE LUIS
1 615=13 3391 = 16
16
29 = 11 26 36
26
36
7
5 10 1466=1981 =18=9
5 10 1966 =28 =10   2100 =3
1844 1981 =2008 =10

step one: use your full name as it is found on your birth certificate (excluding titles, family lineage: Jr., Sr., Dr., II, III, Esq., etc.; and with businesses, no extensions: LLC, Inc., Co., Corp., Ltd., etc., unless it is part of the recognized name)

If you were adopted as a baby and your name was changed early in life, you may want to compute both names. If you have undergone a name change, you will want to compute the Environmental Influence for your new name as well. However, the birth certificate name stands as the original imprint.

step two: attach a numerical value to the vowels of each name

The vowels are A, E, I, O, U. Y can be a vowel or a consonant. When Y is used as a vowel, it is counted as a vowel. *Examples:* Mary, Barry.

(handwritten, top of page)
$$10$$
$$15$$
$$\underline{-2}$$
$$27$$

Rule to Remember: If the Y follows a vowel, it is not a vowel. It becomes a consonant. Example: Carey. The "y" is essentially silent because it duplicates the sound of the "e." In such cases the "y" should be calculated as a consonant.

step three: **add the vowels and arrive at a vowel sum for each name separately; take the numerical sum of each name and reduce it to one digit**

If it comes out to 11 or 22, however, leave it.

Example #1

G e o r g e	L o u i s	S m i t h
e + o + e	o + u + i	i
5 + 6 + 5 = 16	6 + 3 + 9 = 18	9
1 + 6 = 7	1 + 8 = 9	
(7)	(9)	(9)

(handwritten) 10 = 1   15 = 6   2 = 2   9

step four: **add the sums of each name**

Assuming the outcome is a double-digit, it will serve as the Compound Number (top number).

$$7 + 9 + 9 = 25$$

The Compound Number is 25

(handwritten) 1 + 6 + 2 = 9   9/

step five: reduce the Compound Number to find the Base Number

If it comes out to 11 or 22, leave it.

$$2 + 5 = 7$$

The Base Number is 7
The Outcome number for the vowels: $25/7$

step six: attach a numerical value to the consonants of each name

step seven: add the consonants and arrive at a sum for each name separately; reduce it to one digit

If it comes out to 11 or 22, however, leave it.

G e o r g e	L o u i s	S m i t h
g + r + g	l + s	s + m + t + h
$7 + 9 + 7 = 23$	$3 + 1 = 4$	$1 + 4 + 2 + 8 = 15$
$2 + 3 = 5$		$1 + 5 = 6$
(5)	(4)	(6)

step eight: add the numerical sums of each name

Assuming the outcome is a double-digit, it will serve as the Compound Number (top number).

$$5 + 4 + 6 = 15$$

The Compound Number is 15

step nine: reduce the Compound Number to find the Base Number

If it is an 11 or 22, leave it.

$$1 + 5 = 6$$

The Base Number is 6

The Outcome of the Consonants: $15/6$

step ten: add the Compound Numbers of the consonants and vowels outcome

$$25 \text{ (vowels)} + 15 \text{ (consonants)} = 40$$

step eleven: add the Base Numbers of the consonant and vowel outcomes

Remember to reduce the Base Number to a single-digit
unless it is an 11 or 22.

$$7 + 6 = 13$$
$$1 + 3 = 4$$

The Environmental Influence Number is: $40/4$

The 11, 22 Exceptions

Master Challenge Numbers, 11 or 22, *must* be allowed to accurately surface.

Rule to Remember: When you arrive at an 11 or 22 sum in any of the individual names, let it stand. Do not reduce. When the possibility appears that a Master Challenge Number might come up as the outcome (you end up with a 2 or a 4), you have to go back into the individual name numbers and reduce any 11 or 22 sums to a 2 or a 4, to see if it alters the outcome into a Master Number.

newmerology

Example #2

Shakira
real name: Shakira Isabel Mebarak Ripoll

step one: attach a numerical value to the vowels of each name

S h a k i r a	I s a b e l	M e b a r a k	R i p o l l
a + i + a	i + a + e	e + a + a	i + o
1 + 9 + 1	9 + 1 + 5	5 + 1 + 1	9 + 6

step two: add the vowels and arrive at a vowel sum for each name separately; take the numerical sum of the each name and reduce it to one digit

If it comes out to 11 or 22, however, leave it.

S h a k i r a	I s a b e l	M e b a r a k	R i p o l l
a + i + a	i + a + e	e + a + a	i + o
1 + 9 + 1 = 11	9 + 1 + 5 = 6	5 + 1 + 1 = 7	9 + 6 = 15
			1 + 5 = 6
(11)	(6)	(7)	(6)

step three: add the sums of each name

Assuming the outcome is a double-digit, it will serve as the Compound Number (top number).

$$11 + 6 + 7 + 6 = 30$$

The Compound Number is 30

step four: reduce the Compound Number to find the Base Number

If it comes out to 11 or 22, leave it.

$$3 + 0 = 3$$

The Base Number is 3

The Outcome number for the Vowels: 30/3

step five: attach a numerical value to the consonants of each name

S h a k i r a	I s a b e l	M e b a r a k	R i p o l l
s + h + k + r	i + s + b + l	m + b + r + k	r + p + l + l
1 + 8 + 2 + 9	1 + 2 + 3	4 + 2 + 9 + 2	9 + 7 + 3 + 3

step six: add the consonants and arrive at a sum for each name separately; reduce it to one digit

If it comes out to 11 or 22, leave it.

S h a k i r a	I s a b e l	M e b a r a k	R i p o l l
s + h + k + r	i + s + b + l	m + b + r + k	r + p + l + l
1 + 8 + 2 + 9 = 20	1 + 2 + 3 = 6	4 + 2 + 9 + 2 = 17	9 + 7 + 3 + 3 = 22
2 + 0 = 2		1 + 7 = 8	
(2)	(6)	(8)	(22)

newmerology

step seven: add the numerical sums of each name

Assuming the outcome is a double-digit,
it will serve as the Compound Number (top number).

$$2 + 6 + 8 + 22 = 38$$

The Compound Number is 38

step eight: reduce the Compound Number to find the Base Number

If it is an 11 or 22, leave it.

$$3 + 8 = 11$$

The Base Number is 11
The Outcome of the Consonants: $38/11$

Special Note: If we reduced the 22 to a 4 in the consonants, the outcome number
would have been $20/2$.

step nine: add the Compound Numbers of the consonants and vowels outcome

$$30 \text{ (vowels)} + 38 \text{ (consonants)} = 68$$

step ten: add the Base Numbers of the consonant and vowel outcomes

Remember to reduce the Base Number to a single-digit unless it is an 11 or 22.

$$3 + 11 = 14$$
$$1 + 4 = 5$$

The Environmental Influence Number is $68/5$

Example #3
Lowell George Elliott

step one: attach a numerical value to the vowels of each name

L o w e l l	G e o r g e	E l l i o t t
o + e	e + o + e	e + i + o
6 + 5	5 + 6 + 5	5 + 9 + 6

step two: add the vowels and arrive at a vowel sum for each name separately; take the numerical sum of each name and reduce it to one digit

If it comes out to 11 or 22, however, leave it.

L o w e l l	G e o r g e	E l l i o t t
o + e	e + o + e	e + i + o
6 + 5 = 11	5 + 6 + 5 = 7	5 + 9 + 6 = 2
(11)	(7)	(2)

step three: add the sums of each name

Assuming the outcome is a double-digit, it will serve as the Compound Number (top number).

$$11 + 7 + 2 = 20$$

When the possibility appears that a Master Challenge Number might come up as the outcome (you end up with a 2 or a 4), you have to go back into the individual name numbers and reduce any 11 or 22 sums to a 2 or a 4, to see if it alters the outcome into a Master Number.

newmerology

step four: reduce the 11 in the individual name to 2

L o w e l l
o + e
6 + 5 = 11
1 + 1 = 2
(2)

G e o r g e
e + o + e
5 + 6 + 5 = 7
(7)

E l l i o t t
e + i + o
5 + 9 + 6 = 2
(2)

step five: add the sums of each name

Assuming the outcome is a double-digit, it will serve as the Compound Number (top number).

2 + 7 + 2 = 11

step six: because the Compound Number is an 11, we leave it

The Outcome number for the Vowels: 11

step seven: attach a numerical value to the consonants of each name

L o w e l l
l + w + l + l
3 + 5 + 3 + 3

G e o r g e
g + r + g
7 + 9 + 7

E l l i o t t
l + l + t + t
3 + 3 + 2 + 2

step eight: add the consonants and arrive at a sum for each name separately; reduce it to one digit

If it comes out to 11 or 22, leave it.

L o w e l l	G e o r g e	E l l i o t t
1 + w + 1 + 1	g + r + g	1 + 1 + t + t
3 + 5 + 3 + 3 = 5	7 + 9 + 7 = 5	3 + 3 + 2 + 2 = 1
(5)	(5)	(1)

step nine: add the numerical sums of the each name

Assuming the outcome is a double-digit,
it will serve as the Compound Number (top number).
If it is an 11 or 22, leave it.

$$5 + 5 + 1 = 11$$

The Compound Number is 11
The Outcome of the Consonants: 11

step ten: add the Compound Numbers of the consonants and vowels outcome

11 (vowels) + 11 (consonants) = 22

The outcome is a 22
The Environmental Influence Number is: 22

Note: As we move into the Environmental Influence Compound Numbers and their information, I want to say that it is extremely rare due to number combinations from adding the consonants and vowels that we would have numbers above the 50s. Therefore, you will not see any Compound Numbers with information listed here of 60 and above.

the environmental influence number

newmerology

compound numbers in relation to environmental influence

The Environmental Influence 10s

The Main Influence Number dictates the theme of the Compound Number and strongly colors the entire triad of numbers, meaning the entire identity and character.

When the Main Influence Number is a 1, this puts emphasis on the self. This gives the person more control in situations. For individuals with a number 1 as the Main Influence, it is often better for them to own their own business. They tend take a direct approach and their opinion is important to them. They make good attorneys and good writers. When the number 1 rules in the Environmental Influence, the father's impact is strong.

10/1

People perceive you as individualistic and independent, perhaps narrow-minded. People may misunderstand your sense of humor, as it may be dry or sarcastic. Others will seek your opinion since they see you as direct. Others will *see* your sense of urgency. This position reflects a strong influence by the father. You are considered to be creative, especially as a writer.

11/2

You are inspirational to others and attract many people, although some may see you as high-strung. Some may want to partner with you. Some may see you as codependent or possibly psychic. You may be perceived as selfish or self-centered. People will try to pull you into the media.

111

12/3

Men and women alike admire you; therefore, you are seen as social, friendly, and outgoing. Your mother and father have a big influence on your life. People will seek your leadership abilities. People will see that you have an interesting approach to problem solving. Others may say or feel that you may be overbearing.

13/4

People see you as logical, analytical, and pragmatic. They see you as a leader but also as someone needing to get their way. If you work at a company, you will be pushed toward management and viewed as a hardworker. But due to do your independent nature, you could be perceived as somewhat of a loose cannon. You definitely will be seen as having alternative approaches to problem solving. People see you as having the ability to bring about change that is ultimately good for the situation. As change is hard for some to cope with when it affects the structure, you may be perceived as cold and uncaring. You may come off as judgmental of people or as categorizing them, possibly prejudiced.

14/5

People see you as multitalented—someone who can do many things. Some people see you as impatient and trying to get the job done. Thus, you may come off as a taskmaster. This may be a result of an overbearing parent, especially the father. As a child, one of the parents may have tried to push you into sports. People will perceive you as having a lot of potential. Some will see you as a hard worker, while others will see you as someone who likes to play. This may cause people to be hard on you.

15/6

Your family may perceive you as a gypsy or the prodigal son. Depending on how traditional they are, they see you as somewhat of a catalyst or the black sheep of the family. They will see you as the one who is different which may cause them to completely misunderstand you. People see you as different, and at the same time, a humanitarian. Your peers or superiors may try to push you into a profession that involves alternative methods of healing. Even your own family may use you as a therapist. You may see none of their faults and turn a blind eye, or see too much of their issues. You may confound or frustrate romantic interests as they see you as good marriage material but noncommittal. Be careful as you may get a reputation as a heartbreaker. Others see your home as uniquely decorated and encourage you to be an interior designer or an architect because of your "eye" for fashion and style.

16/7

People see you as a loner, deep, mysterious, and strange. They see you as forceful and dogmatic with a strong ego. Opinions of you are going to be split. Some people will see you as constructive; some people will see you as destructive and fanatical with your beliefs. Be sure that you do not create a reputation as being fanatical. Without effort on your part, some people will follow you blindly. You could create a cult. You must be aware of the perception that people have of you because your reputation is at stake. This coincides with the Tarot card the Tower, the explosion. As the number 6 represents your house and family, your family may feel that you are somewhat of a black sheep.

You do have a strong influence on them, but they may never admit to you that the influence that you have is actually a good one over time.

As a child, you were seen as a kid that's different and doesn't always interact with the other kids. You may go off in a corner and read a book rather than run around with the other kids at recess. You may do the same thing at home. Even from a young age, you may be perceived as having a more serious, instead of playful outlook. People will see you as wise beyond your years, even when you're young. As a child, you may be perceived as simply not getting along with the other kids, or other kids may want to pick on you because they think you're different. So in early years and maybe even into adult life, you may be perceived as somewhat of a nerd or a geek—a loner who is not communicative. It is important to remember that when humans don't understand something, there's a tendency to get a little defensive, feel a little threatened, and ultimately criticize and/or attack the situation or the person. It is something that you need to learn, because this number is all about your individual belief system. However, if people do attack you, you will defend your turf; the 16 means that you will protect your space and home. In conflicts, you are kind of like Switzerland, in that you tend to be neutral. You don't really take sides between people. But on the other hand, if people attack you, they will be in for a real surprise.

17/8

People see you as a star, a leader, influential, and inspirational. They see you as having a unique approach to making things work. You are seen as successful, and someone who has created new and different ways of becoming successful. So people are drawn to you and they will model forms of the way they do business after your actions. Some people may find you a little different in the manner of the way you do things. Some people may criticize some of what you do because they may notice your higher-level spiritual approach or belief system. An example would be Los Angeles Lakers Coach Phil Jackson (although the 17/8 is not his number). A lot of people now criticize his methods and

they did so even when he coached the Chicago Bulls. Some people feel threatened by the fact that others can have such mind control and are successful on that level. Nonetheless, no matter what business you are in, people cannot help but see you as a good "coach." You have the ability to inspire people to be successful. People see you as creative or abstract in everything that you do and will have a tendency to be in awe of you.

18/9

People see you as a self-made person, as a successful individual that has made great strides, achieved on a great level. They also see you as someone they can turn to. If you are in a large corporation, upper management will actually listen to you. People see your compassionate side, your fairness, and understanding. They see you as balanced, strong, and firm. But at the same time, your colleagues see you as someone who has climbed up through the ranks and therefore as someone who appreciates what it's like to be at the bottom or in the middle. On your bad days, people may see you as egotistical and just simply wanting to be left alone.

19/1

People see you as individualistic and compassionate. But in this position, people see more of the individualistic and dependent side. They may see you as somewhat self-serving, or even when you do help people, they may not see you as completely altruistic.

People feel you are a fair leader. However, when you want something done, they feel that you want it done your way. They see that you prefer to listen to your own advice as opposed to listening to anyone else's. So people may get somewhat frustrated with you.

The Environmental Influence 20s

When the number 2 is in the Main Influence position, the number is ruled by emotions, a partnership, or some issue or theme of the mother. Remember that before we have an intimate relationship or marriage, our emotional partner is our mother or representing the feminine energy. Partnership can also represent business. When you have a 2 as the Main Influence, you must take great care in dealing with business and money. Emotions can get involved where emotions shouldn't be.

20/2

In the position of the full name or your label, people see you as the ultimate partner, but also as emotional and sensitive. Since you present yourself as somewhat shy and withdrawn, people may not know exactly how to work with you or communicate with you. On a romantic level, you are the all or nothing partner, sometimes the ultimate partner. You will be labeled as the "marrying type." Because of this perception, you do not attract casual relationships. Romantically, you are taken seriously, maybe even too seriously. Everyone you encounter romantically sees you as a candidate for a long-term relationship. You hear things like, "Well, you know, you're really nice, you're really sweet, but I don't want to hurt you," when, in fact, you're not looking to be nice and sweet at the time. You are just looking for someone to play with. Your relationship with your mother is extreme, as we have the number 2 on the bottom and the number 2 in the Main Influence position. You must look clearly at your relationship with your mother and make sure that she is supportive without manipulation. Since this number is also in the area of how people perceive you, you must be careful that people don't view you as a doormat.

21/3

People will like you and see you as friendly. Your shy side or naïve side is endearing. You draw partners to you who wish to be supportive, but be careful you do not take too much of a subservient or back seat position as you can leave yourself open to being manipulated by people who are controlling, or who would seek to take advantage of you. Your mother had more influence on you than your father, and she also had influence over your father. People will want to draw you into sales positions or leadership positions in order to make you more vocal, at the same time recognizing that you have a shy side. If you find yourself having this number in your full name, and you do end up in a managerial position, you must be strong, as your employees may feel that they can get away with things or take advantage of you. People may feel that you are passive-aggressive.

22/22 or 22/4

It is possible when we have done the math to have a Birth Path Number that is 22/22 or 22/4. Your mother has been a major influence in your life. You must be completely certain that what your mother does and says is for your benefit, and is not a form of manipulation. Your mother may influence you with her behavior, which you may or may not agree with. You must find it within yourself to extract from your relationship with your mother only what you feel will help you to do whatever you need to do. In different periods of your life, others will see you as someone with a lot of potential, especially in school. You may be criticized for not living up to that potential. At times, you may find that people put more pressure on you than you feel is necessary, or you may simply feel that you cannot live up to the expectations of those around you. If a company name has a 22 in it, you would be drawn to it as an investor. You must be careful that the company can perform based on its own abilities, not your perceptions.

23/5

Socially, people may see you as somewhat fickle. You may frustrate people who are looking for a commitment from you. You may be just too noncommittal for their liking. You may be susceptible to an overbearing partner who may try to manipulate you and your friends. Or your partner may simply try to tell you whom your friends should or should not be. On a professional level, you may be seen as somewhat undependable or simply as someone who wants to break tradition. Some of the scattering that you experience on an emotional level may be due to having an unclear or undefined relationship with your mother. Maybe your mother presented herself as a friend more than a parental guide.

24/6

The 24/6 represents a partner who is supportive, becomes part of your structure, or one who tries to control you. People that come into your life could trick you. They could present themselves as supportive, but really want to take over. If you have this number in your full name, I greatly advise you not to cohabitate before marriage. You could get someone into your space that takes over, and you may have a hard time getting rid of him or her. If you are a woman, you are seen as somewhat maternal or, if you are a man, paternal. People will see you as family-oriented. If you are somewhat mature, you have probably heard many times, "When are you going to settle down and get married? You'd make a great mother or father." Be careful that you do not invite people into your life that need help. You must say no to individuals that need therapy and use you as a therapist. Later in life, your mother, depending on her health or financial situation, may try to wish to, or need to live with you.

25/7

Those who are interested in you romantically find you deep. They are curious about what makes you tick. But because you have a tendency to pull back, your partner changes or moves away. You are perceived as someone who goes inside your head so much that it frustrates someone trying to get close, and you passively drive them away, even if that is not your intention. Others may see you as eclectic or eccentric. But they will respect your wisdom. Some may see you actually as a teacher.

26/8

You're seen as a leader, and as moral and ethical. People see you as someone who is successful and they want to be like you. You attract a partner who is not only a loving spouse, but also a good business partner. In the negative, this number represents being on the losing end of the alimony. If this is in your name, make sure that your spouse is interested in you for love and not your money, for the two of you will acquire wealth together. You may be seen as easily taken advantage of when emotions get in the way of your business decisions. People see you as someone they can turn to for emotional support. You also find, as you go through your life that money may come to you in unexpected ways. You must stay clear on what your intentions are toward money, especially when it involves marriage.

27/9 ✓

People see you as soft, caring, wise, and spiritual. You attract someone special whose belief system helps to complete you. It may be difficult for people to get to know you, but once they do and understand you, it brings you to a place of completion.

Some people may see you as soft or a bit of a target—easily taken advantage of. They should not mistake your kindness for lack of strength. Be careful that you do not attract people who are in need of therapy unless you are a therapist yourself.

28/1

This number can be fortunate, especially to women. This is the partner helping you to be successful and allowing you to retain your independence. I have seen this bear out many times in case studies. On the down side of this, you could find yourself victim to someone who is involved with you for your money. People see you as independent and individualistic but having a fair side too.

29/11 or 29/2

You attract a lot of suitors and people who are meaning well. You also attract people that may play upon your sympathies or compassions, or people that may have a lot of emotional pain. Your energy is so soft that people may view you as completely shy and retreating, as well as kind. This may draw pity, so people may look at you and say poor so and so. However, you should avoid drawing pity from people because that only pulls you down. Ideally in this situation, starting with your mother and then moving into an emotional partner, you want someone that has compassion for you. Others, especially in a job situation, may see you as sensitive and nervous. They feel that just by coming up and approaching you, you jump out of your skin as if you are surprised by every casual encounter. Think of the ever-nervous Barney Fife character in the *The Andy Griffith Show*, and you will get the idea of people's impression of your temperament. The people that you do draw into your life will take you seriously, however. On one hand, no one will mistake you for a one-night stand. On the other, you will not be seen as gentlemanly or very ladylike. You are viewed as helpful, caring, and charitable.

The Environmental Influence 30s

When the number 3 is in the Main Influence position, communication and dealing with people is key. No matter what the Base Number is, we must remember that when we are ruled by the 3, we must be optimistic and positive, and never involve ourselves in any negative communication, such as gossip or lies. People are your natural resource, and if you mistreat it, that resource can run out. People and communication are synonymous with each other. Because people do talk, your reputation is always at stake.

30/3

People perceive you as extremely social, friendly, and downright gregarious. They are drawn to you, but because of your exuberance, there will be those who feel you are a bit over the top. You always have something to say. Some people will wish you were less verbal in your opinions. Others hang on your every word waiting for the next thing that you have to say.

People may see you as somewhat of a motivational speaker or a priest, a preacher, a minister, or someone who inspires. People have the utmost faith in you.

Because of the way that you draw people to you, there are those who feel that you command such stage presence that you should either be on stage literally, or you may draw people to you that simply bring a lot of drama into your life. You could find yourself literally in the entertainment business without even trying.

31/22 or 31/4

People are drawn to you, but they can be overwhelming. The people may tell you what's good for you or what you should do. People see you as hardworking, and as a leader, and they push you into leadership positions that you may or may not want.

In the workplace, people will be turning to you incessantly to get your opinion or to see how you would solve certain problems.

Some people see you as logical, some people see you as abstract. People like to talk to you because they see you as a good listener, and as having the ability to logic out and break down what they are saying to you. People also see you as someone that they simply want to do business with because they trust you.

32/5

People see you as easygoing and cooperative. They also may have a lot to say about your romantic life, or they may try to influence your romantic partner.

You must be careful that even your friends do not unintentionally drive a love interest out of your life. People may see you as so cooperative to the point that they can push you around or cause you to do things that you normally wouldn't do. Yes, your friends can definitely get you into trouble.

Because of the mercurial feel of the number 5, and the friendly influence, if you are married, or in a committed relationship, you must make sure that a night out on the town with the guys or the girls does not get out of hand. You may be seen as just a good time gal or a good time Charlie.

In the work place, your playful side may be seen as unnecessarily flirtatious. Or you may be seen as someone that everybody likes but doesn't always live up to work expectations and does not do the best job. They may see you as a little bit of a loose cannon that comes and goes as you please. This creates problems for management, for they may like you, but may have to come down hard on you.

Your home life may have been somewhat dysfunctional as you may have a single parent that had a lot of friends of the opposite sex, or was somehow noncommittal. This parental example will highly influence your noncommittal side.

Make sure that your reputation is not of someone who is so flirtatious that you are perceived as being loose. People get a mixed read on you as being sometimes a talker, but also at times withdrawn.

33/6

This number makes you invisible, and invisibility can be a target. People recognize you through your work, but may criticize you while others praise you. People see your life as being dramatic, even if you're not on the stage. People are always going to have something to say about you. Your own family, parents, spouse, or children may have comments or criticisms about you.

They may recognize in you that you're the kind of person that turns the other cheek, and take advantage of your good nature. Or they may simply look to crucify you or victimize you.

The people that really appreciate you will praise you and respect you. You will be seen as a leader and an innovator in whatever field you find your occupation. People will be drawn to hear your voice and your healing words. And even if people do criticize you at some point in your life, they will recognize that you've made an impact on everyone around you.

34/7

The more you try to pull away from people, the more they're drawn to you. It's your mysterious side that attracts them. If you simply come forward, and confront people, it will create equality in the relationships. At that point, you will need to learn to trust people.

This may create the feeling in you that people are trying to manipulate you, which isn't necessarily the truth.

35/8

People are drawn to you as a leader. They'll see you as an example of someone who has earned everything that they've got, and people will respect you. But by the same token, if you're going out to dinner with a bunch of people, they may expect you to buy. People have the perception of you being a big spender or wealthy. This can be a problem, especially if your Birth Path Number is a conservative number like 4. You are cautious with money so the perception of you as a big spender is going to create a lot of conflict. People have high expectations of you. By the same token, people are going to jump on the bandwagon and want to work for you or work with you.

If you're not a leader as a 35/8, then people will want to hire you and put you into that position, or people will want to hire you as an agent or some kind of personnel manager, as in human resources. They see that you have the feel for getting people to change and grow. On the other hand, people may simply try to get you to change, so you can be more successful. People may see you as someone who just has the ability to make money and want to learn from it.

36/9

People turn to you for healing and compassion. People, especially friends, will see a special side to you where they trust and confide in you. They feel that you're honest, and that you take responsibility of teaching people how to heal. You may also have to learn that not everyone is your friend. You may need to keep business as business, and not do therapy on your friends if they don't want to heal.

Because of the way you live your life, you have the sympathy of family members, but by the same token, you may be misunderstood.

37/1

People are drawn to your mind and your belief systems. People will see you as different, abstract. They want to know not only what it is that you think, but also why you think it. People will see you as very forthcoming, brutally honest, or dogmatic. People will urge you, or maybe even insist, that you write about your belief systems. Sometimes people will feel that you're being evasive. They may make the mistake of pushing you for information, causing you to lash out.

You also may have had a father who is very dogmatic in his belief systems, who did not allow much room for argument or even discussion.

38/11 or 38/2

People are drawn to your success and everything you accomplish. As a **38/11**, people see you as somewhat of a star performer, someone that they can turn to for inspiration. People may turn to you in need of money since they feel that you have plenty.

You must be very careful how you portray yourself if this number is in your name, because the perception is that you may have money to burn. And you must not lend money to needy people.

You present an interesting dichotomy to people, so some of them will see you as very dynamic and others may see you as very reticent

As this number is in the label or an Environmental Influence, you may find people pushing you into positions of leadership that you really don't want. Some people will definitely try to push you into the performing arts, or simply try to make you into a star. Also, you may present yourself as some kind of financial guru. People may feel that you have very good predictive powers when it comes to money. Others may urge you to be a motivational speaker.

39/3

People may be very critical of you, or think you're not very loyal in friendships. As a **39/3** there are going to be very diverse and maybe conflicting opinions about you. If you are in the public eye as a **39/3**, the press may be very hard on you. Your fans may adore you, or at times, be very upset with you. If you are in the artistic/creative world, or a performer, you keep people interested in you by reinventing yourself, even if this goes against the grain of who you are. Or people may simply see you as diverse.

People will be drawn to everything that you have to say. By the same token, they may dissect everything that you have to say as opposed to hearing the complete message. For the most part, people will

see you as someone that they are drawn to because you like to have fun. They will see you as social, playful, and maybe even flirtatious.

People will see you as innovative and inventive. You may come off as very popular and some people may feel that your social schedule is so full, they may back away, thinking that you don't have time for them. You may draw jealousy toward you. People may feel that you have a lot going for you, not on the material side, just rich in friendships. No matter what, people will have something to say about you. You are better off not retaliating, but just simply continuing to speak with compassion.

The Environmental Influence 40s

When the number 4 is in the Main Influence position, you are ruled by the concept of the box, a four-sided figure. A part of you, for better or worse, is contained. You prefer law and order. You are a linear or left-brain thinker. You have a strong need for the feeling of foundation and security, professionally, personally, and emotionally. You are ruled by rationalization, pragmatism, and have a conservative, traditional approach to life.

The number 4 in the Main Influence position controls, influences or even manipulates the number that's in the Minor Influence. The number 4 represents the controlling factor in your life.

40/22 or 40/4

People see you as extremely hardworking, and because of your work ethic people may get the impression that you're not fun loving, or just one-dimensional. Because you are so logical and left brained, you may come across as boring, as if you can't take a joke or don't understand a joke. Because you are perceived as hardworking, you may find yourself being assigned more work than those around you. Be very careful what you volunteer for, because people will give you all the work that you ask for and more.

27

You are seen as dependable and very conservative in your approach to things, but also very moral, ethical, and hardworking. Because the number 4 represents the system, the legal system or the corporate structure, you may be very influenced by, or succumb to, the influence of the system. Be very careful about being in the wrong place at the wrong time, or inviting legalities that could incarcerate you. In the day-to-day of your life you may simply find yourself constantly receiving pressure from all angles.

People do respect you, though, as someone who can overcome obstacles. They see you as a great lawmaker and respect your ability to organize on a very large level. People may try to push you into work that is heavily linear or angular, such as engineering, architecture, or accountanting.

41/5

Whenever the number 1 sits in the Minor Influence position in the Environmental Influence Number, you are especially affected by the Main Influence Number, in this case, the 4. With a 41/5 in your name, you're very susceptible to the system or the environment around you. It could corral you or trap you, causing you to feel that you are losing your freedom.

People see you as a paradox, or some kind of dichotomy. They see that you can or will succumb to the system and law and order, but also at the same time, they see you as someone with the 5 energy, which may be undependable, or scattered. People around you may try to inflict some kind of system upon you that they feel you need. They may show you how to clean up your desk, how to incorporate a system that helps you be more organized. Others may think you suffer from the messy desk syndrome, or they may see you as someone who has a way of doing things that they just can't figure out. You may know exactly where a file is within the piles on your desk. But other people don't, and it may frustrate them. So with 41/5 as your full name, it is important that you demonstrate to people that you are reliable and dependable, so they do not try to box you in.

On a personal level, the 41/5 means that you're susceptible to being manipulated. The 41/5 means the system controls the individual. Now when I say the system in this position, I do mean legalities. Marriage is a legal arrangement. So you must be very careful that you are not conned in any way, shape, or form when it comes to marriage. You could find yourself with someone who says they are going to be very supportive of you, when instead, you end up stuck in a situation which compromises your freedom. The solution to these Perils of Pauline predicaments is to structure yourself. That way the world will leave you alone, and you won't lose your freedom. You are very good at dealing with the public and have the ability of doing things in a nontraditional way in a traditional business. People will see you as versatile and talented. And if people leave you alone, you actually do much better.

42/6

People see you as family-oriented, a caretaker, and someone who has very traditional family qualities and standards. However, a prospective spouse or business partner will see you as needing control. This creates a certain amount of confusion on a partner's part because you are also seen as responsible, hardworking, loyal, honest, and sincere. You may need to give up a little bit of control and allow a partner to have more influence and more insights into situations. Because the number 4 represents structure, your children or people that work for you, may see you, at times, as somewhat of a task master, or a bit too strict. They may feel that you are so organized about the way things go in the family or the workplace that they may feel micro-managed.

Because we associate the concept of interior design or things that go on in the house physically with the number 6, the 4 on the 6 may mean that your style is somewhat rigid. People see you as having a traditional style. If you were an architect, you would come off as not very adventurous, but still a very good, solid person that does good, honest work. People feel that you are honest and trustworthy. This is a good number to have in the full name, because it will enhance your reputation.

People also see you as a healer or a fixer, someone they can turn to. People feel very comforted by you. Because of this, people may suggest to you that you become someone in the medical or psychological profession.

43/7

People see you as a loner, but they also see you as somewhat friendly. However, they may sense that you try to block them or hold them back. Some people will see you as logical, and some people will see you as more creative. It will depend on the group of people that you interact with. People will see you as evolved, and because this is where your label is, you do have an effect on people. They may see that you try to pull back so much that you're absolutely stubborn or resistant to others.

People will seek you out for your ability through reason to solve problems. People see you as not just wise, but also actually sage. They see your mind as having a very mechanical side, not just in wisdom but also in the ability to figure things out. People see you as curious, as not always saying what's on your mind. People know just by looking at you that the wheels are turning. People notice that when you are really focused on something, it's really hard to interrupt you. The funny thing is, people will try to interrupt you because they are so curious about you. You have a way of drawing people in. If you're looking up in the sky at something, they're going to look up too. People may try to push you into being a teacher because they see in you the ability to organize communication.

The biggest puzzle with any of the 7 personalities in the Environmental Influence is that you are mysterious and somewhat difficult to read. So, if your name contains any kind of 7, especially a 43/7, you will need to make sure that you do communicate who you are and what you want because the possibility of you being misunderstood is very possible and very likely.

44/8

People see you as a workaholic, a workhorse, and a pack mule. In terms of achievement, all of those terms are complimentary. However, people also figure you can shoulder most of the load and are only too happy to give it to you. If you are interested in a stock that has a 44/8 Environmental Influence Number (its name), you must also find out its Birth Path Number because the 44/8 Environmental Influence could fool you. It may seem like the stock is very solid and designed for long-term growth. But as with all Environmental Influence Numbers, that is only the stock's image.

If you are a 44/8 in the full name, people will see your leadership ability and they will trust you based on the 4s. They feel that you can really get the job done. People may also get the impression that you're too organized or too pragmatic about everything, and may see you as narrow-minded, with the attitude that there's only one way to get the job done. They may see you as a strict, unbending kind of a ruler that doesn't cooperate.

The double 4s indicate logic on both sides. People may interpret you as so narrow-minded that they actually may try to pull things on you. They may think you so logical and pragmatic that you will not catch any ulterior or dishonest motives of those around you. However, those who appreciate you will promote you from the bottom up. You have the ability to earn the respect of your superiors with this number, almost as if being promoted through the ranks of the military. Some may interpret you as being militaristic or having served in the military even if you did not. People see you literally as a good accountant or a good handler of money. They may try to push you into being a securities officer or a stockbroker, an investment broker, or something of that nature.

People also will see you as somewhat of a pressured type A personality. People may be concerned about you because you seem closed off. People may be inclined to ask you "are you okay?"

45/9

People will see you as somewhat indecisive, waiting for things to happen. People may feel that you're too soft or too nice, and the system will take advantage of you. When the 45/9 is in this position, job changes may occur unexpectedly. The company you work for could move you. You could be let go. You can be promoted. Whatever, you come off as gracious when these things do happen.

As a 45/9, the perception of you is that you may be fairly hardworking, but not exactly a go-getter. People are not quite sure where you stand. Although the 4 and 5 are at extremes in their approach to life, people may see you as somewhere in the middle, and almost vanilla and not very exciting. They see you as a good person, a person that's easy to be around, but not someone with the charisma that gets people excited.

If your name is a 45/9, you are almost at the mercy of what the system dictates for you because they see you as willing to wait for whatever happens. People also may feel that the way you live your life just simply doesn't make a lot of sense. People may find it hard to understand and wonder what your priorities are. People may feel that the work side of your life is very organized while your personal life is very haphazard.

For the most part, they will see you as tolerant and patient, and people will see you as someone with a shoulder to cry on. People may also get frustrated with what they perceive as your inability to make a decision.

46/1

People will see you as independent, strong, and responsible. They see you as a leader or a boss; someone who obeys the rules, but at the same time, has the ability to break new ground, especially on a business or entrepreneurial level. You are seen as very parental, in that you care for everything and everyone around you. Even though you are caring, people feel that ultimately you are going to take responsibility for whatever happens. Some people may view you as strict, but this attitude grows from care and concern, not from a desire to run over people. Many people will turn to you for your opinion. People see you as having a good sense of right and wrong and know that your advice will be to the point. Some see you as someone they can just simply lean on for support.

With the 46/1 in this position, a parent may want to lean on you a lot. You can find yourself supporting a family member later in life. Other people see you as very parental, and if you are a parent, they see you as a proud parent. However, you could be proud of your child to the point where you may come off as if no one else has ever had a child before.

132

47/11 or 47/2

In this position, which will most of the time show up as a 47/11, instead of a 2, you may draw to you very needy people that end up causing you problems. People may see you as codependent, which causes you to attract codependent people. People may be interested in the structure or the foundation of your beliefs, and at the same time see you as withdrawn or insecure, maybe even paranoid. Some people may try to take advantage of you, and others may pity you. Neither opinion serves you.

Those who see your organized analytical side see you as the perfect assistant, someone that they can dictate to and know will get the job done without putting up much of a fuss. On an esoteric level, you may find yourself on the receiving end of statements like, "Have we met before?" or "I feel as if I know you."

This isn't necessarily a come on, it's simply the vibration that they feel coming from you. Romantically speaking, you may find potential partners want to get serious with you very quickly, sometimes after 1 or 2 dates.

48/3

People will see you as creative and expressive and a bit of a show boater. They may see in you that you have a materialistic side whether it's in your clothes, your car, or your home. You may like to show off what you have. Despite all this, there is usually something that you like about them and that people like about you, which draws them to you. They will know that you have worked for and earned everything that you have. They see you as someone who does talk a lot, but as someone who speaks more about business than anything else.

You may be friendly with your clients, and some of your clients may be your friends. People may not exactly understand where they stand with you in your life. People will seek out your advice for the occupation that you're in, but nothing else. They see you as an expert in what you do, but not an overall open-minded thinker. Some people may feel a little nervous around you when they talk to you, as if they may feel that you have a price for everything, and that it may cost them to be in the presence of your company.

49/22 or 49/4

Those around you see you as someone who very slowly, very cautiously builds in steps. You are very focused on completing the task at hand, and at the same time they see you as someone who is building something that eventually will become very big and very beneficial. You must watch this because the 49 represents working for compassion. You may have a lot of people around you that continually invite you into charity organizations or working for nothing. You must maintain a balance in your life if this happens, because people see you as having the ability to apply a business end to charitable organizations.

In the full name in this position, the 49/22 means your mother had a huge influence on your ability to hold a job, and that may be good, bad, or indifferent. But overall, as people see you as a

49/22, they see that you have the ability to get the job done and that you bring the work to completion.

The Environmental Influence 50s

When the number **5** sits in the Main Influence position, you are ruled by change. You are illustrated by the pentagram, which means you can go five different directions at once. You will have a natural feeling of adaptability and may have an energy that keeps you on edge or even on the move. You may have to learn patience or to stand pat and simply leave things alone long enough to see what can happen without you constantly fueling the fire. You like to be a catalyst.

50/5

People will be very drawn to your charisma and may not necessarily know what they're drawn to. Your star quality has an impact on people, or at least their perception of your star quality. Throughout your life, you will be labeled as having potential. That is your reputation. On the other hand, those who are not taken in by your charisma will want concrete proof from you of your abilities. With your reputation, anything that you accomplish that is less than the best will be perceived that way.

People may see in you that you have a tendency to start a lot of things. They may have an impression with your dynamics that things are in action, but simply it may just be the movement of energy. If people ever feel that you're not dependable, your reputation will be ruined for a long time, and you will have to go to great lengths to undo that undependable reputation. Some people will see you as very magical, which is part of the charisma. Romantic interests will be very drawn to you, but they will be very frustrated by you when they feel that you're not going along with their program. Others may simply find you uncooperative or extremely noncommittal.

When it comes to jobs and occupations, people may not be sure exactly where to place you. You may be seen as overqualified. If your Birth Path Number does not coincide with having **50/5** in the Environmental Influence, the information that people will reflect back to you will completely baffle you, and may cause you to go through long stretches of time being unproductive because you may not be sure exactly what people are asking of you. However, know that people believe that you have the ability to do anything.

Because the number **5** represents movement, there's a certain amount of athletic ability that comes into **5**s. For instance, if you were a professional baseball player, your manager or coach may play you in several different positions, because he believes you are adaptable enough to do that. But this will cause you to feel somewhat displaced or "out of position." This can apply to any kind of job.

51/6

You are seen as paternal and domestic. But you are also somewhat confusing to people. Therefore, people try to change you and make you into something that they feel you should become.

This is the most imposing Environmental Influence Number because the people in your environment do have a major impact on you. People will want to put responsibility on you or may blame you for things. You can be seen as the black sheep of the family. People may tell you many times in your life to "grow up."

Now, there is another side to this. Some people may see you as so responsible that they'll let you do things yourself. They may not lend assistance. They'll see you as doing what you do very well. They will feel that you can handle things on your own. So, it you are married and have **51/6** in the Environmental position, you may have a spouse who lets you handle all the family responsibilities. You may have to speak up if the burden is too much.

People who are very intrigued with your style will insist that you go into some form of design, such as home, interior, or clothing. Some people, even if it's casually, may seek out what they perceive in you as a healing touch. They may just want you to rub their shoulders and neck, but be careful that you don't rub people the wrong way.

52/7

People will definitely see you as a loner. But many times they will see you as cranky. They may feel that when they ask you a question they are bothering you. People get the perception that you're moody, that your mind is always at work. Therefore, people get the feeling that you want to be alone and that you're happier in your solitude.

People see that you think differently, and that you are very wise. But people feel that you get upset or bothered if they ask a question that is mundane or obvious. People see that you have alternative beliefs in philosophy and will be very drawn to your opinion.

On an intimate or romantic level, people see you as downright fickle and become afraid to get involved with you because you have a "love 'em and leave 'em reputation." You may draw to you people that wish to contest your belief system. Some people may see you as just plain unstable and feel your beliefs are radical. Whether they are or not isn't important. This is simply the perception of you.

Your best friends will turn out to be other very intelligent people, because they will want to be able to discuss high philosophy with you. They feel you have the capacity to see things on that level.

53/8

People see you as a leader, but with an unorthodox style. People feel very affected by you and feel your sense of motivation or your ability to motivate them. People feel very inspired by you. They see you as successful, and people may want to be like you. People see you as generous and may feel that you have money to spare. They may seek you out for loans or monetary gifts. They may feel that due to your success they should seek your advice on handling money issues or money problems, or simply how to invest.

You are also seen as a leader that brings change for the good of the people. So, if you are an employer, people will like working for you. But be careful that you do not allow your employees to become too familiar with your personal life. It could cause them to feel lax or feel that you are just one of the guys.

54/9

People read you in two different ways. They will see you as changeable, but also having a certain amount of structure in your life. At times, they will see you as very patient, and wanting to stir things up. At other times, they see you as overly passive, and not being aggressive enough. People recognize your compassionate side. They also see that the changes you make are simply to reform the structure that exists, not to make a whole new structure. This allows people to feel comfortable in working with you. They sense that you are going to take a good situation and make it better. People have a sense that you care.

55/1

People see you as very independent and very changeable. Some people see you as a wild stallion or a bucking bronco that they'd like to tame or corral. A lot of people will see you as your own worst enemy. Some people may want to grab you by the ears and say, "Would you just listen?" They see you as not just independent, but unable to take orders or listen to reason. People will tell you how much potential you have and may get upset with you for not living up to that potential.

You definitely appear impatient, impetuous, wanting everything yesterday. In fact, some people will read your impatient side as you just being a nudge. Others may see you as having a devil-may-care attitude. But because you are somewhat fearless, you may do things that they won't, and people will enlist your services for such activities. Some people may feel that you have a lot of grievances, but that your grievances are balanced and justified, that you're a crusader for a cause. So remember, some people like crusaders and some don't.

If you allow yourself to be pulled into the world of writing and journalism, people will feel that you take a lot of liberties or may not respect boundaries, so anything that you do publicly must protect your reputation, and the reputation of others.

On the romantic side, people will be very drawn to you, but they may not take you very seriously. They see you as fun and not a lot more. But people may see you as having the energy to be the life of the party or have the charisma to light up the room.

56/11 or 56/2

People will see you as somewhat elusive, noncommittal, and highly sensitive, maybe even too sensitive. They may feel that the slightest thing, the slightest upset, or even a movie makes you cry. Your family may see you as disruptive, or as the problem causer. We talked so many

times about people being problem solvers. The perception of you is that you're disruptive.

Ultimately, those around you will see the change that you bring and the disruption for the better. Once you do move away, the family will appreciate you more. People will remark in a positive way about your personal style. They may see you as being somewhat withdrawn or shy but they also sense that you are precognitive. People will feel inspired by you, more by your actions and not by your words. In this position, people will feel that there is a very silent star quality in you where people might try to pull you into some form of the entertainment business.

Be careful about drawing a partner or a marital partner who moves a lot, maybe due to job or maybe because of the military. You can be drawn into a multitude of moves.

57/3

People will see you as a communicator, a teacher, someone with a message to bring. They may feel at times that you may be talking above them. They can't always grasp exactly what you're trying to say, or people may feel somewhat astounded by what you have to say. They feel that you may be saying things, bringing messages, or talking about things that other people wouldn't dare to say, or venture into. People see you as some kind of reformist. At the same time, people may feel that you don't know exactly what you're talking about.

You may invite people into your life who are very skeptical or simply don't want to hear what you have to say. Some people may feel that what you communicate based on your belief system is somewhat troublesome. At the same time, people are left feeling affected by the message that you bring. Because of the perception of your alternative beliefs, you must be careful that you're not perceived as too outlandish. People may think you're nuts, creating stories, or even a liar.

You will draw the right friends to you, so they nurture your mind, and your mind nurtures them. You must be careful that you are not drawn into relationships with people that belong to extreme right-wing organizations, cults, or fanatical groups. People will see you as somewhat mysterious, or mystical. At some point, you may be considered somewhat of a master teacher, and someone who has a great effect on people.

140

58/22 or 58/4

People will see you as powerful, and changing the system as it is. Some people may see you as all about big business and not looking out for the little guy. But people will model themselves after you, even though they may not admit it openly. They may want to have a business that's like yours. If this is the name of a company, people will be very drawn to doing business with it. If it's a publicly traded company, people will want to invest in it. Some people will see this, whether it's an individual or a company, as a money train to success, and they will want to climb aboard. If you are looking to name a business, this is a great name to have, because the **58/22** or **58/4** communicates success and growth.

59/5

People see you as changeable and very impatient. They see you as multitalented and having a lot of irons in the fire. But somehow they have the confidence that you can get the job done. As they see you as changeable, they also see you as compassionate. They see that you are into transformation as opposed to rapid dynamic change. They see you as someone who brings change for a good cause that benefits human kind. They will see you as someone who makes up the rules of the game as it is being played. This also means that they see you as adaptable.

chapter 6

The Conscious Desire Number

realizations of youth

As a child, what did you want to be when you grew up? An astronaut? Actress? Fireman? Doctor? Teacher? Writer? Mother? Musician? Someone of great wealth? Someone of great beauty or dignity? A world traveler?

Whether or not you actually lived out that childhood wish list, think about it again. Did you want to be an astronaut because it was adventurous, involving travel and exploration; an actress because you were expressive or craved the spotlight; a fireman because you wanted to be a hero; or a doctor because you wanted to help people?

Our childhood images of ourselves may have been whimsical, but also quite clear, unclouded by cultural indoctrination. Childhood instincts are simplistic, but often-truthful expressions of what we know we want out of life. These are desires that are obvious and on the surface. No need to dig deep into our psyches on this one. We know what we want and we've always known we wanted it. That's why we call this number The Conscious Desire. Desire is one of the by products of the consciousness. It is something in the forefront of our mind. It's something we know we want.

newmerology

The Conscious Desire Number, calculated from the vowels of the full name, has three defining qualities:

➤ It represents what you consciously want and have known that you wanted since early in life.

➤ It represents how we wish to be perceived by others.

➤ It reveals shortcomings that we acknowledge and wish to overcome so we can get what we want.

So tell me what you want, what you really really want. I'll tell you what I want what I really really want. I want to . . . I want to . . .

The Spice Girls, whose music was so resolutely aimed at the pubescent set, were onto something. Conscious Desire represents realizations about ourselves that we had in youth regarding the situations, people, objects, and events that we feel will make us happy. You've all heard people say, "It was my childhood desire" to: drive a sports car, own a horse, raise a big family, travel the world, work as a nurse, paint, or perform music. Sometimes, we don't fulfill our Conscious Desire Number until later in life. But we first had the yearnings in childhood. The Conscious Desire Number represents the first things in life that we seek.

Celebrity Example
Child Stars

The most obvious examples of the Conscious Desire at work and fulfilled are the child stars of Hollywood. Of course, there are many reasons why very young people may want to express themselves on stage or screen. But one big reason is to be a star. So it is with two very notable child stars: Britney Spears and Gary Coleman. Both have a Conscious Desire of **17/8**, which is the star number in Newmerology.

142

Of course, as with all things from childhood, that early desire may fade and get replaced with adult goals as maturity sets in. This means that when people have a **17/8** as a Conscious Desire, it is very easy for their star to fade. They hit young and it does not continue into maturity unless other numbers in the Numerological Realm support it. That happened with Gary Coleman. We shall see how long Britney Spears lasts.

identifying shortcomings to attain our desires

The Conscious Desire holds the intention to achieve your wish: "I intend to be famous"; "I intend to have a wonderful relationship." From that intention comes the realization of our shortcomings—what you need to learn or do for your earliest wishes to manifest in your lives. Through the Conscious Desire Number, you recognize the obstacles you need to overcome to fulfill our desires.

If your Conscious Desire Number is an **8** that means at an early age you realized you wanted to make a lot of money. However, the Conscious Desire Number of **8** also indicates that you need to learn to manage money in order to have more of it.

As a mature adult, you may have already realized your Conscious Desire, and worked on your shortcomings. If you are younger, your Conscious Desire Number can reinforce what your inclinations have been telling you all along.

One more aspect of the Conscious Desire is that it expresses how you want to be perceived by others. There's something about this number that undoes the misidentity that is often a consequence of the full name.

parenting your child's conscious desire

If you are a parent, your children's Conscious Desire Number can help you guide behavior and indicate where they may need help. For instance, a Conscious Desire Number of **35/8** may want money, but spend it too freely when it is around. As a parent, you could set up a savings program

newmerology

that will teach your child about managing money and watching it grow. Or you could simply ferret it away and hand it over when it is time for college.

The Conscious Desire Number also can raise a red flag for parents. The number reveals an area of life where a child could seek instant gratification and end up making big mistakes. For instance, if the Conscious Desire Number is a 6 or a 2, the child could be dreamy-eyed about marriage and children and try to satisfy that desire at a young age. The Conscious Desire is an area where a child needs guidance. It reveals both wants and shortcomings.

the conscious desire number as an adult

Even though it dawned on you as a child, The Conscious Desire remains with you your whole life. Let's say your Conscious Desire Number is a 30/3. You've always had this itch to perform. You catch yourself saying things like," I always wanted to be on stage." But somehow you ended up in a middle management job. Knowing the meaning of your Conscious Desire Number tells you that the call of the lights and camera is more than just a fantasy. It is a legitimate part of your deepest desires. If nothing else, you may want to join a theater, a musical group, or take acting lessons to satisfy that yearning.

Fulfilling your Conscious Desire makes you happy. When a person's authentic cravings are revealed, release and inner validation follow.

Celebrity Example
Donald Trump

Donald Trump's Birth Path Number is a 40/22. This is someone who builds big things, works hard, and can handle a lot of pressure. His Environmental Influence Number is 50/5, which means he is often seen as reckless and causes changes for the sake of change. His Conscious Desire is 16/7. From the time he was young he wanted to cause change in real estate. His desire is symbolized by the

tower and is his signature piece of real estate—the Trump Tower. By the way, his Missing Number is a **2**, meaning that close relationships can undo him. We'll get into those later.

finding the conscious desire number

10+15+2= 27/9

The Conscious Desire Number is found by adding all the vowels of your full name, as found on your birth certificate. If you have already computed your Environmental Influence Number, look to the Compound Number of the vowels. That is your Conscious Desire Number. If you just want to figure out yours or someone else's Conscious Desire Number, follow these steps:

➤ Add the numerical values of all the vowels of each name separately.

➤ Take the sum of each name and add them together.

➤ Assuming you reach a double-digit number, that is the Compound Number.

➤ Add the digits of the Compound Number to get your Base Number.

The Numerical Values of the Alphabet are:

1	2	3	4	5	6	7	8	9
A	B	C	D	E	F	G	H	I
J	K	L	M	N	O	P	Q	R
S	T	U	V	W	X	Y	Z	

newmerology

step one: attach a numerical value to the vowels of each name

The vowels are A, E, I, O, U. (Y can be a vowel or a consonant).
When Y is used as a vowel, it is counted as a vowel. *Examples:* Mary, Barry

Rule to Remember: If the Y follows a vowel, it is not a vowel. It becomes a consonant. Example: Carey. The "y" is essentially silent because it duplicates the sound of the "e." In such cases the "y" should be calculated as a consonant.

step two: add the vowels and arrive at a vowel sum for each name separately; take the numerical sum of each name and reduce it to one digit

If it comes out to 11 or 22, however, leave it

Example #1

G e o r g e	L o u i s	S m i t h
e + o + e	o + u + i	i
5 + 6 + 5 = 16	6 + 3 + 9 = 18	9
1 + 6 = 7	1 + 8 = 9	
(7)	(9)	(9)

step three: add the sums of each name

Assuming the outcome is a double-digit,
it will serve as the Compound Number (top number).

$$7 + 9 + 9 = 25$$

The Compound Number is **25**

step four: reduce the Compound Number to find the Base Number

If it comes out to 11 or 22, leave it.

$$2 + 5 = 7$$

The Base Number is 7

The Conscious Desire Number is $25/7$

The 11, 22 Exceptions

Master Challenge Numbers, 11 or 22, *must* be allowed to accurately surface.

Rule to Remember: When you arrive at an 11 or 22 sum in any of the individual names, let it stand. Do not reduce. When the possibility appears that a Master Challenge Number might come up as the outcome (you end up with a 2 or a 4), you have to go back into the individual name numbers and reduce any 11 or 22 sums to a 2 or a 4, to see if it alters the outcome into a Master Number.

Example #2
Lowell George Elliott

step one: attach a numerical value to the vowels of each name

Lowell	George	Elliott
o + e	e + o + e	e + i + o
6 + 5	5 + 6 + 5	5 + 9 + 6

147

newmerology

step two: add the vowels and arrive at a vowel sum for each name separately

Take the numerical sum of the each name and reduce it to one digit.
If it comes out to 11 or 22, however, leave it.

L o w e l l	G e o r g e	E l l i o t t
o + e	e + o + e	e + i + o
6 + 5 = 11	5 + 6 + 5 = 16	5 + 9 + 6 = 20
	1 + 6 = 7	2 + 0 = 2
(11)	(7)	(2)

step three: add the sums of each name

Assuming the outcome is a double-digit
it will serve as the Compound Number (top number).

$$11 + 7 + 2 = 20$$

step four: reduce the 11 in the individual name to 2

L o w e l l	G e o r g e	E l l i o t t
o + e	e + o + e	e + i + o
6 + 5 = 11	5 + 6 + 5 = 16	5 + 9 + 6 = 20
1 + 1 = 2	1 + 6 = 7	2 + 0 = 2
(2)	(7)	(2)

148

step five: add the sums of each name

Assuming the outcome is a double-digit,
it will serve as the Compound Number (top number).

$$2 + 7 + 2 = 11$$

step six: because the Compound Number is an 11, we leave it

The Conscious Desire Number is 11

Note: In regards to Conscious Desire Numbers, there are rarely any numbers found above the 20s because it would take too many letters in a name. On few occasions I have seen higher numbers in names, such as Asian names, which contain a large presence of consonants. These two regularly come up as single-digits, or teens through 20s, stopping at 29. Companies wanting to find information for investing usually will look to the Birth Path or Personal Year Numbers to see how their cycles are running.

compound number in relation to conscious desire

The Conscious Desire 10s

The Main Influence Number dictates the theme of the Compound Number and strongly colors the entire triad of numbers, meaning the entire identity and character.

When the Main Influence Number is a 1, this puts emphasis on the self. This gives the person more control in situations. For individuals with a number 1 as the Main Influence, it is often better for them to own their own business. They tend to take a direct approach and their opinion is important to them. They make good attorneys and good writers.

10/1

You have a desire for individuality. You want to use creative power, own a business, or something that has your label. You desire to be independent and more individualistic and want to develop more insights into self. You need to develop more will power and recognize any imbalances between ego and insecurities. You have a desire for comfort and a strong male energy.

11/2

You need to learn the difference between self-empowerment and draining yourself. You desire to be in the media or to gain attention. You need to overcome your shy side so you can become the inspirational leader that you know you can be. You possess a deep interest in the psychic world. You need to learn to self-empower and overcome the inner conflict between giving to others or yourself.

12/3

You want a partner who is also a friend. You learn at an early age that every time you leap without consideration into relationships, you get into trouble. You want a balanced amount of male and female friends. You want a partner that can be supportive of you because you may have had a father that was too strong or a mother that was too passive. Because of a need for approval, you may try to sway your friends too much. Because the number 3 represents communication, be careful that you do not fish for or solicit compliments from people. You wish to use your voice so you can be heard. You have pure creative abilities that you wish to express.

13/4

You want to be seen as fair to people so you can gain popularity. It is important to you to be able to use your voice, especially to influence people and to take leadership. There is a desire to develop and use your artistic talents as your form of work as opposed to them being a hobby. You want to keep a few people as close friends that you can count on and vice versa. You want people to come to you to solve problems.

14/5

You have a desire to work for yourself or create your own structure so you can come and go as you please. You'll recognize that you can be scattered and can cause changes in your life haphazardly. Thus, you want to develop a system of organization that keeps you from sabotaging all of your hard work. You're willing to work hard in early life so you can travel later on. Your desire for movement translates directly into the athletic arena and you may play several sports. You'll want to develop a patience level that allows you to grow and see the fruits of your labor. You need to be more patient with yourself and others.

15/6

You want to be married and have a family, but you recognized dysfunction as a child in the family of origin. You know that it's better that you marry later in life or not at all. You may move a lot in trying to find the perfect home. You have an interest in anything that involves houses or homes, especially anything in design or architecture. You want people to trust you and see you as responsible. You want to be able to influence people to make the changes necessary to get the appreciation they deserve.

152

16/7

You desire to quiet your mind and, at a young age, you recognize the need for rest, relaxation, and meditation. Because you discover your belief systems early in life, you understand that the more you get inside your head, the more energized you are. At a young age, you may already find that you resist going to a traditional church or following a particular religion. At the same time, you have an interest in philosophy and theology from a more spiritual angle. Since this is also the area of how you wish to be perceived, and any shortcomings that you feel that you want to overcome, you have a tendency in youth to be somewhat of a know it all. This needs to be corrected or else it will carry all the way through adulthood. If you are a parent, and this number comes up in the Conscious Desire area of your child's name, you need to enhance the child's belief system without feeding the ego. This child will have a finger in your face telling you how it is. As a parent, sometimes you need to take a moment and recognize that children come in naturally evolved, fresh from the other side. Just don't allow the child to be bossy. The child may have a bit of anger that needs to be dispelled or the child may know how to manipulate the family. Make sure that this child does not become a con artist or woman. Now if you are an adult and you look back and see this in your own name, you will know what I'm talking about here because you have great power and influence over people, and it's something that you've always wanted.

You've always wanted to tell people how it is and how you feel about the world. You may even have extreme beliefs, such as opinions about UFOs. You may desire to visit interesting, mysterious places, such as the Bermuda Triangle, Stonehenge, and the Pyramids. You're not going to be the kind of person that will want to go lie on a beach and waste time, even though unplugging is the best thing for you. However, you will go somewhere where you can study and gather information. Any place you go, even if it's just a regular vacation, you are likely to keep a journal of your days and make notes about whatever it is you've seen. At times you will just have a desire to be left alone. The concept of marriage and family appeals to you, but you must accept at the same time that you must be active in the family. You could be the invisible or ghostly parent, and instead of nurturing a child, you may be more admonishing or come off as more of a guidance counselor. You need to develop a sense of warmth, so that when you tell people something that really is for their own good, you express your thoughts with compassion rather than with an air of "I told you so." You need to understand that sometimes all people need is a hug. Your ability to have a great affect on people comes at a young age. Couple that ability with the great wisdom that you also possess.

17/8

You have a desire to be creative in the pure sense and to explore the depths of your mind. You're interested in exploring your spiritual metaphysical sides. You're interested in using the occult, meaning something hidden or secret, not black magic. You use deep methods to become successful. But because your tendency to study the deep mysteries of life is realized in youth, you must make sure that whatever you do comes from the light. Do not allow yourself to get caught up into the concept of trying to work spells or magic. Do not allow yourself to be disillusioned by " the dark side" as in *Star Wars*. Do not be drawn in by the ego's desire for power.

Simply allow yourself to reach within to find the strength to be successful. You have a desire to be the star—to be unique, where you can stand-alone and be successful. You are not interested in copying anyone, but you know from a young age that you want to attain a level of success that will have an influence or be seen for years to come. So the possibility of becoming a child star is great. But as a child, you have to learn and understand the concept of money and power, which is a little much to ask of a child. If any of the money you earn as a child goes awry, it could create a pattern of money problems all through your adult life. Even as a child, you must understand the value and appreciation of material things.

You need to understand that just because you may have done something to attain money, doesn't mean that you should abuse that privilege or power or feel that you are above everyone else because of your level of attainment. If you use this energy correctly, you could parlay your early successes all through life. As you get older, you will learn that maintaining a balance between your spiritual and material side will help you to get to where you want to be. Your desire to do big things will exist throughout your life. By increasing your spiritual awareness, material gain will follow. For you, it is purely a matter of trust or blind faith that all will go well. One last note: In your desire for notoriety, you must make sure that you keep the drama in your life on the stage. You must be careful that you do not become a tabloid target.

18/9

From a young age, you want to build a big business that helps people. You want to put your name and your label on some venture that has a lasting effect. You want people to see you as patient and tolerant and glad you want to build a business. You want to be able to help other people to be successful too. In early life, you desire to teach, be a counselor, or be a good consultant. You also recognize that you may mishandle money. You can actually be so generous with it that you help other people before you help yourself. You must be balanced in your dealings with money.

19/1

You want to own your own business, do something individualist or independent that helps you to feel complete. You also need to teach yourself compassion toward others, while letting go of any harshness or cynicism. You need to learn how to unload so that unnecessary anger does not get in the way of you completely loving yourself or loving others.

The Conscious Desire 20s

When the number 2 is in the Main Influence position, the number is ruled by emotions, a partnership, or some issue or theme of the mother. Remember, before we have an intimate relationship or marriage, our emotional partner is our mother or representing the feminine energy. Partnership can also represent business. When you have a 2 as the Main Influence, you must take great care in dealing with business and money. Emotions can get involved where emotions shouldn't be.

20/2

Since this is the area of the realizations of youth, you must be careful that you do not go through the early part of your life looking for that ultimate partner. You could find yourself in and out of relationships, wasting time, wasting energy, and getting hurt if the thrust of your desires becomes all about relationship and emotional fulfillment. If you place too much emphasis on relationships at an early age, you will find yourself disappointed. Take a good look at your relationship with your mother and make sure, especially if you're a man, that you do not "marry your mother." You will need to take the time to see if your spouse embodies your mother's attributes. You may have a strong desire to assist people and to be of help because you want to please people. You also may have a desire to play a musical instrument or take dance lessons. You could also have a desire for feminine energy that becomes your own. Even if you're a man, you may find yourself out of balance and looking for your own feminine energy. This can go as far as to exploring and discovering homosexual tendencies. As a woman with this number, your desires may lead to being too subservient in your relationships.

21/3

From a young age, you wanted to have a supportive partner. You learned repeatedly, maybe even with bitter lessons, that your partner must be someone who is a friend first, and then becomes a romantic interest. Every time you have put on the rose-colored glasses and fall head over heels in love, you get burned. At a young age, you noticed that you must develop friendships with members of the opposite sex and that not every member of the opposite sex is a potential love interest. Respect and value your friends and let romance be romance. This realization may be confusing to you, for ultimately, it is a friend who becomes a great partner for you. Allow that person to make the transition from friendship to lover. Do not look for it or try to make it happen. At a young age, you realized you needed to learn to overcome your shy side and speak your mind. You have a desire to use your voice in a musical, lyrical, or poetic way, and a desire to be in harmony with yourself.

22/22 or 22/4

It is rare that the 22 would show up in this position, but if it does, it simply means that you want to overcome issues with the mother, or conflicts with the mother that may be holding you back. As a woman, you decided at a young age to go for career advancement and put off family issues and

marriage until later. There is also a desire from a young age to want to do big things that help give back in either a charitable or a philanthropic way.

23/5

You want to balance your intimate relationships and your friendships. Or, you may simply desire to be in a nontraditional or off the beaten path business that deals with people management and staying behind the scenes.

24/6

You want a partner who is supportive without being controlling. You have a strong desire to be a parent, but you also know that you will not settle for just anyone, even though your emotional desires are strong. You recognize at a young age that you are the neighborhood or the high school therapist and that your friends will turn to you to help solve their emotional problems or issues. At a young age, you know that you must keep your emotions and your logic separate and not let one influence the other. Be careful about getting emotionally involved with someone at work. You could have patterns at a young age that create this.

25/7

You will realize at a young age that you were interested in traveling to places of metaphysical interest. You realize that you have a great need to quiet your mind through simple rest, relaxation, or even meditation. You know from a young age that you may be moody and you seek the proper way to control these mood swings. Your desire to expand your mind is great, but you prefer to do it in private. You look for a partner who has an expanded mind and that is not judgmental. You also realize at a young age that you are sensitive to criticism.

26/8

You may be looking for a partner who is going to pay the bills, or you may leave yourself susceptible to just wanting a partner who will manage the funds. You may realize at a young age that your desire to be married and have children is strong, and therefore, you feel that abundance in your life is through love and the relationships of those who are close to you. You may have a desire to collect or obtain collectibles, such as antiques or things that have an emotional and material value. Your interest in making money will come at a young age.

27/9 √

You know from a young age that you are different and need a partner who thinks differently. You want to learn and feel compassion and want people to see you as tolerant, patient, and compassionate. You have an interest in the arts that is somewhat mysterious and different.

28/1

At a young age, you had an individualistic approach. Emotions and the concept of power influence you greatly, and you must keep perspective on power, and not let it go to your head. You have a talent for writing in a musical or a lyrical way, and prefer to be somewhat of a creative force, or a pacesetter in your field of creativity.

29/11 or 29/2

You want a partner who is compassionate. Because this is a realization of youth, you may have felt that your mother was not caring enough, or, to the other extreme, that she was somewhat smothering. You have a desire to be of service to people, although you may take a passive role in any undertaking or endeavor. In any situation, you want to be perceived as helpful and assisting. If your other numbers in the numerological realm indicate over-aggressiveness or if you are over-endowed with money numbers, you may consciously try to present yourself as a "nice guy." You want to get over emotional issues and resolve them so you can become a good partner.

chapter 7

The Subconscious Motivation Number

realizations of maturity:
what's your life's dream?

The Subconscious Motivation is the number of latency—latent talents, latent motivations, and latent desires. "Better latent than never." It is the number of the voice you hear as you drift into the alpha state before sleep, while in the depths of meditation, sitting quietly (if that ever happens), and daydreaming. It is the flicker of a thought, an image, an impression, and an "I want" that flits by too quickly to identify it. If the Subconscious Motivation has a parallel in nature, it is like trying to catch a butterfly in the dark. In a David Lynch movie, it would be the scene where the dwarf whispers the answer to a mystery in the hero's ear during a dream.

When you realize your Subconscious Motivation, it is like waking from that dream and coming into reality. For this is the number of your deepest longings, buried in the recesses of the psyche. The Subconscious Motivation Number identifies those longings, digs them up, and brings them to the surface, so they can be recognized, honored, and transformed into an aspect of the conscious mind and acted upon with intent.

newmerology

Realization of our Subconscious Motivation comes to you in maturity, after the age of 35 or 40. It is most often delayed because a certain amount of life experience is necessary before you realize that the goals and wishes of the Conscious Desire do not fully satisfy you.

With the Subconscious Motivation Number, you realize that there is more—more to do, more you want, and more you can offer. By the time you understand the Subconscious Motivation Number, you have the experience that enables you to go after your heart's most profound impulse.

The Subconscious Motivation is the number of your dreams, but, in the long run, it is the number of your ultimate reality. For few things bring greater satisfaction than to align with your dreams. In doing so, you feel most fully alive.

the backseat driver revealed

The Subconscious Motivation Number reveals what drives your behavior, usually from the backseat of your psyche. You may not be aware of your Subconscious Motivation until later, but it is active— usually *very* active—your whole life, demanding expression and operating in your life unbeknownst to you, sometimes in inappropriate ways. For those 35 and older, this number can result in one of those "Ah ha" moments where you finally understand your past decisions or why you have chased one goal only to suddenly switch to another. If your Subconscious Motivation is a 3, the number of personal expression, you may invite all kinds of personal drama into your life until you figure out you need an outlet that allows you to take center stage. If your Subconscious Motivation Number is a 5, you may find yourself jumping from job to job, relationship to relationship until you finally figure out that you want to be in business for yourself or with a mate who is equally independent and freedom loving.

An undiscovered Subconscious Motivation is often the culprit behind the "midlife crisis." Once the Subconscious Motivation does comes to light, once you acknowledge and decide to do something about it, even in the smallest way, it loses its subterranean grip on you. Its recognition gives it a new home in the conscious mind and may replace the Conscious Desire in your life. After all, what you want as a child is not what you necessarily want as an adult.

The Subconscious Motivation opens the door to the true-life purpose. You may or may not immediately act on it once you realize it. You will take a mature approach to it, inching towards it in measured ways. But once the Subconscious Desire rises to the surface—and it will—it can profoundly change your life and allow you to truly blossom.

Some people realize their Subconscious Motivation earlier than others, especially when the Subconscious Motivation Number matches one of the other key aspects in the Newmerological Realm—either the Birth Path Number or the Conscious Desire Number. When this happens, the individual gains a leg up in life. By the way, the Subconscious Desire Number cannot match the Environmental Influence Number. It is a mathematical impossibility.

when the subconscious motivation and birth path match

The individual can embrace the full range of talents at a young age. Here, the dream is one-in-the-same as the self; the inner motivation aligns with the self-identity. No expanse of time or years of experience must pass to recognize the highest dream. The Dream is the same as the self and therefore immediately apparent.

Celebrity Example
Robert Edward (Ted) Turner

His Birth Path and Subconscious Motivation are both **51/6**, which stands for the ability to change the self and take on responsibility. He knew innately that the more he changed himself and the more he grew, the more responsibility he could take on.

Because his Birth Path and Subconscious Motivation are aligned, Turner had a head start as to where his life was going to go. He didn't have to wait to come to a realization.

newmerology

when subconscious motivation and conscious desire match

This creates the potential to achieve a dream early in life. The earliest wants and deepest inner drive coincide, eliminating the push-pull between the Conscious and Subconscious. Desires and motives are in agreement. These individuals discover a deeper part of themselves earlier in life.

Keep in mind that the Subconscious Motivation does not necessarily apply to the career. If your Subconscious Motivation is a 9, you may come to realize that you are very empathetic to people's pain and experience a sense of well-being and fulfillment through volunteer work. If it is a 7, you may come to decide on a spiritual path or pursue meditation.

Knowing your Subconscious Motivation helps you gain control over your life, because, in fact, you gain control over your behavior. For those in their 20s, this number is especially important. Knowing your deepest dream ahead of time affords a distinct advantage over its own mastery and unlocks a key to an individual's most vital goals.

For those 35 and older, this number offers great insight on how to proceed into the future unencumbered by the constraint of the unconscious past. It can inspire you to take action toward true fulfillment. The Subconscious Motivation Number steers you into the healthiest direction for future happiness. And, it offers more fun in the process.

finding the subconscious motivation number

The Subconscious Motivation Number is found by adding all the consonants of your full name, as found on your birth certificate. If you have already computed your Environmental Influence Number, look to the Compound Number of the consonants. That is your Subconscious Motivation Number. If you just want to figure out yours or someone else's Subconscious Motivation Number, follow these steps:

164

➤ Add the numerical values of all the consonants of each name separately.

➤ Take the sum of each name and add them together.

➤ Assuming you reach a double-digit number, that is the Compound Number.

➤ Add the digits of the Compound Number to get your Base Number.

The Numerical Values of the Alphabet are:

1	2	3	4	5	6	7	8	9
A	B	C	D	E	F	G	H	I
J	K	L	M	N	O	P	Q	R
S	T	U	V	W	X	Y	Z	

step one: attach a numerical value to the consonants of each name

Rule to Remember: If a Y follows a vowel, it is not a vowel. It becomes a consonant. Example: Carey. The "y" is essentially silent because it duplicates the sound of the "e." In such cases the "y" should be calculated as a consonant.

12   +   13 + 28 =

step two: add the consonants and arrive at a sum for each name separately; reduce it to one digit; if it comes out to 11 or 22, however, leave it

G e o r g e
g + r + g
7 + 9 + 7 = 23
2 + 3 = 5
(5)
3

L o u i s
l + s
3 + 1 = 4
(4)
4

S m i t h
s + m + t + h
1 + 4 + 2 + 8 = 15
1 + 5 = 6
(6)
10 = 1+0=1
17/8

newmerology

step three: add the numerical sums of the each name

Assuming the outcome is a double-digit,
it will serve as the Compound Number (top number).

$$5 + 4 + 6 = 15$$
The Compound Number is 15

step four: reduce the Compound Number to find the Base Number

If it is an 11 or 22, leave it.

$$1 + 5 = 6$$
The Base Number is 6
The Subconscious Motivation Number is 15/6

The 11, 22 Exceptions

Master Challenge Numbers, 11 or 22, *must* be allowed to accurately surface.

Rule to Remember: When you arrive at an 11 or 22 sum in any of the individual names, let it stand. Do not reduce. When the possibility appears that a Master Challenge Number might come up as the outcome (you end up with a 2 or a 4), you have to go back into the individual name numbers and reduce any 11 or 22 sums to a 2 or a 4 in order to see if it alters the outcome into a Master Number.

step one: attach a numerical value to the consonants of each name

S h a k i r a	I s a b e l	M e b a r a k	R i p o l l
s + h + k + r	s + b + l	m + b + r + k	r + p + l + l
1 + 8 + 2 + 9	1 + 2 + 3	4 + 2 + 9 + 2	9 + 7 + 3 + 3

step two: add the consonants and arrive at a sum for each name separately; reduce it to one digit

If it comes out to 11 or 22, leave it.

S h a k i r a	I s a b e l	M e b a r a k	R i p o l l
s + h + k + r	s + b + l	m + b + r + k	r + p + l + l
1 + 8 + 2 + 9 = 20	1 + 2 + 3 = 6	4 + 2 + 9 + 2 = 18	9 + 7 + 3 + 3 = 16
2 + 0 = 2		1 + 8 = 9	1 + 6 = 7
(20)	(6)	(9)	(7)

step three: add the numerical sums of each name

Assuming the outcome is a double-digit,
it will serve as the Compound Number (top number).

$$2 + 6 + 8 + 22 = 38$$

The Compound Number is 38

step four: reduce the Compound Number to find the Base Number

If it is an 11 or 22, leave it.

$$3 + 8 = 11$$

The Base Number is 11

The Subconscious Motivation Number is 38/11

Note: In regards to Subconscious Motivation Numbers, there are rarely any numbers found above the 20s because it would take too many letters in a name. On few occasions I have seen higher numbers, such as Asian names, which contain a large presence of consonants. These two regularly come up as single-digits, or teens through 20s, stopping at 29. Companies wanting to find information for investing usually will look to the Birth Path or Personal Year Numbers to see how their cycles are running.

compound number in relation to subconscious motivation

The Subconscious Motivation 10s

The Main Influence Number dictates the theme of the Compound Number and strongly colors the entire triad of numbers, meaning the entire identity and character.

When the Main Influence Number is a 1, this puts emphasis on the self. This gives the person more control in situations. For individuals with a number 1 as the Main Influence, it is often better for them to own their own business. They tend to take a direct approach and their opinion is important to them. They make good attorneys and good writers.

10/1

You dream of owning something or developing something that says "me." In maturity, you have comfort with your ego.

11/2

With maturity, you learn that you must self-empower before you can have a working relationship. Prorating time between yourself and others is challenging. Media attention comes later in life, as does the discovery of your psychic abilities. The more you love yourself the easier it is to love others. Love relationships can be like walking on a razor blade. You learn later in life that your abilities can inspire the masses. Because of the 2 vibration, you may have a dream lover that you seek.

12/3

You discover communicative abilities in maturity, and that your parents heavily influenced your communication. You have latent talents in creative writing.

13/4

Your dream is to make use of your creative talents after another career. You ultimately build and save for security in the golden years and are willing to earn everything you get.

14/5

You ultimately want the freedom to travel the world without worry. You realize in maturity that you have to create your own structure or foundation to do so. You also may want businesses in more than one location. You learn later in life that patience pays off.

15/6

You ultimately seek love, home, and family as your reward in life. But you realize in maturity that you have to go through many changes and sow many seeds before you can settle into a committed relationship. Somewhere between ages 35 and 40, you will learn that you need to heal yourself instead of trying to heal everyone around you. You are able to take on responsibility as a mature adult that can be the head of a household.

16/7

As you mature, you develop the ability to affect people. You discover that your belief systems are different than what you grew up with, and your dream is to share this wisdom with those around you. You are happiest when yakking about philosophy and spirituality. You might find, as you get older in life that you may pull away from responsibilities and go off and be alone a lot. If these feelings become extreme, this could create a mid-life crisis where you actually abandon a job situation or family and go off and explore the world, but in a more reclusive way, almost becoming a hermit. In maturity, you may simply become interested in spirituality or the metaphysical arts. Or you may

go back to school and look to change jobs. Try and explain the yearning for self-discovery and your search for a belief system to those around you, especially if you are the head of the household. Otherwise, you could cause a lot of upset to the people around you. After age 35 or so, you discover that you have the ability to affect change and heal people. You may discover that you are a pretty good therapist and may switch into that field as the rest of your life's work.

17/8

It is your dream to become inventive, creative, and to do something that does create royalties. You may find the success that you've been looking for comes later in life. It's a dream to do something or have a business that speaks to you, one that does become big and influential. Possibly, a project that you have been working on for a long time comes to fruition after age 35.

18/9

You dream of building a business or becoming successful, and helping people to become successful as well. You know how to handle success and keep your ego in check, and that usually comes with maturity. In maturity, you may decide to quit working for others and go into business for yourself. This allows you to feel complete.

19/1

You accomplish what you've been wanting to for some time at a mature age. Then, you breathe a sigh of relief and experience a level of attainment and accomplishment to help others.

The Subconscious Motivation 20s

When the number 2 is in the Main Influence position, the number is ruled by emotions, a partnership, or some issue or theme of the mother. Remember, before we have an intimate relationship or marriage, our emotional partner is our mother or representing the feminine energy. Partnership can also represent business. When you have a 2 as the Main Influence, you must take great care in dealing with business and money. Emotions can get involved where emotions shouldn't be.

20/2

You discover that marriage or partnership should come a little bit later in life. You are patient and wait for the right person to come into your life. It is much more advantageous to have 20/2 in the maturity number versus the Conscious Desire Number. You are less prone to make relationship mistakes early in life. You have peace and harmony in maturity.

21/3

You realize in maturity that friendships of the opposite sex are valuable. You learned through some difficult lessons that it is better to allow a friendship to evolve into romance as opposed to falling head over heels in love repeatedly. Ultimately you understand and appreciate what a good spousal partner can do for you, and you appreciate having a partner that sees you as attractive and appreciates you in return. You have a blatant urge to do something musical or something vocal.

22/22 or 22/4

There is a latent urge in maturity to go on and do good things. Usually in this position, especially if you are a woman, you had your family early in life. You have the ability and maturity to not only be successful, but the maturity and grace to understand and appreciate what it takes to be successful.

In maturity, you develop the ability to organize large projects, and to be a part of a large charity or foundation that benefits people in need.

23/5

In maturity, you get the urge to travel, to see people that maybe you have lost touch with, and see people that are geographically distant. You want to be able to make those travels without worrying about money or responsibilities that may hold you back. If you've been married for a number of years, your spouse or partner becomes a great friend and that relationship eases your mind.

the subconscious motivation number

24/6

You have the knowledge and maturity to know that marriage for you should either come later in life or not at all, and you accept that. However, you view a wonderful loving partner as your reward in life.

25/7

Your dream is to ultimately spend time in old age or maturity studying with masters or to even be reclusive, spending your time alone.

26/8

In maturity, you balance materialism and family values. You may become a parent at a more mature age. Your dream is to obtain the material wealth so that you can pass it on to your heirs, establishing a legacy for yourself.

27/9

In maturity, you realize that being kind and compassionate has helped you to understand people to the point of understanding why they suffer and why they experience pain. You must be

careful that you do not develop emotional attachments to needy people in an effort to satisfy your need to be needed.

28/1

You have a latent desire to write and be creative and to make money at it. In maturity, you allow someone close to you to help you to be successful.

29/11 or 29/2

Because of the musical rhythmic side of the 2, you may have latent musical talents that you experimented with as a child but never really put to use. So at age 40, you may want to take musical lessons or dance classes again. At this point, on an emotional level, the 29/11 or 29/2 means bringing emotions to completion. If a partnership or a marriage fails, you may not marry again.

chapter 8

The Dharma Number

there's strength in your numbers

Sometimes, people don't know their own strength. That's why the Dharma Number is important. It is your source of power, your natural drive. The Dharma Number *is* your strength number. So, as we go forward in this chapter, think of those two as interchangeable.

Dharma is just as important as Karma, but it is a lesser-used term. Dharma is conforming to your own path and duties. It keeps you on the path of doing what is right, versus what is wrong. It is your innate strength, so you know what you are supposed to do in this lifetime. It is *not* your purpose in life, but the strength to find it and accomplish it. It is the ability to do what is right because it *is* the right thing, not because the law tells you that it is right.

When you live your Dharma, your life goes easier. Why? Because you are making the right choices and you are faced with less critical choices that border on crisis. Conversely, when you take the easy way out and give into immediate gratification, you are weakening yourself. Ultimately, the poor choices that you make lead to problematic situations that throw you into crisis for long periods of time. The poor choices that you make do not seem significant at the time. But those choices add up. What are they?

Procrastination is a big one. How many times do we say, "I'm going to start working out next week?" Another simple example is diet choice. Do you have fast food or a healthy salad? Do you try hard enough at work? Are there times when you can offer someone assistance and don't? Do you simply shrug responsibility when no one is watching? If you see trash on the ground that you did not leave there, do you pick it up? What is the right thing to do? Can we achieve greatness without doing the little things too?

When you get used to making good decisions, it sets you up for an inner knowing of how to make the right choices in a crisis, because you have practiced simpler matters and circumstances.

To get the Dharma Number, you add the Birth Path Number, which represents who you are, with the Environmental Influence Number, what people think you are. When you blend these elements together, as keeping them apart and in conflict, you get strength.

The Dharma Number can serve as a touchstone, keeping you aware of your greatest assets for accomplishing your purpose in life.

Celebrity Example
Bill Gates

His full name is William Henry Gates. His Birth Path Number is **58/22**. His Environmental Influence Number is **41/5**. This makes his Dharma Number **99/9** (58/22 + 41/5 = **99/9**). His strength, that which will allow him to accomplish his purpose in life, is actually based on peace of mind that comes through to serve humankind.

That may seem unusual given what we know about Bill Gates, the mogul. But consider his philanthropic efforts, which continue to grow in importance to him. To achieve his peace of mind, he will need to give away a lot of money in a way that will serve humankind.

As you will notice in the Bill Gates example, the Dharma Number enables you to accomplish your purpose in life, which is not necessarily related to an occupation. Although we are conditioned to think otherwise in Western culture, our purpose in life is about more than accomplishment on

the material level. Your Dharma Number helps you accomplish your soul purpose and destiny. The Dharma Number gives you the strength to be who you are and fulfill your destiny.

Celebrity Example
President George W. Bush

Bush is a $33/6$ in both his Birth Path and Environmental Influence Number. That makes his Dharma Number $66/3$ ($33/6 + 33/6 = 66/3$). He has the strength and ability to heal and help people in a humanitarian way. It is very important for him, as president of the U.S., that he truly helps people. If he doesn't help people, he will dishonor his Dharma and create a major crisis in his life. Remember, the negative side of the $66/3$ is the victimizer, the one who does people in. Businesses have strengths too. How many times have you heard that a business was faltering because "it got away from its strengths?" When you are looking to invest in a business, find its Dharma Number. Is it still leading with its strengths? Or is it diversifying away from its source of power?

Example
IBM

IBM's Dharma Number is $65/11$, which means it finds its inspiration through humanitarian changes. The Dharma of IBM is to set a good example and find ways that create positive change in people's lives. They are supposed to help or undo problems.

newmerology

finding the dharma number

Add the value of the Birth Path Compound Number and the Environmental Influence Compound Number. The sum is the Dharma Number.

Example #1

Birth Path Number is 37/1
Environmental Influence is 33/6

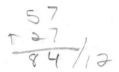

step one: add the Compound Numbers of the Birth Path and Environmental Influence Numbers

37 + 33 = 70
The sum of 70 is the Compound Number

step two: add the 7 + 0 to reach the Base N umber

7 + 0 = 7
The Dharma Number is 70/7

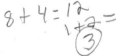

Rule to Remember: Sometimes the Dharma Number sum can be high, in the triple digits. If you reach a triple digit when you add the Birth Path and Environmental Compound Numbers, only add the final two digits. Let the first digit stand.

Example

Birth Path Number is 55/1
Environmental Influence Number is 60/6

step one: add the Compound Number of each

55 + 60 = 115

step two: let the 1 stand and add the two final digits

1 + 5 = 6

Taking the first digit (1) and the sum (6) from above, the Compound Number is 16

step three: add the 1 and 6 to reach the Base Number

1 + 6 = 7

The Dharma Number is: 16/7

compound number in relation to dharma

The Dharma 10s

The Main Influence Number dictates the theme of the Compound Number and strongly colors the entire triad of numbers, meaning the entire identity and character.

When the Main Influence Number is a 1, this puts emphasis on the self. This gives the person more control in situations. For individuals with a number 1 as the Main Influence, it is often better for them to own their own business. They tend to take a direct approach and their opinion is important to them. They make good attorneys and good writers.

10/1

You have extreme power of the self and will.

11/2

Your strength lies in psychic abilities and the ability to inspire the masses. You can empower yourself without your ego getting in the way.

12/3

Your strength lies in your ability to communicate either on paper or by using your voice. You have the power to influence people with what you say.

13/4

Your strength lies in taking leadership and creating new foundations.

14/5

Your strength is in your ability to create security for yourself without getting trapped. You can be structured and at the same time be free-flowing. You have the patience to watch things grow and mature.

15/6

Your strength lies in your ability to change the people around you by changing yourself first. You have the ability to take responsibility for your life's decisions without blaming people for getting in your path. You are innately humanitarian.

16/7

Your innate strength is your wisdom and your ability to heal and help people. Having the 16/7 in this position means you come on with a lot of force, as if blowing down the walls of Jericho. You must recognize within yourself, and for yourself, that the changes you bring must be thought out, so they are for the good of all. At no time can you have any negative or distractive thoughts. Any negativity will cause the walls of Jericho to fall in on you. You have the strength to break away from normal belief systems, and share them with people. Allow people to follow you, do not try to push them or pull them along.

17/8

You have a balance between spirituality and materialism. You know that you are going to do something that lasts possibly beyond your life and you create a reputation for yourself that other people wish to emulate. Your reputation comes from your abilities, not a desire to be visible.

18/9

You achieve a level of balance between spirituality and materialism. You help other people do the same thing. You hone the ability to be successful and compassionate at the same time. This makes you feel complete.

19/1

This is the feeling of compassion and completion on an individualistic level that helps you recognize that you have the ability to accomplish your purpose in life. It's the strength to be strong and fair to others, and still not lose yourself in everything that's going on around you. If you believe in reincarnation, you may feel within yourself that you may have accomplished what you set out to do, and may not have to come back again.

The Dharma 20s

When the number 2 is in the Main Influence position, the number is ruled by emotions, a partnership, or some issue or theme of the mother. Remember, before we have an intimate relationship or marriage, our emotional partner is our mother or representing the feminine energy. Partnership can also represent business. When you have a 2 as the Main Influence, you must take great care in dealing with business and money. Emotions can get involved where emotions shouldn't be.

20/2

Chances are remote that the Dharma Number would be in any of the 20s. It is possible. but the odds are low that it would happen. If 20/2 is your Dharma Number, your strength would be in the ability to partner and not expect anything in return. Your strength and empowerment comes from being completely comfortable with the feminine energy.

21/3

You have the strength to communicate both sides of the issue, to be passive or domineering without upsetting people. You have both men and women as friends, and have a strong relationship with your mother and father.

22/22 or 22/4

If this shows up, this is special. This is the power and strength to create great projects that benefit people long after you have passed on.

23/5

You go with the flow, in regards to people. You extract the best from people. Even if people criticize you, it is the kind of constructive criticism that will help you grow. You will not lose your sense of self.

24/6

You know how to balance the emotions and logic. Your strength is as a natural therapist.

25/7

Your strength is in your solitude, in an understanding of how your own emotions work, so you can understand others.

26/8

You are a leader and yet, sensitive and humanitarian at the same time.

27/9

Strength lies in your compassion. You also teach others to be compassionate and strong in their spiritual belief system. When you talk to people, you come off as sharing information as opposed to lecturing them.

28/1

Your strength is an individualistic approach to put business deals together, or to get partners together that benefits each other.

29/11 or 29/2

You have the ability to be strong, sensitive, and empathetic. You can be a model for how to be a person who is soft, caring, and still strong. An example would be Mother Teresa, who is kind and soft but also intimidating in her strength. She inspires people to be like her.

The Dharma 30s

When the number 3 is in the Main Influence position, communication and dealing with people is key. No matter what the Base Number is, we must remember that when we are ruled by the 3, we must be optimistic and positive, and never involve ourselves in any negative communication, such as gossip or lies. People are your natural resource, and if you mistreat it, that resource can run out. People and communication are synonymous with each other. Because people do talk, your reputation is always at stake.

30/3

You can sell the Brooklyn Bridge to a New Yorker. You are convincing in your communication. You may take on a leadership position that is basically thrust upon you or given to you. You may simply have the ability to be elected to leadership.

31/22 or 31/4

You have the ability to lead people in organizations and create a foundation that people can turn to. You simply have the ability to make people feel secure.

32/5

Your power lies in your ability to cause change, or to blaze paths that help people break from the norm and overcome shyness.

33/6

You have the ability to help people selflessly. You may get recognition posthumously. It is the power of your voice that overcomes obstacles and adversaries.

34/7

Your strength lies in the balance of your mind as both creative and logical, and having the ability to teach and learn from people. The key here is to teach and learn so it becomes a practical part of your life. This is truly practiced spirituality, not book read or book learned.

35/8

You have the ability to be generous and help people make money or help them to be successful. Your strength is in sharing the wealth.

36/9

You are a healer who has the patience to allow people to heal. Your strength lies in waiting for people to get where they need to get to, almost like a bird that simply will have the patience to sit on the eggs and wait for them to hatch.

37/1

You speak the truth and as you do, you find your purpose in life. You must say what's on your mind no matter how hard it may be for the listening audience.

38/11 or 38/2

You have the voice of power. You speak from strength and you inspire those around you. Your strength lies in your pure prophetic, precognitive psychic abilities urging people on into their purpose in life, which in turn will enable you to find yours.

39/3

Your strength lies in dealing with people compassionately, and being a problem solver. You have the ability to help other people without looking for anything else in return.

The Dharma 40s

When the number 4 is in the Main Influence position, you are ruled by the concept of the box, a four-sided figure. A part of you, for better or worse, is contained. You prefer law and order. You are a linear or left-brain thinker. You have a strong need for the feeling of foundation and security, professionally, personally, and emotionally. You are ruled by rationalization, pragmatism, and have a conservative, traditional approach to life.

The number 4 in the Main Influence position controls, influences or even manipulates the number that's in the Minor Influence. The number 4 represents the controlling factor in your life.

40/22 or 40/4

You have the ability to create a new foundation, something that is very strong and powerful, something that creates the feeling of organization on a global scale. You can act as an umbrella of protection for those around you. You are not afraid of hard work on any level. While you create organization or build a foundation on a large scale, you are not trapped by it. You can be part of the organization, without building walls around yourself. You are not blinded by all the rules and laws that you set up. Yet, you are willing to work within that system, playing fair with those around you.

41/5

You have the ability to structure yourself and learn lessons of conservatism and conformity that allow you to grow. You are able to create structure for yourself and take responsibility for yourself so the system around you leaves you alone.

42/6

Your strength lies in your ability to be very structured in very emotional times. You can be a great help to people and soothe them. You have the ability to be calm and compassionate in times of an emergency.

43/7

If **43/7** is your Dharma Number, then spirituality is your strength. You have the ability to be organized and logical in your belief system, and to disseminate that information to people via some form of communication. You are some form of a spiritual messenger.

Your strength is your belief system. And you have the ability to defend that belief system to people. You may also have strength in organized religion as a minister, a priest, or some kind of practitioner, being able to help people in communal practice or organized faith.

You are very dogmatic and you have an impact on people with this dogma. You have the ability to be very convincing. You must be very careful that you do not fall into misuse of power.

44/8

You can manage large endeavors, make a lot of money and to help create structure and foundation via your balanced approach to handling business matters. Your strength is in being a firm but fair leader. You take on all challenges and are not afraid of obstacles. Your strength is in being fearless.

You have the ability to understand all types of businesses, to run them, possibly sell them off, and start new ones.

45/9

The 45/9 represents the ability to organize change on a gradual basis, and bring things to completion. You may be the tortoise instead of the hare, but you do get the job done with compassion and sensitivity to those around you.

46/1

Your strength lies in coordinating humanitarian efforts, being courageous, taking up the cause for grievances, and being supportive of anything that is institutional, or something that society really needs. You have the ability to make good sound judgments for the good of all, while keeping the ego in check.

47/11 or 47/2

You have the strength to structure your belief system and share it with people and help them learn emotional lessons.

48/3

You have the ability to convince people to get involved in business situations that ultimately may benefit everyone, but you really have the ability, as it's said, to sell snow to an Eskimo. You have the ability to get people to invest in you or the endeavors that you're involved in. But ultimately your strength lies in your ability to get everyone into a win-win situation so that they may invest in the endeavor that you're involved in, but benefit from it financially.

49/22 or 49/4

The 49/22 is the ability to look at problems and then turn them into solutions. You not only help the person that you're trying to find the solution for, but it spills over into the lives of others. Everybody benefits from your solutions.

The Dharma 50s

When the number 5 sits in the main influence position, you are ruled by change. You are illustrated by the pentagram, which means you can go five different directions at once. You will have a natural feeling of adaptability and may have an energy that keeps you on edge or even on the move. You may have to learn patience or to stand pat and simply leave things alone long enough to see

what can happen without you constantly fueling the fire. You like to be a catalyst.

50/5

Your strength lies in your ability to manifest in a moment's notice. In this position, this number can be equally destructive as well as constructive. If this shows up in this position, in your numerological realm, you must be extremely careful about what you think and what you do. You have more power than you realize.

51/6

You are somewhat of a chameleon, and your strength lies in your ability to heal in many ways, and help others to heal in a nonconventional way. You have the ability to master healing of the body through the mind.

52/7

Your strength lies in your ability to change your belief system, to see both sides of things, and to discuss different philosophies on an intellectual level. You may love to play devil's advocate.

53/8

You can change people, get the best out of them, and bring them to success without expecting anything in return.

54/9

You combine patience, organization, and compassion to bring moderate changes, expecting nothing in return, knowing that you are helping people and allowing yourself not to become too attached to the outcome. You simply perform the task and then move on to the next thing without waiting around to see the results.

55/1

You can do many different things and pull various projects together so that they form one cause. This is your strength. You have the ability to see issues and aspects from a lot of different angles and make sense of it, so you can present that singularity and purpose.

56/11 or 56/2

You bring change to healing, trying different and alternative methods, experimenting with the

concept of healing, wellness, and health, which is an inspiration not only to yourself, but also to everyone around you. You have the courage to experiment and try something new.

57/3

You have the ability to explore all parts of the mind. You explore different philosophies and belief systems, and are able to communicate those feelings, thoughts, and beliefs to people. You help people gain an understanding of an alternative belief system, or to be more open-minded.

58/22 or 58/4

You can construct an entity or a business that is willing to grow and create a foundation that helps people along the way. You have true power without allowing that power to get out of hand. This number represents true cause and effect and recognizing the consequences that come with it.

59/5

You have the power to make change for human kind that is a transition into security and stability. You bring about change for the good of all.

The Dharma 60s

When the number 6 is the main influence, the issues encompass health, healing, humanitarianism, family, things in the house, dealings with nature, and high standards. A sense of design is strong. The occupation of architect, as well as, real estate and escrow are either a 4 or a 6. Nurturing and being parental, whether maternal or paternal, is part of the 6 as a Main Influence. If the number 6 influences you, you are going to have a load on your shoulders—mostly family responsibilities.

60/6

You have the ability to take on more responsibility than you ever dreamed. You are the ultimate humanitarian and caretaker, but also can employ tough love. Your true strength lies in your healing powers, however you must be careful that you don't give too much and become drained. You are everybody's parent.

61/7

You have the strength to stick to your philosophies and beliefs while everyone is telling you you're wrong. You will find strength in yourself and may have to face your path alone.

62/8

You will reap monetary rewards by helping people. Because the 6 represents humanitarianism and healing, simply do your work without expectations. You must stay away from emotional attachments to money. There is a good chance that money will come to you from unexpected sources as you help people.

63/9

Your strength lies in your compassion and humanitarianism. You see people clearly and can get closure on your personal dealings. You help people by getting them to help themselves. You are open-minded enough to hear your own healing words that are spoken to others, and realize that the message is for you too.

64/1

You have very broad shoulders, or so it seems. Your strength is your independence and sense of self. Your sense of pride allows you to take on more responsibility than most people would think of. You allow people to lean on you in many ways without losing yourself in them or the work. You may ultimately write about your life or your work.

65/11 or 65/2

You have the ability to adapt, especially to different living situations. You shoulder responsibilities and you grow and evolve from them.

66/3

This Dharma Number weighs heavy on you and humanity. You have come into this world to heal humanity. Your words are powerful and make a huge impact on mankind. You must be careful though, as this number is extremely constructive and destructive. If you misuse your powers you will incur the same plight as those you adversely affected. This is the Dharma Number of George W. Bush.

67/22 or 67/4

You are a natural humanitarian and healer. If you have a 67/22 here, you could forge a humanitarian and healing institution.

68/5

You could be involved in medical innovation or research that breaks new ground or takes medicine or healing to the next level.

69/6

This is the strength of humanitarianism and compassion. You are born with healing feelings that help you first heal your own family dysfunction. This awareness allows you to pass on your experiences as a therapist to understand and help those of a similar plight. You have the ability not to turn a blind eye to the faults of those around you. You have come into this world to help people. You also have very high standards.

The Dharma 70s

The 7 is the higher mind, a situation where you are both the student and teacher. These numbers tend to show up in the Dharma Numbers for multi-name corporations.

70/7

Your strength lies in being both teacher and student. This is the number of unlimited spirituality. You have the ability to attain knowledge at many levels without becoming a know-it-all. You must stay spiritually balanced to avoid fanaticism or becoming a cult leader. At times, you need to ground yourself and spend time alone to quiet your mind.

71/8

This number contains the strength to balance spirituality and money. You can be a spiritual leader and at the same time run a large business. You understand the meaning of power. You have

prophetic or precognitive abilities that translate directly into everyday business. But remember that your talents are purely god-sent and you must meditate for the sake of meditation and to give thanks. The flow of money that you enjoy must be shared.

72/9

Your spirituality influences your emotions and influences your partner. Your spirituality also can balance out your emotions. You are a very, very sensitive person. Like the 27/9, you acutely aware of the senses: physical pain, emotions, and the intuition or ESP. Your partner can be literally part of the spiritual work that you do. A 27/9 is about finding a partner who is spiritual, and having a relationship on the physical level. The 72/9 is more about spirituality as a shared experience with another individual.

Your strength comes from spirituality with another person, perhaps a business partner or a spouse.

73/1

You are a channeler. If the 37/1 is communicating from the heart and soul, or speaking the truth, the 73/1 is spirit influencing the voice, and coming out of the individual. Spirit speaks through you. You are spirit's voice. Because you are a 1, you, as a person, are a conduit for universal energy.

74/11 or 74/2

With the 7 and 4, there's a certain amount of pragmatism that goes along with your practice of spirit. This means that, at some point, spirituality literally becomes your work. The 11 is a number of high evolution—the psychic level. The 4 actually keeps you grounded and keeps you from literally going nuts. The 4 stabilizes you. Your strength is in your psychic side. Spirituality influences your foundation and your work. Spirituality creates your foundation and from that you evolve into self-empowerment. Your spirituality has to make sense to you.

75/3

You are a spiritual catalyst for spiritual change and you know how to communicate it. This is a great number for a minister, or an evangelist. The 75 is the number of a messenger. The 57 is the bearer of bad news, the person who hands out the news others are not ready to hear. But with the 75, your spirituality causes change that you then communicate. If this energy is negative, you will philosophize about change, but may not put it into action.

76/22 or 76/4

This number is about taking on spiritual responsibilities. Your spirituality influences your family, home life, and your foundation. You could be on the receiving end of epiphanies or revelations. Your spirituality actually affects your physical life. You are a very soft person and a humanitarian. Your presence can be healing to people.

newmerology

77/5

This is the master teacher and the master student, someone who causes change. This is a very powerful number. You could be a real Houdini—an escape artist—literally and figuratively. The 5 is all about change, and sometimes being aloof. You can get so far into your mind that you lose touch with reality and need some sort of medical intervention. The 77 becomes the master teacher and the master student. You really like to go to the mountaintop to meditate. But your energy could be very scattered. You may not be grounded enough.

78/6

Your spirituality brings success in the healing realm. Your spirituality makes money. When we talk about the number 6, we talk about mortality. Because the 6 refers to, among other things, mortality, this number may have to do with crossing over or going into spirit and making money through that ability. You may rationalize or philosophize about money. The number 7, in spirit, has everything to do with crossing over or being *in* spirit.

79/7

You have great spiritual empathy. You could be philosophical. If it goes too far, all the philosophical talk will get in the way of whatever they are trying to do

Spirituality comes to completion. You have a certain amount of skepticism. Skeptics are people who want to believe. If a person doesn't care about something, they don't challenge it. They leave

it alone. But a skeptic prods you because they want to believe. This number could represent someone going off the spirituality deep end. Or, if it's positive, it could represent coming into spiritual power and integration. With the 9 on the back end, it tells you that you have to let go of the results. Something is coming to completion or an ending, so that the next thing can come into being. You may be a channeler that helps people cross over. A 79/7 is a person that will spiritually help people come to completion, especially if the person, say a patient or client, is in pain.

The Dharma 80s

With the number 8, we're talking about money and power. We're talking about someone with a lot of influence, like a CEO, an executive, a high political figure, or a corporate figure. This is someone who has clout, someone who is definitely a leader. If your Dharma Number begins with 8, then your power is being influenced by the concept of leadership.

80/8

If this is your Dharma Number, your power comes from money. Your strength is in working with money. You could throw caution to the wind; someone who throws things against the wall to see what sticks and what doesn't. You could come into power in a corporate structure but you are going to be a bit radical. You are a power seeker. The 8s denote action, putting things and moving things forward. So, there's a lot of action with a number like this. If this is a business name, the business is going to run really hot and cold because of the all or nothing energy of the 0. The business will need to learn to be moderate.

81/9

With the 9, good things come to those who wait. With 81/9, rewards come to you because you have the power to finish what you start; the power to stay within your own compassion and compunction to let it come. With this ability, you are an empowered individual.

82/1

Your money influences or goes to the partner. Your power actually comes in remaining on your own while, at the same time, letting your partner become successful. You can exercise the power to stay out of the way and let that power go to your partner. Keep in mind, when I say the word partner, I am also talking about business partnerships too, not just a wedding or a marriage. What may be confusing here is that your power is within yourself. So you become very empowered by allowing success to go to the partner. That's really stepping out of your ego.

83/11 or 83/2

You are on the receiving end of money via communication. This is a payoff. This number has a lot to do with someone who could be in the entertainment business, but behind the scenes—manager, agent, or a producer. This is money empowering the voice. You could have a lot of clout with numbers and obtain recognition. But because the 3 is in the back end, not in the front end, you are generally not a performer, although you could be if you wanted to.

84/3

Money creates structure in your life and then it is shared and disbursed among people. This makes you a great fundraiser. Money creates the structure. Money influences the structure. You could also be a movie producer, or raise money for businesses. The money you raise provides work for others. The **8** is all about the power of money. You could also have strong political connections as well. You could raise funds for a political campaign.

85/22 or 85/4

You have the power to bring change in the structure or in the foundation. This is a very catalytic kind of number. Remember we said that Bill Gates is a **58/22** (or **58/4**)—growth of money and power in the structure, doing big things. Here, the power is going to cause movement, but if you use it the wrong way it could create an earthquake. You will definitely create a shift in the foundation with this number.

86/5

Doctors might have this as their Dharma Number. The **86** is the power to heal, bring about change, or bring in money around humanitarianism, or an institution. Here, the money also influences things like home and real estate. With this number, you could be a real wheeler-dealer. You could be very charitable, or possibly inherit a lot of money. If used in the negative, the money that comes into the family could make you lazy.

87/6

This is power blended, or influencing, spirituality to bring humanitarianism and healing. This is very powerful, because it is materialism of the 8 balanced with the spirituality of the 7. Put this all together and you have the influence of power and money aimed at the spirituality that affects a healing or humanitarianism institution. This makes you a giving person and very philanthropic. Just don't blow all your money along the way.

88/7

Here we have a Master Challenge, the 88, which is the multiple of 11. You could be someone who has so much money you don't even realize it, like Howard Hughes. You could be reclusive and remove yourself from the world and live in your head. Your money could explode to such a level that you lose consciousness of what you have. Or you could be very fanatical about money.

89/8

Money comes to fruition. This is money over money. The 89 is power with compassion bringing success. This is a very philanthropic kind of number, because the money is the power. If it goes into the negative, however, the money could become a destructive force. You could become power crazy.

The Dharma 90s

This is the number of completion—the number of final empowerment and compassion. The Master Challenge of 11 is substituted for the number 2. The 11 on the bottom is empowerment, not the 2. Anything beginning with a 9 in the Compounds is very empowered.

90/9

This is the all or nothing in compassion. There are times when the number 9 represents a level of empathy that causes you to feel other people's pain. It can indicate a curiosity about why people suffer. It's not always a good thing. You've got to be careful that you do not overextend this capacity.

91/1

This is a very esoteric number. It indicates compassion for the self. You are complete within yourself. This number indicates the completed ego. It no longer needs to be fed.

92/11

This is empowerment or compassion to the partner. It's compassionate giving, which brings recognition. Compassionate emotions. You are a very, very sensitive person. Because of the number 11, this is a number of tremendous self-empowerment, but you could get drawn into crises. You should bring compassion to someone close, but stay out of any crisis. Allow your mind to completely integrate without the left and right brain feeling like a vice is closing in.

93/3

You have the ability to soothe people and make them feel okay with your voice. You know how to verbally express compassion and make people feel good. Your power is in your compassion for people.

94/22 or 94/4

Compassion brings foundation, builds structure, and brings work. Compassion influences the work and structure. The 4 represents logic and pragmatism. So here, compassion influences the logical situation or the foundation. It could apply to a business. It could apply to a town that's very stubborn. Maybe it's the influence to get them to build a community center or a homeless shelter. You put compassion to work.

95/5

You are a peaceful activist, one who looks for change. You are also compassionate—the compassion of passion, which brings about change.

96/6

This represents compassion toward the family or bringing the completion to dysfunction. You probably have a huge history of family problems with siblings battling it out and possible fights over inheritance. The **96** brings this to an end.

97/7

Your belief system is based on compassion. This is also a very elevated belief system. You believe that if you leave others alone, they will leave you alone.

98/8

You use compassion and patience to create money. This is similar to the **89**. But this time the **8** isn't in the lead. The power isn't in the lead, the compassion is. You may have a psychic feeling, like you're going to get money.

99/9

This is the number that ends the system—completion of completion. People with this Dharma Number are very peaceful.

chapter 9

Missing Numbers

karmic lessons

If you have noticed that certain areas of life create consistent challenges for you, you may be unconsciously sensing your Missing Numbers. Missing Numbers are any of the digits from 1–9 that do not show up in the Compound or Base Numbers of your Newmerological Realm: Birth Path, Environmental Influence, Conscious Desire, Subconscious Motivation, or Dharma Numbers. When you are missing a number, you are missing the essence of that aspect, as defined by that number. Also, you don't have a karmic lesson on the Master Challenge Numbers of 11 and 22.

Missing Numbers represent your greatest karmic lessons and challenges. Many of you are already cringing at the sight of the word "karmic" because of its negative connotations. But, *Karma* is the most misused spiritual term used in modern New Age lingo and in everyday language. First of all, Karma is translated directly from the Sanskrit language as work, act, or deed. There is no such thing as paying past life Karmic debts or inherited bad Karma. Your deeds create your fate and destiny.

Your Missing Numbers identify what areas of your life contain shortcomings and need your "act or deeds," your focus and attention most. This knowledge allows you to fill in your own numerological "personality gaps," so you can acquire the knowledge needed to become whole. The Missing

Numbers identify what you must learn to complete yourself.

If you are in your thirties, forties, or beyond, you may have already identified missing aspects of yourself and learned your karmic lessons. But for a person who is not mature or self-aware, Missing Numbers can delay progress in life. This is often true for someone who has a wide spectrum of Missing Numbers and, therefore, a wide spectrum of challenges.

One client of mine, Matt, is missing 2,4,5,7, and 9—more than half of the nine main numbers of the realm. He clearly has lived out struggles and challenges in the areas of partnership and emotions, consistent work ethic, adaptability, spiritual foundation, money awareness, and a system of values. When I shared this information with his wife, a friend of mine, she laughed out loud and stomped her foot, which I took as a confirmation to the facts. His progress in life has been delayed because he is constantly putting out the fires caused by his Missing Numbers.

We've all met people who seem to have it all. These are people who have all the digits from 1–9 represented in their numerological realm. Madonna has all the numbers. These individuals however, are the exceptions. Most people are missing at least one if not several numbers. Rather than look with dismay over our Missing Numbers, we should see them as opportunities, clear indicators of what we need to work on to progress in life. By working on our Missing Numbers, we too can complete our Newmerological realm and "have it all."

Example

Debbie is a young woman in her 30s. Her Birth Path Number is 57/3; her Conscious Desire is 11; her Subconscious Motivation is 11; her Environmental Influence is 22; and her Dharma is 79/7. She is missing 1, 2, 4, 6, and 8. Debbie has to learn lessons in individuality, partnership, emotions, consistent work ethic, love, family, money, and a value system. Not only is she missing five numbers, she has Master Challenges in all three aspects of her name, which means that not only does she have many lessons to learn, but she also has resistance to learning them. So her Missing Numbers become even more problematic. Since she is missing the number 2, she is continually frustrated in relationships and can be rather cold emotionally. Every time she comes for a reading, the issue is a

new guy she is dating. But because she is missing the 6, she is prone to dysfunction and gets involved with men who aren't good for her. She is also missing the number 8, which means she has gotten into power struggles at work. Since she is missing the 4 (lacking ethics and a sense of boundaries), she gets involved with men at work.

Not many people are missing as many numbers as Debbie. The average is two. I have seen as high as six. Moreover, there is no surefire way to incorporate the elements of the Missing Numbers into our personality. It differs for every person. However, the timing aspect of Newmerology, which will be discussed in subsequent chapters, can indicate the most advantageous time to seek out knowledge and help in certain aspects of our lives. One consistent and important characteristic about Missing Numbers is that *you must make the effort to acquire the aspects of life that the Missing Numbers indicate.* They will not just come to you. They are challenges you must meet.

Donald Trump and Ted Turner are good examples of Missing Numbers. Trump is missing the number 2 and 8. As we all know, his relationships have been a disaster and nearly his downfall. He and Ted Turner are both missing the number 8, which means the possibility of the misuse of power. Have they learned their lessons? Only time will tell. Even though someone has money, the 8 is also the proper use of that money, giving back and not manipulating people with less money.

how to find your missing number

Look at the 15 digits (Compound Number, as well as the Base Numbers of Birth Path, Environmental Influence, Conscious Desire, Subconscious Motivation, and Dharma Numbers) in your Newmerological Realm and see what you are missing. Those are your Missing Numbers.

Rule to Remember: Keep in mind that you can only miss numbers from 1–9. You cannot be missing an 11 or 22. Conversely, if you have a 22 and you are missing the number 2, the 22 does not reduce and become a 2 or 4. You are missing a 2. The same holds true for an 11. You can have an 11 and still be missing the Number 1. An 11 is not two 1s. It is an 11. You can't cheat.

newmerology

meanings of the missing numbers

1

You need to learn lessons of independence and individuality. You may lack a certain aggressiveness or raw creativity. You may not be a self-starter and may have low energy. You may lack a sense of individual intention or purpose. You will need to develop a sense of urgency.

2

You need to learn about the emotions. You need to learn how to be sensitive, how to incorporate the feminine or yin energy, and how to partner and do for others. Because the number 2 represents being shy or in the background, the person missing the 2 may not know how to pull back when necessary. This person doesn't know how to coast. Think of it this way: you can drive your car from stop sign to stop sign, gas to brake, but that's a waste of gas and energy. Sometimes, it is better to take your foot off the gas and coast to a red light. You may need to learn the value of being passive sometimes. There may be unresolved issues with your mother. Also, you need to learn to sing and dance, to be more rhythmic and melodic.

3

You need to speak up. You may lack tact in dealing with people. The number 3 represents optimism and a positive outlook so, the Missing 3 person could be pessimistic or morose. You may lack pure artistic ability and inventiveness. You may not realize the natural intuitions that most people possess. The major issue here is learning how to talk to and deal with people.

4

You may lack a work ethic or any ethics, as well as certain moral standards. This person needs to develop an understanding that they need to work for what they get. You may need to develop logic and analytical abilities. You could lack a certain amount of accountability and, therefore, you may need to work on your memory. You may have to learn to save something for a rainy day. This person needs to learn how to obey orders and the law.

5

You are a person who resists change and does not readily go with the flow. You may have to learn to be more adaptable and spontaneous. You may need to learn to be more adventurous when it comes to travel and seeing more of the world. When missing the number 5, which involves the ability to go in different directions, you may have trouble multitasking and may not know how to do two things at once.

6

Since **6** represents the healthy, happy family, the Missing Number **6** person has to unlearn the dysfunction found in their family of origin. You have to discover the comforts of home, how to nest, and feel safe at home. You may not have that much of a design flair and may not relate well to plants or animals. You may not have children or relate well to them, unless you really work on it. It may take this individual a long time to settle down, whether that means where to live or who to marry. You need to learn humanitarianism. Don't take your health for granted.

7

This person is missing a belief system or a philosophy of life. You no longer identify with the religion in which you were raised. You may feel a spiritual void until a suitable spiritual belief is found. You may be naturally agnostic, atheistic, or resistant to anything like meditating, or having peace of mind. You may need to learn how to be alone.

8

You have to learn how to identify with money, what it can get, what it can do for you. You have to learn how to manage money or acquire a value system. A Missing **8** means that you need to learn the flow of money—that as you give, it comes. How can you spot someone with a Missing **8**? They will say things like "Money doesn't matter," or "Money is not important to me." The number **8** also means power on a big level. So you may be resistant to corporate politics or politics in general. What you may want to do is work within a larger company for a while, until you can understand how it is run. Then, corporate politics or the workings of large organizations will no longer be part of your fears.

9

The lessons here are learning to be compassionate and finishing what you start. You may have to learn how to be of service to people. Learn how to be more patient and tolerant.

chapter 10

Personal Year Cycles

your metaphysical clock

In numerology, your birthday heralds an abundance of new energy and new possibilities for the 365 days ahead. It rings in your individual New Year, or what numerology calls your Personal Year Cycle.

Your Personal Year Cycle begins on your birthday and continues until your next birthday. It does not begin on January 1. This birthday-to-birthday "new year" number is the best, most accurate numerological indicator of what is to occur and at what age. Your Personal Year Number constitutes your individual metaphysical clock, which started ticking on the day you were born.

So what does the Personal Year Number tell you? It tells you what is most difficult for psychics—it tells you when. When it is a good time to start things or finish them. When it is the best time to buy a house, get married, start a business, take an extended trip, seek out a spiritual path, go back to school, concentrate on finances, start a family, or redecorate the house. Your Personal Year tells you when an event, in any specific area of your life, is likely to happen and what the conditions around it are likely to be. Your Personal Year allows you to go with the natural forces at work in your life.

newmerology

By following the numerological indicators of your Personal Year, you are plugging into a universal energy that supports certain efforts and aspects of yourself at specific times.

working with the personal year energy

The more time and attention you invest into the aspects indicated by the Personal Year Cycle, the better your results.

Rule to Remember: On the other hand, if you decide to ignore your Personal Year aspects and make decisions or take action that actually oppose your prevailing energy, be forewarned, it will take nine years before you can undo the effects. The reason being that we live in nine-year cycles.

Personal Year Cycle's relate to the idea of process in life. Let's say you want to do something really big, but you are currently in a $12/3$ year. The time to do something *really* big would be a $17/8$ year, but that is still five years down the road. Each of the five years is actually a step in the process toward doing something big. The $12/3$ year is a time to develop communication with other people. The following $13/4$ year is working hard and creating a foundation. The following $14/5$ year might present the opportunity to quit a full time job, yet have enough security to give you freedom.

Our Personal Year Cycles are all steps in a process that get us where we want to be. It's actually a very wonderful thing. But oftentimes, people do not want to go through the process. Your Personal Year Cycle lights up different sectors of your life at different periods of your life. Go toward the light. It will serve as your beacon for the timing of major and minor decisions and a guide for focusing your efforts to gain maximum results.

Example #1

Georgia got married when she was in a 5 Personal Year Cycle. A 5 year is associated with freedom, independence, and being footloose and fancy-free. But her boyfriend was about to move out of town and she did not want the relationship to end. So, against her instincts, she married at the exact time of her life when she should have been single and exploring her own independence. The marriage was unhappy. From the beginning, she felt tied down, almost suffocated. She subconsciously fought and undermined the union, even while her conscious mind attempted to keep it together. She stayed with her husband for nine years, finally ending the marriage when her 5 Personal Year Cycle came around again and gave her the courage and impetuousness to leave what was an unhappy and premature union.

Example #2

In 1996, Emma entered a 44/8 year, a year of hard work. Emma is in her 40s, and loves to travel. She had a history of taking long weekends. I specifically told her to keep her nose to the grindstone in her 44/8 year. But she did the exact opposite. She has been in a money nightmare since then. It will take her until 2005 to break that pattern.

energy flow and the personal year

Keep in mind that Personal Year Cycles relate to the energy flow in your life. And I do mean flow. Your Personal Year Cycle is not a curtain that goes up and down on your Birth Date. It is not that one day you are in a happy-go-lucky 5 year and the day after your birthday you are calling the realtor because you have entered a 6 year, a time of settling down and nesting. Personal years have an overlapping effect. If your birthday set off sudden, violent changes in your life, the shift in energy

would be too traumatic, akin to throwing your car into reverse while driving at **50** mph. It would be a jolt rather than a natural evolution in your progress.

The energy of any particular cycle tends to build as your personal year continues. On the other hand, you may begin to feel the energy shift as early as six weeks before your birthday and the start of your next cycle. It depends on the importance or strength of your Personal Year Cycle. Yes, some Personal Year Cycles are stronger and more impactful than others, especially if they match any of the numbers in your Newmerological Realm (more about that in upcoming chapters).

One other consideration: As stated, your Personal Year begins on your birthday. However, whatever occurs in the new calendar year before your birthday is like a preview of your year to come. So, if you birthday is in May, the months of January through April will serve as previews of the numerological trends in your year ahead.

This is a very important notion for investors. It is why investment wisdom says that the way January goes, so goes the rest of the year for the stock market. The Nasdaq has a very short preview period since its birthday is in February. The New York Stock Exchange birthday is in May, so the preview period is longer. Therefore, if January is positive, that means those indices are going to be up. If it is slow or if it is a bad January, that means the market is headed down.

compound numbers and the personal year cycle

Like the numbers of your Newmerological Realm, your Personal Year Cycle is likely to consist of a triad of numbers, the Compound Number (top two numbers) and the Base Number (bottom number.) The Base Number identifies the issues of that year. The Main Influence Number (number to the top left) provides a theme that impacts those issues. The Main Influence Number of your Personal Year Cycles tends to remain the same for several years at a time. So the Main Influence theme shifts gradually, forming a natural progression in life. However, the millennium change caused an energetic shock for everyone on the planet.

When the calendar year went from 1999 to 2000, the Main Influence Number changed—suddenly—for everyone. It was a collective shift. Therefore, here we are going along with 1998 adding up to a 27, 1999 adding up to a 28, and then we have 2000 which drops us to a 2 once it is added. This is the reason people were so on edge starting with the year 2000 because of the huge jump in number difference. Everyone on the planet experienced a Main Influence Number shift on his or her birthday in that year that left him or her feeling unsettled. There was an atmosphere of anxiousness that prevailed. The new millennium indeed ushered in a new numerological era.

single-digit personal years

The millennium also created, for the first time in many centuries, the possibility of a single-digit Personal Year Cycle. This is especially true for people born in the first six months of the year and in the early days of those months. When this occurs, it indicates a year of simplicity, with fewer dynamics in place. For instance, if you have an 8 Personal Year, it means that your year is all about the money. If you watch how you manage your money, you will do fine.

calculating the personal year

Once again, follow the instruction exactly, although finding your Personal Year is very simple. Take the calendar year (called the Universal Year in numerology), find its sum, and then add it to your month and day of birth.

Rule to Remember: Your Personal Year Cycle begins on your birthday, not at the beginning of the calendar year—January 1—and does not change until your next birthday. So, if today is August 28, 2002 and your birthday is September 19, 2002, you would use 2001 in your calculations because you have not completed your Personal Year Cycle.

Example

Personal Year for someone born on February 17

step one: find the sum of the current year

$$2 + 0 + 0 + 3 = 5$$

The Universal Year is 5

step two: add the Universal Year sum and the birth month and day

5 (Universal Year) + 2 (February) + 17 (day) = 24 (2+4=6)

The Personal Year Cycle, starting on February 17, 2003, is 24/6

Notice the Personal Year Cycle began on the birthday.
For the month of January and February, this person would still be in a 23/5 year.

compound personal year cycles

Personal Year Cycles are too complex and too important to limit them to Base Numbers. Life and life events simply have too many complications and dynamics. Therefore, like the Compound Birth Path Numbers, Personal Year Cycles are composed of a triad of numbers—Base Number, Main Influence, and Minor Influence. Although the Base Number determines the arena of life where the action occurs, the Main Influence Number will denote the dominant theme, with the Minor Influence and the Base Number on the receiving end of the Main Influence.

That is why the Personal Year Cycle descriptions are organized according to the Main Influence Number, beginning with 1. Remember that the Personal Year goes from birthday to birthday, not the calendar year.

1

New beginning, fresh energy, letting go of what didn't work; modifying what did work.

2

Partnership, cooperation, emotions, relationship issues, marriage, or divorce.

3

Social, entertaining, assuming leadership, using voice, having fun.

4

Being logical, busy, watch legal affairs, hard work, organizing, maintaining security.

5

Change, movement, scattering, promoting self for growth, travel.

6

Responsibility, family matters, house and home issues.

7

Wisdom, learning, going back to school, introspection, planning, spiritual revival.

8

Money matters, taking action, balancing the material and spiritual.

9

Compassion, completion, finishing what has been started, being of service.

11

Gaining notoriety, crisis if you let it, psychic awareness, anxiety, tension.

22

Hard work that is the foundation of big things to come, dealing with mother issues.

compound personal years beginning with 1

The 1 in the Main Influence position of a Personal Year represents a cycle where the self, meaning the individual, can exercise some control over circumstances.

10/1

The number 1 represents the self and the ego and the 10/1 represents the all or nothing of the ego. Always remember that 0 is God's number, meaning the all or nothing. This is a time when you definitely come into your own. A 1 Base Number year, with any Compound Number sitting atop of it, represents new beginnings. But in a 10/1 year, you put your label on everything that you do. This is a time when you can be very "into yourself" to the point where you may not notice other things going on around you. If your Birth Path Base Number is a 1, a 10/1 Personal Year will accentuate your native individuality, independence and raw creativity. You must be careful in a 10/1

year that you do not become too selfish or too self-centered, or take on an attitude of wanting too much too soon. Remember the 1 year is all about new beginnings and fresh energy. A 10/1 year follows a 9 year, where the energy has been waning and you may have felt tired. By contrast, the 10/1 year will feel like an adrenaline rush. This is definitely a time to get to know yourself, discover your raw creative abilities and make a fresh start in your life.

11/11 or 11/2

Here we have the Master Challenge of 11 versus 2. When we do the math, it may show up in some numbers as purely an 11 year, where you must face the Master Challenge, or it may show up as an 11/2, where you're facing the aspects of partnership versus being completely self-centered. In either example, we visualize the number 11 as two 1s, and illustrated as an individual or a stick person looking at himself in the mirror. This indicates self-empowerment, giving back to self, turning love back to self, as opposed to the vibration of the 2, which is more about being emotional, giving love away, doing more than your fair share for other people. The number 11 represents the left and right brain coming together to form the intuitive abilities. This does not refer to the left and right brain in terms of creative versus logical. Instead, the 11 brings high intuition, precognition, or, of course, psychic abilities into action. If the person in an 11 year does not subscribe to using their abilities in this way, the 11 energy simply creates higher mind activity, which translates into anxiety. Thus, an 11 year can be a crisis if you let it. In an 11 year, you must learn to vent energy so it does not build up too much. Because 11 sits in the path between 1 and 3, where 2 would normally sit, people around you will perceive the number 2 energy and want to partner with you. Or they may try to engage you in the co-dependent side of the number 2. The worst mistake that you can make in an 11 year is to do too much for other people, or allow other people's needs to come before your own. This is truly a time to focus on yourself, much more than even the 10/1. This is a time to learn about yourself and do for you, while, at the same time, becoming such a good example of caring and doing for yourself that you are an inspiration to those around you. In an 11 year, you may also find yourself interested in the media in some way, shape, or form. Or, because of the psychic side of the 11, you may simply become more involved in metaphysics.

12/3

A 3 year is all about being more communicative, social, and friendly. It's a time of involvement with the environment and people. In a 3 year, you must always take note and take responsibility of what you say, because your words, in this time, affect those around you. When we look at the compound form of 12/3, we see 1 in the main influence affecting the minor influence, which is 2. So we have the individual influencing a partner, the male influencing the female side. This is a time to balance the yin/yang energies within, creating harmony. That harmony translates into the 3 energy, which is happiness. We also see the number 1 influencing the 3, which is the individual influencing the surrounding social structure or friendships. Because of the romantic implications of a 12/3 year, it is very important not to fall deeply in love right away. Instead, allow someone you like or admire to be a friend first and evolve into a partner. Remember with 1 as the Main Influence, you have the ability to influence the partner and the emotions. You have the ability to influence friends. This is also a time to use your raw creative ability to work on anything artistic that you feel you want to do, or any artistic abilities that need to be developed.

13/22 or 13/4

The 4 year is about new foundations and structure. A 4 year is always a time to work, to be logical, to be pragmatic, and to use street smarts and common sense. A 13/4 year involves expressing creative

talents and making use of these creative talents as a form of work, not a hobby. With the 1 influencing the 3 in this year, the individual influences people, so this may be a time that you may feel you want to segment your friends. You may be doing just a few little assessments, not necessarily weeding out, just taking note of who your close friends really are. You may have a lot of influence on your friends this year to the point where you actually may become bossy, or may say something to them that could be offensive.

14/5

This is a time of change and movement. The previous 13/4 year involved a lot of hard work and structure. In the following 14/5 year, the individual solidifies that structure so it creates a strong basis for security and affords a little more room to move around and experiment. Be careful, however, not to undo in the 14/5 year any hard work that you did in the 13/4. As the number 1 influences the 5, you may feel inclined to create more change than normal in everything around you. This is also a time as the number 4 influences the 5, to have a good balance between structure and freedom. You are still working hard, but you have the opportunity to take some breaks here and there.

If used wisely, the energy of the 14/5 can mean that while you work hard, you obtain solid growth and true expansion in life.

15/6

The 6 year represents family issues, issues of house or home, and a time of taking on responsibility. As the number 1 influences the 6, you recognize how trustworthy you are and how much responsibility you can handle. You may be very influential in family issues. As the 1 influences

the 5, you may find yourself going through a lot of changes that allow you to be more responsible or more committal in terms of family. Because the 5 (number of changes) influences the 6, you may be in a time that you are disrupting your family, if this energy is not used correctly. That includes the family you grew up with, or within a marriage situation. If you are married and are in a 15/6 year, pay a lot of attention, and take responsibility for your behavior. You could change residence in the 15/6 year. Make sure that any changes that you make on the home front in a 15/6 year are for the right reason with healthy intention. This is a good time to make changes on the existing home, such as redecorating or remodeling. If you are a female in a 15/6, you can become pregnant, as in a 15/6 year, the individual grows. Do keep in mind that in a Personal Year Cycle where the number 1 is the Main Influence, you, the individual, are the one who is dictating the action. You have a choice in everything that you do. You cannot blame anyone else for anything that happens while the number 1 is in the Main Influence.

16/7

This can be an ominous time of high construction and destruction. As President Bush was about to be inaugurated, I predicted we would go to war after his birthday on July 6, 2001. Why? On that day, President Bush entered a 16/7 year. Those of you familiar with the Tarot may know that the number 16 card is the explosion in the tower. Many times I had spoken of the explosion in the tower with reference to President Bush, prior to September 11. Here is why: The number 7 represents a time of philosophy, belief system, and spirituality. The number 1 influencing the 7 means the individual has very strong beliefs or dogma. The number 6 represents responsibilities, the home, the homeland, and any kind of holdings that exist. Since the 1 affects the 6, the individual is influencing those he is akin to, related to, or shares responsibility with. So the 16/7 translates directly into philosophical differences with those with whom you have some kind of entrustment. If you are simply in a family situation in a 16/7 year, you will be very dogmatic about what you believe. You will be telling your family how strong you feel about certain things. This time may find you breaking away from your own traditional religion and going into a time of self-discovery. Because of the power of change that the 16/7 delivers, we must be very careful of our actions at this time for we can create a lot of disruption. At the same time, we can go into a state of healing, especially healing of the mind. Remember the number 6 also represents our physical health, so we're having a big affect on our body and our mind in a 16/7. The 7 energy represents going up into our head a lot, which is very easy in a 16/7 to neglect the body when we need to have a balance between the body and mind. So if you are in a 16/7 year, because of the time that you may spend in mental work, get out and exercise and use your body. Take time to reset, relax, or even meditate. Calm the mind. A 16/7 can definitely cause you to fly off the handle. If you experience frustration in a 16/7 year, you must vent it in a very healthy way. Also in a 16/7 year, in regards to philosophy, you may feel that you are so right, or become so opinionated in what you believe, that it could have very destructive effects on those around you. After the United States birthday in 2003, the country goes into a 16/7 year. This is a time where the country represents the people as a nation. So, there could be an uprising, and a change in the way the country does things, with long-lasting effects.

17/8

The 8 year always represents money issues, money management, and doing things in a big way. In this year, you must not allow the desire to be successful or to rule too much to overtake the other issues in life. I like to equate the 17/8 year with The Star card in the Tarot. It is a time of great possibility, notoriety, success, or attainment. The number 17 in numerology has been known as the number of royalty. The number 1 represents the individual and creativity. Since the 1 influences the number 7, which is the mind, the 17 relates to something created in the mind, the heart, or the soul. Over the number 8, which is money, we translate the definition of royalty and pluralize it into royalties. So this is an opportunity to do something very creative that continues to remanifest

itself and pay big dividends. This is definitely a year of opportunity for success, definitely a time to be in the limelight. But it can also, as any 8 year goes, bring a certain amount of pressure to perform. If you are in a 17/8 year, be as creative as possible, as the 7 represents the higher mind. Be as dreamy as possible, because grounding that dream into reality or manifestation is the number 8. This is your year to shine.

18/9

If you are in an 18/9 year, this is where you, the individual, must use your strength, attainment, earnings or power and turn it back into some kind of service or give back to anyone who has helped you or anyone who is in need. The 9 is the year of completion, it's a time of compassion, a time of service. Because 18 is very powerful (the energy of the 1 and the strength of the 8) it would be very difficult to weaken yourself to anyone around you by giving. Yet, this is not a time to be greedy because the energy of the 9 represents "what comes around goes around." The 9 year is a time to be compassionate, tolerant, and patient. Because the 1 and 8 in the Compound Number can be very self-absorbed and obsessive, there may be a tendency to mistreat people. Don't. If we mistreat people in a 9 year, it will take 9 years to correct. We may find ourselves being mistreated by people until the next 9 year appears so we can undo that.

19/1

Here we have the number 1 on the top, and on the bottom again. But the number 9 represents compassion. In a 19/1 year, you are more compassionate, empathetic, and feeling. It also means because the 1 is on the bottom, you are more compassionate to yourself. You are a big influence on yourself,

but not with the same ego theme as with the $10/1$. This is a time where something you are looking to do comes to fruition or completion, almost as if closing a chapter on this project, or creative project or business that the individual has been working on. The $19/1$ simply provides the circumstances where the individual is coming to completion. This may be a time of maturity and of growing up. The $19/1$ also represents looking at any clinging issues from the past year that still need to be finished up, cleaned up, and gotten rid of, so we can move forward.

compound personal years beginning with 2

During these years, the 2 is in the Main Influence position, representing the partner, emotions, and feminine energy. When I say a partner, I could mean marital partner or a business partner. If it is a young individual that has not been in a romance yet, then the emotional partner represents the mother.

20/11 or 20/2

This is the all or nothing of partnership. In a $20/2$ we find our emotions very high. At this point in time we are looking for Mr. or Ms. Right, and can very easily throw caution to the wind when it comes to anything beyond our emotions. It is very easy in a $20/2$ year to get caught up into feelings, and because this is the all or nothing partner, it is very easy to become extremely codependent or needy in a cycle like this. In a $20/2$ year, one must learn to deal with their emotions effectively, and not give love away to the first person who comes along. This is also a time of emotional highs and lows that have nothing to do with romance. In a $20/2$ year the slightest rejection or disappointment could send you to the brink of despair. You must guard against not overreacting to information that upsets you. This is also a time where you can, or could, meet that someone special. If you are not in a relationship, the opportunity is very strong for one. If you are in a relationship in a 20/2 year, your emotions, codependency, or neediness could drive a partner away. Remember the 20/2 is the all or nothing of emotions. The number 2 in the Main Influence position also represents a certain amount of reserve or just plain shyness. You could also feel more rhythmic, musical, or melodic. If you are in an occupation that involves dance or music, this is a time to really go for a job in that profession.

21/3

Once again, this is a time to take care of what you say, your dealings with people, and to express yourself. The number 2 influences the 3, meaning the emotions are affecting or influencing communication. With the 1 in the Minor Influence, this means that a partner and emotions are influencing you. At the same time, the partner may be influencing your friends or social structure. This is also a time that you may meet a partner that evolves from friendship, presenting the opportunity to be romantically involved. Once again, as this is the reverse of the 12/3, this is not a time to fall head over heels in love. Simply take things one-step at a time, and get to know that person. In a 21/3, as 2 is female, and 1 is male, your mother may have issues with your father. Occupationally, this may be a time when your musical side influences how you express yourself. If you are creative, you may be performing musically in a 21/3.

If you are in a relationship in a 21/3, you must take care that your partner does not try to influence you in terms of the people with whom you socialize. Remember the number in the Main Influence position is the number that's in control of the cycle.

22/22 or 22/4

In a 22 year, which is the master challenge of 4, it is a time to roll up your sleeves, go to work, and know that you are building a foundation for the future. We know 22 is the number of the master builder, the master architect. It is simply laying the groundwork brick by brick of your own pyramid that eventually comes to the apex or the point of success, the point of culmination. In a 22 year, there is a lot of hard work, but do not expect to reap great benefits in a 22 year. If you're in a company or a corporate situation, you may get promoted, but it will be up one notch. It's not to the top. Working hard in a 22 year has long-lasting benefits. You simply will not see them at this time. However, if you are the kind of person that needs evidence, take good care and do not be lazy or succumb to the pressure of hard work in this time. Otherwise, you will pay a big price. A 22 does not present itself in every 4 year cycle. This could be a rare opportunity to really create something big. If you are successful, and financially well off while in a 22 year, this is a time to be charitable, or even philanthropic. It may be a time to create a new foundation, a charity, or something from which other people will benefit. This is not a time to get involved in anything like a pyramid scheme, or in any kind of get rich quick program. It's not a time to gamble or do anything foolish. It is a time to use a lot of common sense, recognize your intention for the long haul, and build for the future.

23/5

As always, a 5 year is a time of change. And you must make sure that in a 5 year that change is productive and done for the right reason and that you do not cause change just for the sake of it. With a 23/5, the 2 influences 5, which means the emotions or an emotional reaction can bring about change, or someone very close to us that we are partnering with can bring about change. As the number 3 influences the 5, friends can bring about change. A partner influences our friendships or a partner influences what we say and how we deal with people. So changes that come in a 23/5 year are greatly externally influenced, because the 2 and 3 represent the people who are the closest to us.

This is also a time when the people who are closest to us can help us to grow. If you are in a business partnership with someone at this time, you must allow yourself to be focused on your partner's dealings. They could possibly have business arrangements with other people that you're not aware of. In a 5 year, the possibility of scattering does exist, as well as fragmented platforms. On a romantic level, if you are not in a relationship, this can be a time where dating seems to be like a revolving door for most of the year. In this time, the possibility exists to meet someone special, someone that you may have a long-term relationship with. No matter what the circumstance, it is a time to have fun and enjoy your freedom.

24/6

This is the cycle that the New York Stock Exchange went into on its birthday on May 17, 2000. That was the time that the stock market began to drop drastically. If you are looking at the Personal Year Cycle of a stock, be very careful if it's in a year that is influenced by the number 2, because the number 2 does mean pulling back, staying in the background. The 24/6 represents partner or passivity influencing the structure, which is the number 4. Remember 4 represents contracts. The number 6 has nothing to do with earned money, but in a 6 year, money can appear or disappear mysteriously. It is very wise in any kind of business to be more conservative and prepare for hard work in a 24/6 year, because the 6 also represents responsibilities. On a personal level, 24 represents a partner being supportive, or a partner trying to control a situation. It also represents a partner looking for a legal arrangement and since it is over the number 6, it can represent love, home, family, and marriage. So a 24/6 year is an opportune time to enter into a marital contract. Because the partner is doing the influencing, be careful that the partner is truly supportive and not manipulating, or you could find yourself deep in a relationship that could be binding you literally, not just on paper. If you are in a business partnership or in a marriage, this is also a time that you would want to know what your partner is trying to work on or doing. Your partner could be getting stronger this time in regards to whatever he or she is working on. It is very important to keep balance in your partnerships at this point in time. You could become very passive instead of staying in balance.

240

25/7

2003

The **7** year is a time of pulling back, being alone, and going into your head quite a bit. And because the number **7** represents spirituality, if we translate that literally, if we go into spirit, then we do become invisible. The **25** means the partner changes, the partner moves, or the partner goes away. You must be very careful in a **25/7** that you don't become so removed, so passive, so uninvolved in your relationship that the partner gets fed up and moves on. The **25** also means that your emotions go through changes. And because it is in a **7** year, you may have mood swings or feelings that you don't completely understand. When the number **2** influences the number **7**, the emotions or the spontaneous side is influencing wisdom. As the **5** influences the **7**, the **5** means that there are changes in the way you think. Any energies or situations that seem to be stuck or stagnant in the **24/6** year begin to move in the **25/7**.

26/8

2004

This can be a time of abundance in a family way. The **26** means the partner is facing family issues. Since the **2** influences the **8**, the partner is influencing your money. And as the **6** influences the **8**, the family situation, the home, has an influence on your money. In this cycle, if you are married, and have children, you may face a lot of expenditures on the home front. This is a great time to save for your children's college education. Always remember that an **8** year involves money management. This is also a time where pregnancy is very likely. This is a time where emotions and hormones are running high and have a strong effect on family issues. In a **26/8** year, it's very easy to get caught up into spending money on the home or spending too much money on the children. If your marital situation is weak or if you are in a time of divorce, this is a time where you could lose a lot of money through alimony, because the partner is influencing the money. If you're in a divestiture of a corporation or a business arrangement, you stand the chance of losing money in these kinds of business ventures. On a positive note, this is an excellent time, if you have a partnership or if you are married, to buy real estate and invest. The key to a **26/8** year is to manage money and invest for the future.

This is also a time where your partner may be succeeding financially. Whenever the number **2** is influencing the number **8**, it is very easy to be spontaneous with money because the emotions are influencing the money.

27/9 *2005*

This is a time when a partner may become more spiritual, may influence how you think, or may influence your feelings and empathy. This is also a time when you will be much more sensitive to everyone and everything around you. You may find yourself lost in thought. Because it is a **9** year, a time of completion, this is a good time to become introspective and sort out your feelings. And if anything has been bothering you over the past **9** years, it is definitely a time to let it go and move on.

28/1

2006

In this year, the partner becomes more successful, and in return, helps you with money that creates your independence, perhaps allowing you to start your own business. The partner is definitely more supportive in this year. If it goes into the negative, this year could see a partner taking control of your money, which isn't necessarily negative, but it does put the control in the other person's hands. Because of the energy of the year and the spontaneity of the 2 in regards to emotions, it is possible to be very compulsive with money. Be very careful what you commit to in a 28/1 year, because the energy is fresh and ready to go. If you are working on a new project or starting a new business, this is a time that a backer may come into the picture and help you get going.

29/11 or 29/2

2007

This is a partnership coming to completion, or a partnership coming to fulfillment. You must manage the partnership and your emotions very well in this cycle because there will be a lot of highs and lows emotionally that could make your partnership either very good or bring it to it's knees. If you are in an 11 cycle with the 29, you will feel the pressure of a partnership while you were trying to get in touch with the deepest part of your own feelings. Any partnership formed in this cycle will come to an end. It will not be long-term.

compound personal years beginning with 3

When the number 3 is in the Main Influence position, the main themes are communication, use of the voice, and people. And when I say people, I mean the social structure such as friends, not an intimate partner, or a family member. When the number 3 is in the Main Influence, this is not a time to be reclusive or turn away from people. Yet, at the same time, what you say affects everyone around you. So, when you are in a Personal Year beginning with a 3, you must pay attention to what you say, and employ people as an asset at that time. The number 3 represents optimism and being positive, so if you are negative, or get involved in gossip or rumors at that time, you work against the 3 energy and could very easily alienate people. If you do fall into a cycle where 3 is the Main Influence for a period of time, I highly urge you to be social, friendly, and choose your words wisely. Since the 3 also represents happiness, you can have a good time, without feeling guilty.

30/3

The 0 is the all or nothing number and since it is paired with the 3, this is an all or nothing aspect in regards to the voice and friendships. In this year, our dealings with people are very extreme, either really good or really bad. But with the number 3 on the top *and* bottom, communication and dealing with people is affecting our social structure and our ability to use our voice. In a way, one affects the other. For the most part, because a $30/3$ follows a $29/11$, this cycle follows a time that could be upsetting or very intense emotionally. Maybe a partner prior to this year has gone away, or, at the opposite end of the spectrum, there has been great fulfillment with a partner. But now with a 3 in the main influence, the attention is turned to having a good time. If a person is single and dating in a $30/3$, it can be a real circus. People come and go. This is a time where I would advise you not to get serious. But because every Personal Year Cycle is a reflection of your metaphysical clock, you are probably not in the mood for anything serious. You'll just want to play and have a good time, and have a plethora of social contacts. If you are in a business that involves communication on any level, such as sales, this is a time for you to use your voice and flourish. But if you are in sales, remember you must back up what you say. If you schmooze people to get what you want, or to manipulate them during this time, it will backfire on you. Such behavior could ruin your social structure, social standing, and your reputation. If you are creative, the number 0

represents an explosive energy, representing an opportunity to use the voice, or to express yourself in whatever you do artistically. If you are your own business, or your business is in a **30/3** year, it's a great time to advertise and get the word out that you are open for business.

31/22 or 31/4

2009

The **4** represents logic, pragmatism, and hard work. The **31** means people advising you or telling you what to do. Thus, this is a good time to listen to people and what they have to say. Take their advice, but at the same time be careful that people do not manipulate you. Remember, in a **4** year, you may look for security, but also risk getting boxed in. Be careful what you do contractually at this point in time. The **31** represents communicating the self. At this time, you may be communicating who you are and what you want, so that you can establish the security that you need. As the **3** influences the **4**, people will also try to influence your work, how you work, or whatever you're trying to accomplish. This is also a good time to identify yourself in the work force with a new logo. Remember the number **1** as it influences the number **4** may mean new work or new beginnings around your work. The **3** represents communication in the form of advertising or creatively expressing yourself with your work. This may be a good time to hire that ad firm that your business really needs. If the **4** year does not represent new beginnings, it will bring a recreation of the foundation that you're building upon. Just imagine a high-rise building that is already there. You're just building floor by floor. In every **4** year, you're laying another strong foundation.

32/5

This is the reverse of the 23/5 where the partner may be influencing the social structure. Here, we have friends or people in the social strata influencing a partner, creating a change in our lives. If you are in a romantic or business partnership, be very careful that your friends are not trying to talk you out of or into a situation that they think is good for you, or not good for you. Friends mean well, but they don't always know the whole situation. Because the 5 represents change and movement and 3 is fun, friends could be encouraging you to go out and have a good time. A cycle like this combining the 3 and 5 represents a lot of pleasure. Be sure you do not scatter yourself in the good time and undo the foundation that you created in the previous 31/4 year. A cycle like this could represent a lot of laziness or distractions. In business, a 32/5 may be a time where your clientele or customers may be changing or rotating. If that is the case, do not be afraid of losing people. Sometimes a space has to be created to allow new people to come in. In this cycle, you could get so playful that you may neglect a partner. The positive energy applied to this socially is to include your friends and your partner in social get-togethers. This cycle is also the prelude to the social life getting ready to evolve into a partnership or a marriage.

33/6

The 6 year involves responsibility, trust, honesty, and loyalty, especially in family and home matters. If you're in a business that is service oriented, you will become very, very busy at this point in time. It's very easy to bite off more than you can chew in the 33/6 because you will feel that it's your responsibility to take on responsibility. When we get the 3s on the front and back, we have the double influence of people. The 33 is the Christ number, as represented by Christ supposedly living to 33 years old. This is a time where one could be crucified, so we must take good care in a 33/6.

This is a year where people have something to say. In a time like this, with the number 3 on the front and back, some people will praise you; some will criticize you. In a time like this, it's as if half the world loves you and half the world hates you and you must hear the cheers and cover your ears to the boos. If you are married or have a family in a 33/6 year, everybody will want your time. Yes, definitely you'll feel very wanted in the 33/6. But where do you find time for yourself in this cycle? This is also a time to inspect your health. The number 6 or a 6 Personal Year represents health and in the negative, morbidity or mortality. This is not a time to take careless risks in any aspect of your life, whether with your health, engaging in a sport that could endanger you, driving recklessly in the car, or being reckless with money. We do not usually associate the 6 year with money, but in this year, money could come and go unexpectedly. Normally, it is money that could appear from an inheritance, some kind of legacy, or an insurance settlement, but it also can go away due to unexpected situations. If you are in this cycle or know this cycle is coming up, prepare for it. If you are creative, this is a time to put your creative voice out there and say what's on your mind. This is the time of healing words, and even though Christ was crucified for the work that he did, he's remembered in a positive way. So even though there may be people that criticize you in this cycle, you still must do what you need to do. I do not advise buying a stock that is in a 33/6 year because the company could come under scrutiny and criticism. Even if it is profitable, people can find something wrong with it. The stock could drop drastically if it's in a 33/6 year. I advise everyone that goes through the 33/6 year to think of it in a positive way, even though the energy can be somewhat ominous. Do not be fearful, especially of people. Think of it as having a positive effect on yourself. This is a great time to design a home or redecorate a home. If you do feel that people are overwhelming you, this is a time to simply disappear a little bit. The 6 represents returning to nature, so go to the ocean, to the woods, or the mountains, whatever is close to you that represents a getaway.

34/7

You may pull back or want to be more of a loner in a 34/7. The 34 represents people coming into your space. In a 34/7, people will be curious about you because you are trying to be mysterious. It draws them to you. This is also a time where the creative mind influences the logical mind (the 3 influencing the 4). The right brain influences the left-brain. It's also a time where they are balanced. The 7 year is a form of going back to the drawing board. This is a great opportunity to rethink and take a look at both sides of whatever you are working on. If you have your own business, this is a time to look at recreating or excommunicating your strengths, or your foundation, but not to put it out there. This is simply a time to redraw it. The following year is when you put it into action. So it is a time of planning. It's a time of thought. If you see a stock that's in a 34/7 year, they are planning something. This is a good time to buy that stock. They are planning to do something big. They are planning to move forward. If you work for a large corporation that's in a 34/7 year, keep your ear to the railroad tracks. Something big is in the works. If upper management seems somewhat quiet right now, it means they are up to something. This is a time where no news does not represent good news.

35/8

The 8 year represents money and growth. In the 35 year, people cause changes. People help you to grow. As the 3 influences 8, it represents people helping you to be successful or influencing your money. A 35/8 year is a good time to invest. It can represent rapid growth, especially if you're looking at a stock. But because the 5 represents quick change, the movement on a stock in this Personal Year can be very rapid. It can almost be violent. If you are investing in a stock that is in a 35/8 year, watch it, set a goal for yourself that you are going to make X amount of dollars or percent, and then move on. This stock may move faster than you can watch it. Always remember any 8 year involves money management. It is not a guarantee that you're going to make money. It's how you play it. If you manage a company or are in charge of hiring, this is a time to grow with people. The 35 is people growth. You also may see people coming and going. People may suddenly quit or you may have to hire new people. Remember when it comes to money, the number 3 as the Main Influence makes you optimistic about money, success, and career. This is also a time where you may be promoted, so make yourself visible in some form in this cycle. Promote yourself. If the boss invites you out to lunch, accept that invitation. He or she is most likely feeling you out, to see where you stand on certain issues. The 8 year represents leadership. The 8 is the number of the executive, so this is a good time to grow a business.

36/9

The 9 year is the time of completion and endings, but it's also the number of compassion. I want to address that first because 3 is people and communication, 6 is humanitarianism and healing and 9 comes back to service to people. This is a good time to be of service and to help people. And because the 3 represents people, people will turn around and help you. The 9 always represents "what comes around goes around." The completion in a 36/9 is friends and family. You will be inclined to eliminate people from your life in this cycle. And you will see it from a good one to six weeks prior to going into this year. You will feel the energy shift to wanting to remove people. Because the 6 also represents your home, you will feel strongly inclined to throw away possessions and clean out closets, literally and figuratively. If you're in business you may feel very inclined to let people go, to downsize, or to even fire people. If you buy a stock or you own a stock that had a very strong 35/8 year, the strength will continue part way into this cycle. But watch it very closely because that strength and this cycle will start to come to an end. This is a good time to sell a stock that has grown up to this point. The 36/9 represents the endings of people. Because you are in a time of completion,

you will communicate that ending to those around you with such finality and possibly venom, that they will feel that you truly do not want them around anymore, and they will leave permanently. So if you are not in a good mood in this time, know that you could create endings that you will not have the opportunity to think twice about down the road. Be careful that you do not make enemies in this cycle.

37/1

The 1 year is about new beginnings. The 37 is about speaking the mind. I like to call this cycle the "being brutally honest" year. The communication is coming from the heart 1 and soul. It is a matter of speaking wisdom. It's communicating what you have learned. It is also about people trying to get into your head. People are very curious about you. This is also a time as the 3 influences the 1, that you could express yourself very easily through writing. This is a very dogmatic personal year. You will express what's on your mind very clearly. This is also a good opportunity to take classes or seminars around spirituality, metaphysics, or anything that interests you very deeply. Therefore, you can discuss it with those around you. In this cycle, you will be very opinionated. If you're looking at a company to invest in, this is a time where a company will be revealing something that they have invented. New products are coming out. It may not be a profitable time for that company, but it may be a good time to jump in on something and just wait for the growth to appear. I'd like to add that the performance of a company does not necessarily reflect the performance of the stock—something that baffles investors.

38/11 or 38/2

The 11 appears as a Master Challenge. The 38 is people helping you to be successful, people backing you with money, people promoting you into a leadership position that makes you very nervous because of the 11 energy. If you are in a 38/11, people can have their hands in your pockets. Do not, and I repeat, *do not* ever lend money in this cycle because you will not get it back. People will steal from you in this cycle if you make yourself vulnerable to it. This is a time to be greedier with your money. The theme here is greedy, not needy. A company or a stock that is in a 38/11 year will have many ups and downs. It will attract a lot of investors, so this may be a cycle that you may want to step back and watch what happens. If you're in a 38/11 cycle, and you're normally a very proud person, allow people to help you in this cycle. The help will take you a long way.

39/3

With the 3 on the top and bottom, along the 9, this signifies friendships coming to completion and a social structure coming to an end. I also call this number the "recycling of people" because the 9 represents "what comes around goes around," so it's very easy in this cycle that people you let go of 9 years ago may reappear. The number 3 also represents fun and having a good time. With 39/3, I have seen in my clients for years, that it's the good times coming to an end. So if there's anything that you want to do in terms of pleasure in a 39/3, do it now. Although this is not a year necessarily that has to do with travel, the number 9 has a minor meaning of travel. This is a good time to take that vacation you've been wanting, because in the next cycle you won't be able to do

it. Friendships will come to an end in this cycle because they were simply "cycling out," not with the intention of elimination as in the 36/9. In fact, if anything, the 39/3 can be a sad time for all parties if endings in the friendship come up because the 39 is the voice of compassion or speaking compassion. If you own a business that is in a 39/3 or are looking to invest in a business that is in a 39/3 year, check very closely into their profitability because the business may be overly generous at this point in time to their people. Make sure the company has not weakened itself financially by being too magnanimous.

compound personal years beginning with 4

When the number 4 is in the Main Influence position, the influence is logic, pragmatism, being more conservative, and looking for security. We always see the number 4 as the four-sided figure, or the box. This can work for a person or work against them depending on their nature. When the number 4 is in the Main Influence, it is definitely a time to use common sense, especially when it comes to matters of work, contracts, or legalities. This is a time to go to work. When the number 4 is in the Main Influence position, it is time to roll up your sleeves.

I caution people who have a lot of number 4 influence in their life (a need for structure), whether they are a 4 personality or their Birth Path Number has a 4 as a Main Influence, even a Minor Influence, they may find themselves feeling very disrupted, like they have no control over anything.

40/22 or 40/4

I call this number the pressure cooker. I've always drawn it out as the stick man in the box, with a box ten times bigger coming down on the little box.

That stick man has his hands to the ceiling of the box, trying to keep it from caving in on him. That is the feeling of a **40/22** or **40/4** year. This number vibrates to most people like a giant monolith just ready to fall over on them. This number causes people to cave in if they are not prepared for it. That's why I always tell people the prior cycle of **39/3** is the good times coming to an end. Because in a **40/4**, they must get ready to go to work. A lot of people do not prepare for this number. In a **40/4**, because of the aspects of work coming into play, it is a time that you would be so busy that you may not have much time to do anything else but work. Because you can be so busy, if you are working on anything contractually, whether buying a home, a car, or you're in a business that involves contracts and legalities, have someone else such as an accountant or a lawyer look at those contracts. You will miss the problem if one exists, causing yourself **9** years of legal hassles until the next **4** year comes around so you can undo it. Even though the number **6** represents health, this

is a time that you must watch your health due to stress. It's not a time when the normal nature of the body would create problems, but the stress could create disease. This is also a time, as long as you're willing to work, that you could create strength and a foundation, keeping your focus on the fact that the work is going to pay off. It does depend on your nature as to how you're going to look at this cycle. You just cannot goof off in a time like this. A company in a cycle like this could be subject to legalities or investigations. An individual in a time like this could be prone to legalities. The company may just be under too much pressure at this point in time. If you're looking to back a stock, watch it in this cycle, but do not buy it. Wait until the following year.

41/5

The 5 is the number of change. But with the 4 influencing it, we have a paradox. I say periodically that 4 and 5 don't like each other. The 4 is structure and being boxed in. The 5 is being the star and growing, going in different directions, maybe even scattering. But the 4 influences the 1 or boxing in of the self. This is a time to be very careful about what you commit to. If you are going through some financial instability at this time, this is something that you have to work out. It's very easy to get in too deep in this cycle. Your need for security could compromise the theme of freedom for this year. Take a good look at any stock in a 41/5 year. The New York Stock Exchange's Birth Path is a 41/5, so any stock that's under the New York Stock Exchange, not the NASDAQ, will have a good year because it crosses into the strength of the New York Stock Exchange. I would definitely buy and own a stock in a 41/5 year that's on the New York Stock Exchange. A 41/5 year is not a time to make a commitment, especially into a relationship. Your overall theme at this time is to be able to come and go as you please. It's very easy to get yourself trapped in a situation. Example: If your money is not as good as it should be at this point in time, you may be inclined to take on a roommate or cohabitate with someone. However, you could end up in a worse situation than you were. This is a time to work things out for yourself, not with a partner, legally or romantically. You definitely can go from the frying pan to the fire at this time. Create a foundation for yourself that fosters the freedom that you're looking for. This is a time to strengthen, not weaken.

42/6

This year is about supporting a partner, helping a partner, legalities with a partner while dealing with family matters, and family responsibility. This is a very strong marriage cycle. If you're in a marriage and the marriage is weak, the cycle could bring divorce. This year indicates legalities with a partner in one-way or another. If this is a business partnership you may have more responsibility than your normal share at this time. But somehow it will be okay with you. You're in the time of taking on responsibility and trust. If you own a business, you could go into a merger. If you are looking at a company or stock to invest in, that company may merge, or absorb another company. Be cautious, because most mergers drag down the value of the stronger stock. A 42/6 year is very good for pharmaceutical stocks because of the nature that business deals with is healing and service. This is a time to look at that stock for purchase. This is also a time when you may have to support a female member of the family. It may be a mother who may have to come live with you, or if you're a man and your wife is pregnant you may have to be more supportive of her.

43/7

In a 43/7 year, you may try to control people or keep them at an arm's distance. Once again, we have the 7, which is the loner pulling back, needing space. In the 43/7 year, we have the logical brain influencing the creative brain. The left-brain is ruling. The left-brain is influencing the deeper part of the mind. This is a time where a person will feel that they need to distance themselves from people so that they can learn or take the time to do what they need to do to develop. Be very careful in this cycle on a social level. You may push people away, or forget to return phone calls. You could come under criticism or scrutiny from your friends, even though you don't mean to alienate at this point in time. This is also a time that is very good to literally go back to school because the logical mind is influencing the brain to learn. The ability to assimilate information in this cycle is very strong. The left and right brain are balanced. Also in this cycle, due to the 43, you may find yourself categorizing people, being judgmental of people, or just too hard on people because of your need for perfectionism. Take care of your dealings with people. If you're looking at a stock, or looking at the performance of a company, the company is doing some restructuring. This may not be a good time to purchase a stock.

44/8

I regard the 44/8 as the hardest Personal Year Cycle that exists. It is a factor of 11. It has 4 on both sides, creating pressure. We usually think of the number 4 as work, but the number 4 also represents structures in our life. This could be the need to balance work and family matters. It could be the need to balance two jobs at the same time. It could be working two jobs at the same time to make ends meet, but it is pressure coming from both ends. So instead of the way we drew the 40/4 of the big box crashing down on the little one, this is the stick man trying to balance two big blocks. Or we could also draw it as two big blocks closing in on the stick man. This is a time to manage money very wisely. Be careful of any illegal obligations that you get into. It is definitely a time to roll up your sleeves and work. This is not a time to go off traveling or to be irresponsible. You could cause a lot of financial hardships down the road. I cannot emphasize enough the hardships that this cycle can bring about if the energy is misused. However, as with the energy of 11, the hard work that is put into this cycle will pay great dividends, because the 4s represent foundations or security. You may be working on more than one thing at once, but both entities have the opportunity to be successful. A stock or a company in this cycle will be under a lot of pressure. They may even be divesting or splitting off at this time. If you are looking at buying into a stock that is in this cycle, take great care. Use common sense not intuition. The number 8, because it represents very material things is very evidential. You don't have to read between the lines at a time like this. What you see is what you get. This is also a time when your health could suffer due to the pressure of work and money.

45/9

The 9 energy makes this is a year of completion. But it is also a year of vacillation, since the 4 and 5 collide here. The 4 is structure, the 5 is going in different directions. In a 45/9 year, you'll find imbalanced energies. You may get up Monday morning full of energy. Tuesday you can't get out of bed. Wednesday you're ready to go. Thursday you feel like you haven't had enough sleep. You must balance your energies in a 45/9 to keep yourself on an even keel. Because a 4 and 5 are pragmatism versus scattering or illogic, vacillation occurs. Focus on decisions that need to be made at this time. Do not sit on the fence too long or someone else will make the decision for you. The 45 also refers to work, the system, the structure, and making changes. If you work for a company, this is not a time to be picky or try to stir things up too much, because it means the company will change you or move you. You will either go to another location, another position, or be moved out. As the 45/9 comes after the 44/8, this is a time where some pressure comes off. It is not a time to undo the hard work of the previous year, but you do have the opportunity to take a breath here. It's also important at a time like this to feel compassion. As the 5 influences the 9, which is impatience, the 9 is patience. You will find yourself teeter-tottering in your dealings with people. You want to be nice, but at times you may not be able to help yourself and want to just move on.

46/1

This is a year of new beginnings based on a restructure of responsibility. The 46 is working out of the home or simply starting a home owned or homegrown business. At this time, you may have to take on the father figure or male energy or simply be the keystone of the family and shoulder a lot of family responsibility. If it is a business that you're looking at, the business is going into a time of strength. If it is a stock, you will see growth. This is a good time to buy. Personally speaking, because 4 and 6 are influencing the 1, the load of responsibility on your shoulders will come from work and family. But with the 1 energy, which is new and fresh energy, you have the ability to handle it. In fact, if anything, you welcome the challenge.

47/11 or 47/2

The 47 indicates restructuring of the belief system, where you may change your philosophy of life. You may join a new spiritual organization. Because of the 11 configuration, this may be a time of learning heavy lessons in relationships. If you are not in a relationship or a marriage, be very careful about getting into one in this cycle. You may feel innately that you are working out past-life karma or that you owe a partner something, creating a lot of stress, anxiety, and tension. An 11 year becomes a crisis if you let it. This cycle is mostly about intimate people in your life. If it's a company that you're looking at, they are undergoing a philosophical restructuring. This is not a time for an individual or a company to overextend itself in commitment.

newmerology

48/3

This is a cycle of being very happy in dealing with people. It is a time of communication, being more expressive and creative, bringing about work and structure and also money. If you are a truly artistic and creative individual, this is a time to really go for it—to put yourself out there and not be afraid to work. If you are an artist or an actor, this may be a time where you might have to also work that extra day job to keep yourself going. You never know whom you will meet in a 3 year. That's why you must be very open-minded in a 3 year and always think positive. From May 1997 until May 1998, the New York Stock Exchange was in a 48/3 year. It was a time of great growth, because 48/3 means the people are interested in the security and the monetary possibilities. If you are interested in an individual stock that goes into this cycle, you have found a stock that you should buy and hold onto for a couple of years. It will grow. The 3 makes it attractive. It makes people want to invest in it. The 4 and 8 is the security and the foundation with the monetary growth.

compound personal years beginning with 5

When the Main Influence Number is the number 5, you are now in a time where you are influenced by change, where things have the opportunity to grow at a very fast rate, and where they can become very scattered if you are not used to the 5 energy.

When the number 5 is in the Main Influence of a Personal Year, it means that it will affect or change the Minor Influence number and the Base Number. It is definitely a time to go with the flow. It's a time you may have to learn patience, or tolerance. You may just have to realize that things will not stay the same. The 5 is illustrated by the pentagram, the five-sided figure where energy can go off in different directions. The 5 has an explosive energy, making this a time where you can be a star, or become very charismatic or very visible, or simply have many opportunities. You may have to choose the best opportunity or opportunities, create priorities, definitely focus, and finish and follow through. The 5 energy can get away from you and take you into too many directions at once.

50/5

This is a time of great change. Changes or multiple changes occur at once. I'd like to say that this number represents your changes having changes. We know that in a time of change it is good to be adaptable, and not go in too many different directions at once. But with the 50, the changes are of a very great magnitude. This cycle is very hard on some people, especially those with a predominance of 4s in their numerological realm. If you are a 5 personality, you will flourish in this time, but remember to stay focused and finish everything that you are starting. As we saw in the Birth Path Number, the number 50/5 is the number of the master magician. So this is a time to make things happen. It's a time to manifest, but all thoughts in a 50/5 must be positive. Because of the magic of this number, what manifests will come very soon in accordance with what you were thinking. This number can be very constructive and very destructive depending on the circumstances and the person that has it. This is a time in your life when so many changes can occur at once that you will literally feel as if you are in the eye of a hurricane. Comically, I equate this number to the little Tasmanian Devil cartoon character. When you get out of this cycle, you will feel like that, as if you've been in a spin and needing to ground. With its birthday in 1999, The New York Stock Exchange was in a 50/5 year, and that was a time of great growth. So this gives you an idea of how much can happen in this cycle. Just make sure to manage your time, your money, and your energies wisely. This is a time where you will feel like driving a very high performance sports car. And it can get away from you if you've never driven that kind of energy before. This is also the number that represents a time of being a catalyst for things in motion. In this time you may also affect the lives of other people around you, not just your own.

51/6

This number indicates changes in the home front. This is a time where it can be a change of duties or responsibilities, a change in the home, literally. We must be very careful when we see the 5 and 6 together because this can be dysfunction or scattering of the home. This may be a time when you've been living at home with parents or family and move out. Remember a 6 year can represent getting into a home situation or getting out of one. You may be buying or selling a home at this time, or getting in or out of a marriage. Remember because the 1 is in the Minor Influence, you are on the receiving end of the changes that are coming. You may feel somewhat out of control, or turn around and try to influence things on the home front, or maybe even feel like you must blame those around you for the changes that are going on. In a 6 year, no matter what kind of 6 it is, remember to take responsibility for your actions and deeds. This may simply be a time where you are going through the kinds of changes that allow you to be more of a loving family member. This is also a time for a woman, because 5/1 is growth of self, where you can become pregnant very easily. This is also a time when money that you were not expecting can come your way. The 5 is growth and abundance.

52/7

This is a year of being alone, somewhat deep in thought. The 52 means change of emotions, change of partner, or disruption around the partner. If you are in a marriage or a long-term relationship, you may be feeling as if it's time to get out because of the 52 and wanting to be alone. This is a time when you must manage your emotions and your thoughts very carefully. Do not be judgmental of the person that you're with. Look and see what is bothering you within before you break up a partnership or a marriage. Maybe it's a time where you just need a little more space, and if that is the case, ask for that space. If you misuse this energy in this cycle, you will end up alone. It may

also be a time, because the number 7 is spirit or invisible, and sometimes covert, when you may be tempted to have an affair behind someone's back. Because the number 7 represents the deepest parts of you, you must know your own truths. And in a 7 year, if you are not acting out of integrity in any way, shape, or form, you will have to deal with the ramifications of your actions over the next 9 years. Make sure you act in the truth of your own feelings. When it comes to business, this is a time not to let your emotions cause you to buy or sell stocks haphazardly or spontaneously. If you are looking at a company that's in a 52/7 year, this is a time to watch the stock and not necessarily act upon it. This is also a time where a business may divest of a partnership or undo a partnership that's been in existence.

53/8

The 8 year is always about managing money. But in a 53, you must especially pay attention to the movement of your money. The 5 in the Main Influence can mean the growth of money, or scattering of money. When we apply it to the 3, which represents people or social structure, it's very easy to become too generous with your money at this point in time. This is a time to look at investments very wisely, because the number 3 is people. You may be prone not to listen to what a stockbroker or a financial advisor is telling you, whereas this is the time to do that. For the most part this is a very positive cycle in dealing with money. Stay out of excessive or unnecessary expenditures. It is a time to invest in terms of people and personnel. If you own a business, this is a time to hire people, because people (3) helps the business (8) to succeed. This is also a time to evaluate the performance of the people that work for you. If someone is due or overdue a promotion, pay attention to that. Make the people that work for you feel appreciated and help them grow. In turn, they will help you grow. This is also a time where you may feel inclined to open up a branch office, or just to be more multilocational, or even multinational if that's the circumstance that presents itself. On a more personal level with money, once again, you may have the ability to manage corporate dollars, yet mismanage your own funds, because you are seeing things too much in the big picture, and not paying attention to the smaller details. If you are looking at investing in a company that's in a 53/8 year, the company is in growth. This is a good time to buy that stock. But once again, don't get greedy. If you have set a percentage goal, hit that goal, and then sell the stock.

54/9

This is a time of completing work or structure. The 54 is change of structure, change of work. Now the 54 can mean leaving one job and going to another. It can also mean changing the structure from within so you may move positions within the company. Because of the 5 and the 9, it's also a time when you may have to travel for your business or the company that you work for. As we saw in the 45/9, this number can represent vacillation. The 5 and 4 together do not mix well. But in this case, the 54 means that the changes are affecting the structure or the system as opposed to the reverse in the 45, where the system was dictating. This is where you have the ability to change your work situation and remain in control of it. Remember that because the number 9 represents compassion and being of service to people, whatever changes you make in the structure around you, make sure to keep one eye on how you are affecting the people. Because the 4 affects the 9, you could bring about an end to other people's jobs too. The 5 and 9 together represent the battle of being impatient versus patient. You want to make a lot of changes but the 4 energy will make you think. This better defines the reason for vacillation. This is also a time, as in the reverse of the 45/9, when energies will fluctuate. You will be full of energy one day, low energy the next, full of energy the next, and lower again. You must manage your energies and be careful of burnout. Any time 5 is in the main influence position, the possibility of overgrowth, burnout, or growth at too fast of a rate is always there. If you are looking at investing in a stock or a business that's in a 54/9 year, they may be thinking of, or it may be on their calendar, to split the stock. This is a good time to see when the split occurs and take advantage of that situation.

55/1

This is a time of new beginnings. But because of the 55, it's a time of many new beginnings. So instead of just going 5 different ways with the number 5, with the double nickels it's a time when you can go in ten different directions at once. This is a multiopportunity year. It doesn't mean that all the opportunities are good. It means that you must prioritize everything that you are working on, and not chase pipe dreams or fantasies. Have a good sense of what will work and then go after it. You can work on more than one thing at once because we have both 5s. But the 1 energy represents the self and not to take on too much. The number 1 represents a lot of pride and wanting to do it yourself. You may have to defer somewhat in this time and enlist help. When it comes to businesses, or the stock market, this is also a time where growth can go through the ceiling. A 55/1 is a very positive time. But mete out that energy. Envision being on a stagecoach with a team of fast horses in front of you pulling 5 reins in each hand. This is the power of the 55/1. It's a lot to handle and as long as you're focused, you can handle it. Remember, in a 1 year you are in fresh energy, so you have the energy to handle it.

56/22 or 56/11

The number 11 being affected by the 5 and 6 can be the crisis or crazy making due to changes in the home. The 56 can be moving homes, "running away from home," or trying to get out of a circumstance that is creating crisis. It can be a change of responsibility. The 56 is growth of responsibility which may be creating anxiety and tension. The number 11 affects people in a couple of different ways. It can be an evolution or a growth in the psychic abilities. The two 1s represent the left and right brain coming together on the intuitive scene. But it can also go into crisis mode where time just creates anxiety and tension that affects the person greatly. In any kind of an 11 year I always caution people, whether individually or in a business, that it's only a crisis if you let it be. If you manage this time very wisely and stay calm, the   energy makes you an inspiration to those around you. Because an 11 year sits in the position of the 2 year, you have a choice. You can operate in the 2 energy, which is giving it all the way, or empowering other people. Or you can operate in the 11 energy, as drawn as a little stick man looking at himself in the mirror. This is the image of self-empowerment.

If you let people drain you in an 11 year, and especially where the number 6 represents family matters, you find yourself at times upset with the family situation. If you are a mature adult, you may not even feel like going home after work due to whatever the disruption is. Be very careful about this cycle, because the 5 and 6 can indicate a change of relationship. It can mean getting in and out of a marriage due to a crisis of self. If this Personal Year Cycle hits in a very mature adult, say mid-40s, 50s, or at a time when the marriage is on the rocks, this can create the mid-life crisis that breaks up that marriage due to anxiety. If a stock or a business that you're looking at is in a 56/11 year, be very careful as there may be things about the business that may be changing. There may be a changing of responsibilities, or movement of the people within that isn't always communicated. The business itself may be in some kind of crisis. Do a lot of investigating before buying into a stock that's in this cycle.

57/3

This is a time when the year's events will change how you think. You will change your philosophies of life. You will change your mind a lot. The 57 can also mean you are scatterbrained, with too many scattered thoughts. Because 3 is the Base Number, you may internalize this energy as mind chatter and may simply have too much on your mind. The 3 energy represents communication. So the way to remedy the mind chatter is to share this with people. Now 57 also represents a change of philosophy that you communicate. This is definitely a time where you may be communicating thoughts and feelings that upset people. They may want to shoot the messenger either because you are changing your mind or communicating things to people that they are not expecting. Nonetheless, because you are in a 3 year, which represents a time to deal with people and communicate in a positive, optimistic way, you will see this as doing something good. But the reaction that you get from people may bring a lot of criticism. Your actions may seem good to some people and not so good to others. You may also want to be careful in this cycle, not only with what you say, but how you say it. Because in the 5/3, the 5 influences the 3, which means you are a catalyst to people. If a business is in a 57/3 year, they may be making an announcement that doesn't sit well with the stockholders or the people involved in it. I would not buy into a stock that is in a 57/3. If a stock is in a good position in a 57/3 or the 57/3 cycle is coming, I would sell it and move on, because they may not meet expectations in this cycle.

58/22 or 58/4

This is a time of stability, money growth, and great business growth. The number 4 represents stability and foundation. The 58 means a change in the business structure, a growth of money. If you are the sole proprietor, a solely owned business, or a company that's not incorporated, this is a good time to incorporate and gain strength. If you are incorporated, this is a good time to go public with your stock. In any kind of business that you have, this is a time to grow, make purchases and prepare for growth, or to buy products or add to your product line. The 5 and 4 once again are the paradox of growth and stability, but this number means the more you grow, the more you change the way you attain money—the more stable you become. This is a time of great opportunity to build. It's hard to find anything negative with this cycle. However, a company could over buy or go beyond the bounds or the advice of the accountants. On an individual basis, if you are in a company, you could be promoted. It's also a time where you could be somewhat of a workaholic. It may be hard-earned money, but there's definitely more money. It's a time to be somewhat of a cautious risk taker. Take some chances but don't be foolish. This is not a time where relationships will flourish. If you are in a relationship, you will create a great foundation for your family. You just may not have a lot of time to play. In fact, if you're not in a relationship you won't have the time or energy to get into one. But as the 8 represents growth and money, always remember to give back. Do not be greedy. Help other people out, and say thanks.

59/5

Whenever the number 9 is in the Minor Influence, we know that something is about to end. In this case, the 59 means changes are coming to an end, or changes are coming to completion. This is a time that if there is a long sequence where the number 5 has been in the Main Influence position for a number of years, meaning changes are ruling, this is the time when those changes are coming to a culmination. This allows the person to settle in or be able to be more responsible in the situations that call for trust, loyalty and responsibility. Because it is a 5 year, which obviously designates change and adjustment and the need to be patient, the 9 in the Minor Influence over the 5 means that level of patience is there. Even though a 50/5 and a 59/5 look very similar, the 59/5 means that there's some form of stabilization that's about to come into play. This is a time to make sure that any changes that need to be made are made. This is also a time, especially in a single person if you have more wild oats to sow, to do them now, because when the number 6 moves into place in the next cycle, family responsibilities and loyalty are needed. This is a time to learn and find out what's left inside of you that may be unsettled. This is a great year to travel, to come and go, to see what's out there. Because of the year ahead, this year once again calls for responsibilities that may even be in a job situation. If you are in a job such as a traveling sales person, simply on the go or on the road a lot, this may be a time where you are preparing to take more of a position that's settled, that is in an office, or a management position. If you are on the road, this year teaches you great experience of how to manage being your own boss. The 59/5 lets you know that it's time to settle down, or settle in. If you are looking at buying a company that is in a 59/5 year, this signifies that the rapid growth level, where a company has been expanding rapidly is about to come to an end or come to a completion. They have come to the end of a growth phase. On a personal level, this is a time to learn to be more patient with people, more patient with yourself, to let things come to maturity, and for you to come into a place of maturity.

compound personal years beginning with 6

When the number 6 is in the Main Influence position it indicates a time where family matters, health, responsibility, and issues in the home or the physical house are influencing the areas of our life. When the number 6 is ruling in Personal Year Cycles, this is a time when we must take care of our physical body, because the antithesis of health is mortality. It also represents a certain level of morbidity. We have to watch where our thoughts go in a 6 year. The thoughts can be very healthy, or they can take us into the depths of problems with our mental health. I emphasize that in a 6 year it is very important to take an overall healthy approach to life and make sure that you are solving any family matters that need to be dealt with. Also, because the number 6 is in the Main Influence, depending on the number that's in the Minor Influence, which we will see below, your family itself may be influencing you or part of your life. You may not always look squarely at the family's faults and turn a blind eye to other people's faults. Make sure that you objectively evaluate the family influence. It could be negative, or it could be positive.

60/6

I call the 60/6 year, the *explosion in the house*. The 0, as we've said many times, is the all or nothing. So we're dealing with family matters in the Main Influence, and in the Base year. The reason I call this the *explosion of the house* is because a 60/6 really can bring family matters to a head. If you are married, and either you or your spouse go into a 60/6 Personal Year Cycle, take great care of your marriage because things can get blown out of proportion. You can find yourself in arguments at the "drop of a hat" in this cycle. Conversely, if you are not in a relationship, this is a time where you can get into one very quickly. If either you or a mate is going into this cycle, you must be careful of pregnancy because of the ability to grow in a family way that is inherent in this number. And because the 0 represents God's number, miracles do happen. Remember the 6 also represents nature. In the first *Jurassic Park,* as Jeff Goldblum's character warned, nature does have a mind of it's own sometimes. So take care in the 60/6—nature could wreak chaos. Because the 60/6 is so extreme in its energy, health can fluctuate in this cycle. You must take extra good care of your physical body. In a 6 year, unexpected things can happen with money that is not earned. It can be an inheritance, a legal settlement, an insurance settlement, or an investment that you have not been counting on for income. In a 6 year, all of a sudden circumstances around it accelerate. Now when I say the word "inheritance," a lot of people grow nervous because they infer a death in the family. This is a possibility. Sometimes, there is money that has been buried in paperwork for years, that's been tied up in probate even though the individual may have passed on years before. So please do not assume that there is a death in the family at this time. It's your own health that you have to take better care of. In a 60/6 the issues of the house take precedence.

Also you may look at redoing your home by reconstructing or remodeling. The tension in the house can be very extreme, causing a lot of arguments. If the energy in your home does not feel right, this is an excellent time to Feng Shui it. This may also be a good time to make sure that your own will is current. This is not to say that your death is imminent. Rather it is a matter of dealing with responsibilities, no matter what kind of 6 year it is. It is very important to be loyal, honest, sincere, and fully responsible for everything that you do. On the job level, you may find a lot heaped upon your shoulders at this time.

And if you are not careful, you may find that you are doing a lot of work, but feeling unappreciated. You may also find that this is a time where you may be called upon to do very humanitarian deeds. The people in general around you may be in a lot of turmoil. They may turn to you for your humanitarian or compassionate side. Just be careful that your own mental health is not affected at this time. You are rather suggestible and may take on other people's problems. You definitely can attract psychic vampires at this time. People around you are so needy that they simply drain you.

It's paramount at this time to take care of yourself. Get away from it all, go to the mountains, a lake, the ocean, or whatever is near you that allows you to get back to nature. You may also feel very inclined to have a child or a pet that you've always wanted. In this cycle, a company should be very careful about how it expands or merges. If you are playing the stock market and a company is going into a 60/6 year, and they absorb a company or merge with another, the stock of the company in this cycle could go down drastically because of taking on too much responsibility. Now, because the 6 and the Main Influence represents family, we have to think of the shareholders of a company as family in this situation. It means the shareholders through all of these numbers, where they are positioned, will have a lot of influence in whatever the company does. This is true for any year with the 6 in the main influence position.

61/7

In this cycle, a family may be trying to put a guilt trip on you and your belief system, or you may be in total disagreement with what you believe. This number is the reverse of the 16/7, where the individual was telling the family how it is based on philosophical differences. Here we have the family admonishing the individual. If you are in this cycle, you will want to retreat and get into your own headspace. You can feel very pursued or persecuted for how you think and feel. On a positive note, this is a period where a lot of healing can take place for the individual mentally and physically. This is a time where you may feel overworked or everyone needs you too much. You may need

to get away even more so than in the 60/6. The 7 year is always a time for a certain amount of rest, relaxation, and meditation. At this time you may feel that your family has turned their back on you. But with the 1 in the minor influence you will have to ask yourself: Who is really influencing you? The people around you or is it yourself? When a company is in a 61/7, a lot of responsibility is falling back on the shoulders of leadership. The company may be in a certain amount of upheaval based on the employees or the shareholders, or both. This is a time where a company is planning to rebuild and pull back. If you have a stock that is going into this cycle, it is wise to have already sold it and made your money. If you're well into the cycle and the stock is dropping, at this point you might as well hold on and wait till it goes back up.

62/8

With a 6 in the Main Influence in an 8 year, investments or other business opportunities that have been just kind of lingering or hovering come to fruition. This is when a company would find it advantageous to merge or take on a partner because the responsibilities fall on the shoulders of the partner. The 6 influences the 2. If you are a man on a personal level, you will feel very inclined to start a family with your partner because the 2 is in the minor influence. This puts you into a potent position. The 6 impregnates or acts in a family way with a partner. And if we look at the number 8 drawn as 2 circles, one above each other in simple script, note that if the bottom circle of the 8 is drawn bigger than the circle on top, it can look like a pregnant woman.

So this is definitely a cycle where it's advantageous to be abundant in a family way or to start a family business with your marital partner. This is a time when home expenditures may be bigger than normal. It's very important to manage the household money in this cycle very wisely. If you are going to do major renovations on your home, you must plan this out carefully.

The number 6 represents unexpected events with money, so what you plan to do could cost you more than you thought. You may also learn things about your home that need repair. When we talk about the number 6 representing health, the health of your physical house comes into play in this cycle. You may discover that the heating system, the wiring, or the plumbing needs a major overhaul at this time. This is also a good time to look at the performance of your stock portfolio. This may be a good time to sell after extended growth. Since the number 6 represents the family, your family or your in-laws may be influencing your spouse or partner to get pregnant. Whenever the number 2 influences the number 8, there are always a certain amount of emotions or spontaneity that influences the money. Be very careful in this cycle that you are not compulsively spending. The number 2 represents pulling back or being passive. It could mean that your funds start to pull back due to the emotional attachments that you have toward money. This is also a time not to allow fear to influence your money. Your negative thought forms could cause your money flow to slow down or cease completely.

If you work for a large company or a corporation, this is a time where responsibility will be thrust upon you, and there is more money coming with that responsibility. This is a year to say yes and thank you to the responsibility and the opportunity to perform as a leader. The desire to be successful at this time will create a lot of pressure, which could impact your health. This is a time to take good care of the body and stay away from as much stress as possible. The 6 influence also represents humanitarianism. Whatever you achieve at this time monetarily, financially, superficially, you must give back in some charitable form. This is not a time to be greedy, but to be appreciative for everything that comes your way.

63/9

Whenever 6 and 3 influence the number 9, as we saw with the 36/9, this represents endings with people. The 6 is family, 3 is our social structure. This is when you may feel inclined to do a major house cleaning, literally and figuratively. Clean out closets, throw away things. We may also discard people, friendships, or relationships that have outlived their usefulness. In a 63/9, you may find that you want to wean the people who have been needy of you. At the same time, because the 6 and the 9 are together here, your compassion is needed greatly at this time and your humanitarian side, or your ability to heal people comes out in a very strong way. Now is when you can really shine through your deeds. But do not look for anything in return at this time. What matters now is how you affect people. This is not a time to have expectations of the people around you. Your family may have a lot to say about the people that you hang around with, or try to get you to end a friendship or a relationship. A company that is in a 63/9 is bringing a certain level of responsibility to an end, or a relationship with a company with whom they do business may come to an end. You may see a stock drop in this cycle. Or a company may allow itself to be bought out by another company.

64/1

As your energy comes up in this 1 year, a time of new beginnings, responsibility in the form of work is your fame. You also may find that the level of responsibility on the home front takes equal precedence to the responsibilities at work. You may wish to start a business out of your home. You may be moonlighting or have another business in addition to your regular job. You must be careful in a 1 year, which represents the self, so that you do not become greedy or selfish or fool yourself that you can do more than mere mortals. You may need or receive the support of family, people that are close to you. If you are a single parent, you may find yourself a little more stressed in this cycle, needing to work as opposed to being a stay-at-home parent. You will also feel kind of boxed in or hemmed in by

the level of responsibility that's in your life at this point. The solution is to face the responsibility and not to run away from it. This cycle is the result of choices that you've made. This may be a time where it's very necessary to completely organize your life and set priorities. A family member who is in need may want to come and live with you. A company or a stock in this cycle has recently shed some dead weight, and has restructured itself for the new road ahead. If you buy a stock that's in this cycle, buy it for the long-term, not for short-term goals. Be careful of legal commitments that you make at this time, because the number 1 energy is also very potent. If you're not careful, especially if you are a man, you could find yourself in a paternity suit due to your sexual escapades. This is also a great time to start a new exercise regimen so you can work off the stresses and pressures of the 64/1 year. It's a cycle of new beginnings, new responsibilities, and new forms of organization in your lifestyle.

65/11 or 65/2

This is a cycle where the family dysfunction can create major changes and stresses in your life. The 6/5 means the family or responsibility begins to grow. If your life up to this point has allowed your family situation to go in the wrong direction, this can be a year of crisis. This is a year when the family and family responsibilities have a great effect on you, which can either bring you closer to them or make you very distant. The 65 means the house goes through changes. Your physical home may be disrupted due to renovation. Also in this time, the potential of a negative 65/11 can be an intruder or a burglar. Take good care of your personal possessions in this cycle. Depending on your own behavior, a 65/11 means the family moves you out. Maybe it's a time to let go and move. Maybe you're holding on too tight. Because of the number 6 in the Main Influence position, over the 11, which is the master challenge of 2, this is period that could throw you into the relationship of a lifetime or break up a marriage. Look at yourself and your own responsibility in any family matters. This is also when a company can be very strong. It's not a good time to partner, because any partners that would be taken on at this time would be weak, and weaken the stronger company.

This is a cycle for personal growth, especially on an intuitive level and not let your emotions get the best of you. Do not let people guilt-trip you into taking on more responsibility than you should.

66/3

This cycle is either very constructive or very destructive. We saw the **33/6** as the Christ number in a cycle where you can be victimized or crucified. Here the energy is reversed. This is the crucifier. This is a time when communication is very heightened. And the humanitarian energy of the **6**s can be very healing words. You can have a great impact on everyone around you in this time. But if you choose a negative path, the energy becomes so destructive that you can affect people around you and their well-being, not just on an emotional level, but on a physical level too. You must be careful in this cycle that you are not filled with anger, vindictiveness, or seeking revenge, or also looking to blame people. Plus, the **60**s indicate unexpected sources of money. This is when you can rise to prominence or notoriety based on your actions and your willingness to take responsibility and help those around you. This is when you may have the opportunity as an individual or as a company to make acquisitions that create a lot of jealousy. A stock going through this cycle is very powerful. You would want to own a stock in this cycle. On a physical level, you are very potent right now, both in terms of your stamina but also in terms of your sexuality. You can become very popular in this cycle, but in a position of notoriety that may draw attention that you don't necessarily want. Protect your private life and your reputation at this time.

67/22 or 67/4

A 4 year represents logic and reason and going to work. It's a new foundation or new structure. The configuration of 6/7 is healing of the mind. This is an opportunity to heal your own mind, an opportunity to bring physical healing into mental or spiritual healing. This is a time to develop a very healthy belief system and put it into practice. This particular cycle is not about high ideals that never materialize. This is a time to go into a workable, grounded belief system that creates a foundation or a structure that you can rely on. This is when you wake up every morning knowing that you are solid and well situated in your life. On a business level, theories that you have been working on may be put into action. The company is forming a new foundation. A business could also develop theories now. This is a time of trial and error for a business and if a business does not experiment, it could miss some opportunities. This is also a period that can be taxing on the health due to pressure of the body and the mind. However, it's not a time to shy away from work. A stock in this cycle is in a developmental stage, and any stock bought should be considered a long-term investment. This may literally be when you change your religion or break away from religion. But it is not leaving one belief system and then being left empty handed. It is a transition from one belief to another.

68/5

This is a period of growth and responsibility of money. A company or stock in a 68/5 is in a time of rapid growth. Buy it! If you own a business, or company, grow it and do not be afraid of responsibility. As your company grows, give back to the employees or give to a charity. This is when you should purchase real estate or move into that dream home, or turn a profit by selling real estate. You may be so busy that you want to remember not to neglect family responsibilities. You may travel extensively and spend as much time away from home as they do at home, or they may purchase a second home or a vacation home. It's when you must learn to go with the flow and not take things too seriously or get too caught up in your material endeavors.

69/6

In this year a responsibility or a family situation comes to an end. It is also humanitarianism coming to fruition in the form of compassion. You may be called upon to take responsibility for a situation or situations that you did not create, but you are needed desperately. As long as you do not expect anything in return in a 69/6, you will be honored for your achievements and contributions. But, beware, in this cycle it could be posthumously. This is a time where health must be managed. It could be a health situation that is finally coming to a healing. This is a good time to allow yourself to trace what has been on your mind that has created a distress or a disease. This number also represents responsibilities coming to an end, which means you could retire in this cycle, or relinquish certain duties. On a personal level you may also witness a family member or family members moving away.

compound personal years beginning with 7

In Newmerology, the highest number that a Personal Year Cycle can go in our lifetime is 71/8. That is the highest number of the twentieth century, which was on December 31, 1999. We will not have 72/9 until December 31, 2999. With the number 7 in the Main Influence, spirituality, gaining wisdom, and learning are the theme. In these cycles, your deepest thoughts influence your day-to-day life. Remember to stay grounded in these cycles.

70/7

This is the all or nothing of spirituality. This is when your mind could go into the light or into the darkness. It is when you must manage your thoughts in a positive way. It is a time when your channels are opening up to higher belief systems to receive information that will take you through the rest of your life. It is not a time to think negatively in any way, shape, or form, or be fearful. You do not want to draw anything negative to you. You may literally go back to school and learn whatever it is you feel that you haven't learned in your lifetime. You may feel inclined to travel to mystical places of the earth such as Stonehenge, the Pyramids, or places in South America. Your dreams may be very vivid, revealing information that you need. But you may feel even in the waking state that there's an extra form of guidance. There's an extra energy that is assisting you along your path. As you grow and evolve in this cycle you must avoid any intellectual snobbery or being judgmental of those around you, if you do not share the same belief system. On a business level, this is a time to regroup and recreate the business. This is a time when a company may choose to reorganize or maybe file bankruptcy. A company that files bankruptcy in this cycle will reorganize for the better, having learned it's lessons and come back stronger.

71/8

This is the student and the teacher. This is when the information that influences the individual influences people. This is when you become more of a leader and help people to achieve and get on their path. This is not a period to seek your purpose in life, but to help others around you find their purpose or path. Detach from money and material needs and simply manage what you have. This is also when an individual may feel very inclined to start a business, especially one of a spiritual, educational overtone. As you guide other people and help them, you will rise to the top in this cycle. If it is a company, it is a growth cycle. This is a good time to own stock or own this company, as the company becomes a leader in its industry.

72/9

Even though most of us will not see the year 2999, I still would like to talk about that. The 9 is a year of completion. The 72 is the spiritual partnership that is the coming together. I would like to believe that at the end of the twenty-first millennium, the world will have come together brother with brother, instead of brother against brother. This is a year where spirituality affects their emotions. The mind, the deepest part of the mind, the intuition, affects their decisions, and they do everything with compassion and caring and patience. Any company that would be in a 72/9 year would truly care about what happens to its people, and to anyone involved in the business. This is truly a number of spiritual power and fulfillment.

single-digit personal years

Because the calendar year 2000 only added up to 2, some individuals in the twenty-first century will experience Personal Year Cycles that do not have a double Compound Number on the top. They will have a Personal Year Cycle where they are vibrating solely to the Base Number. When there is no Compound Number in a Personal Year Cycle, it simply represents that there are less dynamics that the individual can truly focus on the day-to-day matters at hand without the distractions that come from the Main and Minor Influences. This is a time of simplicity. It is much easier to maintain a focus when the top number matches the bottom number. So, we look at the Personal Year Cycles 1–9, 11, and 22 in great detail.

When we start with the date January 1, 2000, the lowest simple Personal Year Cycle an individual, company, or entity can have is a 4 year. It is mathematically impossible to have a number 1–3.

4

In a simple 4 year or a 4 Personal Year, this is a time of truly being logical, pragmatic, and analytical. It's a time to create a new foundation and to simply be willing to work for everything that you get and attain. It is a time when you feel that everything needs to make sense and you'll try to make sense of everything. It's a time to be conservative, to be held in account, or to account for everything in your life. It's a time to take into account your friendships, to look at everything personally and professionally, and bring stability into your life.

In a basic 4 year you can be very busy. So be very careful about any legalities, or contracts that you may enter into. You may be so busy that you may miss something such as a typo or a mistake. So be sure to have another set of eyes, such as an accountant or a lawyer, looking at anything that involves a contract in this cycle. It's a time to establish a foundation in your intimate relationships, to make sure that everything is grounded, and going on an even keel. It's a time where moderation is necessary.

5

This is a time of change. Things may feel as if they're going in different directions. You may feel a little impatient, or you may bite off a little more than you can chew. It's a time to make sure that you're not scattering your time, your energy, or your money. It is a time to promote yourself or to advertise your business. It's a time to be a moderate risk taker and break away from tradition just enough to break some of the patterns. Still, you must be careful that you do not undo all the hard work of a 4 personal year in the cycle of 5. A 5 year can actually make you lazy if you're not careful. It is a time to simply stay focused and grow at a moderate rate.

It's also a time where opportunity presents itself. Simply go with the flow or travel where it's affordable. The urge to try something different will hit in this cycle. In a simple 5 year it is not a good time to make a commitment, such as sign a contract in a partnership or marry. It's a time to maintain your freedom.

6

In a 6 year, it is the time to look at family responsibilities, to help those around you who deserve appreciation. It's a time to be a humanitarian. It's a time to look at the conditions of your house. It's a time for being loyal, honest, and sincere with yourself and anyone around you.

In a simple 6 year, money may flourish when it's unexpected. You may find yourself wanting to literally beautify your home or buy a new car. You may feel inclined to want to get a pet, or simply get back to nature. It is a time to reconnect with the simpler side of life.

7

In a simple 7 year, this is the time of rest, relaxation, meditation, and learning. In a simple 7 year, it's time to take a look at your life from a spiritual, philosophical level, to look at what is important to you on a nonmaterial level. As this number applies to business, it is a time of going back to the drawing board and coming up with new plans for improvement.

In a simple 7 personal year there are no influential circumstances or extra influences to confuse your thoughts. This is a time when you can be very clear about what you feel, what you think, and what your philosophy of life is.

8

In a simple **8** year, it is a time of money management, a time to take leadership, and a time to take action. All the plans that you made in the **7** year now begin to come to fruition. This is no longer a time to be dreaming. In a simple **8** year it's time to keep money matters very simple. This is not a time to overextend yourself no matter what kind of business you're in or extend yourself in your own personal finances.

It's also a time to recognize what you've learned on a spiritual level in the **7** year and allow it to balance out the material side of the **8** year, so you feel very clear on spirituality and material issues, allowing them to stay in balance.

9

A simple **9** year is a time of completion and compassion. It's a time to acknowledge very simply that others may be in need of us. It is a time to tie up loose ends. In a simple **9** year we may start to think of issues, things that we want to begin and start anew. It's very difficult to start new things in a simple **9** year. It actually can feel as if you are trying to run on a treadmill. It is better to complete and finish any projects and start them when you go into the next **1** year. This may be a time where you simply may have to teach or show other people how to do things, and not expect anything in return. It is truly a time of giving of yourself.

11

A simple 11 year without the number 2 is truly a master challenge because the 2 vibration does not mathematically exist in this. The person is highly challenged to self-integrate and to find their true self. It is a time that you may spend alone. It is a time that is so important that as you learn to be self-integrated and love yourself, it opens the door for love coming from another person. As you teach yourself to love yourself, this teaches you how to love someone else and how to receive love. It is a time when your psychic abilities manifest, creating a lot of new thoughts and wisdom, visions, or if you are not inclined, to higher beliefs. It can create a lot of tension and anxiety, feeling as if your head is in a vise. This may be a time you may want to seek counseling or therapy to help you understand yourself better. It is literally a time that you will be looking at yourself in the mirror of self-discovery. From this self-discovery, you may become powerful and an inspiration to everyone around you. You may even gain a certain amount of notoriety that puts you in the media, or just gains a lot of attention.

22

This is the cycle of the master builder. It is a time to create a new foundation, to create big projects that benefit many people, and a time to give back. It's also a time when issues, conflicts, or tensions with your own mother may come up. It is a time to resolve all these issues. This is a very rare cycle to have a pure 22. It is something that you must take advantage of. If a business is in a 22, it may be entering a time that is very special, that it may not hit again. It may be involved in projects that benefit the company itself and the community.

personal month and personal day numbers

Your Personal Month Number is a more tailored vibration within the Personal Year Number, serving as a mini-cycle. It further fine-tunes and defines the timing of occurrences in your life. The Personal Month Number can tell you what your month is likely to be about, and what area of your life you should focus your energies. When a Personal Month Cycle matches a Personal Year (an 8 month in an 8 year), this is a time that the issue at hand is accentuated, where you can really take advantage of the energy. It can be a time of great opportunity, but also a time when you must take great care of those issues. If you have the 8 month in an 8 year, you could make a lot of money, but you would also need to take care of your money.

You also have Personal Days, which function like the Personal Year and Month, only on a more minute scale. But keep in mind: Do not make yourself crazy attempting to figure out every personal day. Save Personal day calculations for the big events in your life like getting married or starting a new job.

Your Personal Year Cycle is the strongest vibration, but Personal Months and Personal Days can have very profound effects, especially for rare or once in a lifetime occurrences that only take place on a specific day.

Example
Michelle Kwan at the Olympics in 2002

Michele Kwan was born July 7, 1980, making her a 32/5. She is a 5, which is all about being free and easy. In 2002, she was in a 17/8 year until her birthday. The 17/8 year is the star. In February of 2002, when the Olympics were going on, she was in a 19/1, month, which is herself coming to completion. But her final performance occurred on February 21, which made it a 40/4 day, a number of tremendous pressure. The pressure was too much for her and it cost her the gold. The day offset the year and the month. Why? Because Kwan was on the ice for only ten minutes. So the exact day was everything. And a high-pressure 40/4 day for an easygoing 5 is tough.

newmerology

finding your personal month

➤ Follow the instructions exactly.

➤ Obtain your Personal Year.

➤ Add the month to the Compound Number of the Personal Year.

Example
The Personal Month Number for July, for a person in a 28/1 Personal Year

step one: add Compound Personal Year to the month

$$7 + 28 = 35$$

35 is the Compound Personal Month Number

step two: add the Compound Personal Month Number to obtain the Base Number

$$3 + 5 = 8$$

For someone in a 28/1 Personal Year, the Personal Month Number for July is 35/8

finding your personal day

This is very simple. Find your Personal Month Number. Add the day to the Compound Number of the Personal Month. That is your Personal Day.

Example

The Personal Day Number for March 30 for someone who is in a 37/1 Personal Month

step one: add the Compound Number of the Personal Month Number with the day

37 (the month's Compound Number) + 30 (the day) = 67/4

The Personal Day is 67/4

personal year cycle in business

Like people, businesses have Personal Year Cycles, times in the life of a business that favor certain activities over others, including growth, moving, research and development, creating charitable foundations, adding new people, creating alliances or partnerships with other businesses, cutting back, and reestablishing its foundation. Knowing and understanding the Personal Year Cycle of a business is important if you own a business so you can foresee what years certain aspects of the business are likely to take center stage, as well as, where to apply resources.

The Personal Year Cycle of a business is equally important if you want to invest in a business by buying its stock. *A company's Personal Year provides the important factor of when—when to put your money into a business for the greatest financial gain.* An investor who understands Newmerology would be smart to consider a company's Personal Year Cycle as much as its P/E ratio in deciding when to buy a stock.

Example
IBM

IBM's Birth Path Number is March 17, 1960. On March 17, 2002, IBM entered a 24/6 year. That's a conservative number, not good for investments. A few days after it went into its 24/6 year, its stock dropped.

investing and personal month and personal day numbers

Does a business's Personal Month or Day play into investing? If you are investing for the long term, the Personal Year Cycle number will probably suffice. However, if your investment depends on the events of a particular month or day, as in the case of short terms trades or options, the month and day will have an effect.

Example

How I predicted the first time the New York Stock Exchange would hit and close above 8,000 on July 16, 1997.

At a meeting I attended with 25 Los Angeles business people in February 1997, a stockbroker predicted that the Dow Jones Index would eclipse 8,000 in May of that year. A woman asked if I agreed, based on my knowledge of numerology. I knew the NYSE was founded on May 17, 1792. I calculated that after its birthday in 1997, the NYSE entered a 48/3 year. Then, I searched for a period of growth within that year. I found that the month of July for the NYSE was a 55/1 (7 + 48 = 55 / 5 + 5 = 1, creating a 55/1 month.) The number 55/1 indicates growth in new directions. The 1 is new beginnings. The two 5's indicate new directions.

Then, I looked for the highest number possible in the twentieth century. The highest number that existed in the twentieth century was 71/8. So, I looked for a day in July of 1997 that would

come out to a $71/8$. And that was July 16. (55 [Personal Month] $+ 16 = 71 / 7 + 1 = 8$, creating a $71/8$ day.) So I predicted that the first time the stock market would hit $8,000$ and close above it would be July 16. And it did.

finding a business personal year cycle

Calculate the numerological cycles of a business the exact same way that you would calculate it for a person. Use the date the business started (incorporation date, date of business license). If you are *investing* in a stock, try to find the day the business went public (this can be hard to obtain) as the public Birth Date of the company. If you cannot find the IPO date, the date of incorporation will suffice.

chapter 11

the chance to start again:
calculating the rebirth year

A Rebirth Year occurs when your triad of Birth Path Numbers reoccurs. You stop Rebirthing when you have a year that has the same Base Number as your Birth Path, but a different Compound Number.

Example

A person born on September 19, 1944 has a Birth Path Number of 46/1. This person would have four Rebirths. That is, four Personal Year Cycles that matched the Birth Path of 46/1/7. They would occur in 1953, 1962, 1971, and 1980. We live in nine-year cycles, so from your birth year you will continue to add nine years until the outcome does not produce the Birth Path Number.

$$09 + 19 + (18) \ 1953 = 46/1$$

$$09 + 19 + (18) \ 1962 = 46/1$$

$$09 + 19 + (18) \ 1971 = 46/1$$

$$09 + 19 + (18) \ 1980 = 46/1$$

$$09 + 19 + (27) \ 1989 = 55/1$$

The Rebirthing stops here because you no longer have a **46/1**

By the example above, you can see that this person, with the Birth Date of September **19**, **1944**, would have four Rebirths.

A Rebirth Year is the opportunity to learn who you are. It creates the chance to make the necessary adjustments in your life so you can grow into your true character and personality. You enter a Rebirth cycle when your Birth Path Number recurs mathematically as your Personal Year. So if you are a **34/7** Birth Path in a **34/7** Personal Year, you are in a Rebirth Cycle. I call it Rebirthing because it is the reoccurrence of the theme of your Birth Path Number. The Rebirth Year is a new addition to the practice of numerology, a pattern I discovered after years of tracking clients' lives. The Rebirth Year is one of the "new" elements about "Newmerology."

A Rebirth Year sets the tone for the next nine years. It is one of life's pivot points. The energy of the cycle affords the opportunity to find your path if you are not quite there yet, or to get back on your path if you have strayed. Sometimes that energy takes the form of a shock to the system, a significant change, or a major adjustment in the life. Always, it is another opportunity to get to know yourself better, understand what you have to deal with in life, and how you can work with your tools.

Exactly how does a Rebirth Year work in the overall scheme of life? Think of your life's path as a straight line, until you hit a Rebirth Year. It stops you. It makes it difficult to continue in the way you have before. Something happens like a marriage, divorce, job loss or job opportunity, a child

coming into the family, or a move. Life sets a barricade on the path you have been traveling and points you in a different direction. With every Rebirth, the life path line takes a jog. Several Rebirths can cause a zigzag pattern that sends you in one direction for nine years, then stops you and sends you in another direction. Each Rebirth is an adjustment that forces you to start again.

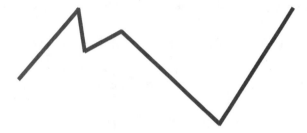

So it will go until you stop Rebirthing and your life is set upon an even course. When you get on that straight line, your life moves forward and gains momentum. You no longer need to worry that you are going to hit a wall in your progress. In a Rebirth Year, you encounter life experiences equivalent of a cosmic neon sign—sometimes large, sometimes small—depending how difficult it is to get your attention. The sign says: "Not that way. *This* way." It is best to follow directions.

If you refuse to face up to the message of a Rebirth Year, you will go afoul. That is true with any Personal Year Cycle, but it is especially true in a Rebirth Year. A Rebirth is a time when you don't take chances with your life. It presents a door of opportunity that you could pass through if you are being unnecessarily risky. This is a time where a person is supposed to find strength, reach inside themselves, and flow with the energy at hand. If you do, each Rebirth will be easier, and by the time you get to your last Rebirth, you have smooth sailing. If you are not doing what you're supposed to do, the last Rebirth is a kick in the pants.

The number of Rebirths any one individual might experience in a lifetime differs depending on the year of birth. It also determines the path and pace of the life.

rebirth years

no rebirths during the life

Anyone born in a year ending in a **0** or between the years of **1990–2000**, will not experience a Rebirth. People with no Rebirths tend to be conservative. They can be cautious and insecure, always looking over their shoulder, wondering if they are doing okay, and seeking approval. They tend not to be risk takers until they get into adulthood, when perhaps the Subconscious Motivation comes into play. They move slowly because they are always looking back at their point of origin, which is mom and dad, asking, "Am I doing okay?" A need for approval and reassurance persists until later in life. On the plus side, these people have an awareness, a grounded-ness, and a common sense from early on. They can go from being very conservative to a huge risk taker later in life. Their approach to life can be very extreme.

one rebirth in the life

These people tend to have extra responsibility at a young age. They hit their one and only Rebirth at age nine and at that point they acquire a level of maturity. Often, they are old before their time. There's usually something that went on in the family that put more of a load on them early in life. People with one Rebirth have a tendency to be rather serious or somber.

two or three rebirths

Two Rebirths is ideal. Then, a Rebirth occurs at age 9 and one at age 18. At age 18, these people are on their path. If there are three Rebirths in the life, that means they will be 27 at the last Rebirth and still young enough to get on the right path relatively early in adulthood. They have stopped hitting walls. They are on their way.

four or more rebirths

These people are late bloomers. This many Rebirths makes it difficult for them to find their path early on. With four or five Rebirths, making the person 36 or 45, there is still enough time to get things done. In fact, people with several Rebirths tend to have more energy, look younger and act younger than their counterparts. This youthfulness gives them the extra "oomph" they need to play catch-up on their path. But if people face seven Rebirths (age 63), their life may not really get off the ground until retirement, which can be tough.

Multiple Rebirths, especially those that occur late in life, can create a lot of pressure. Rebirths, after all, can be a slam, a time when you have to start over and that can be a shock to the system. When you're younger, you're resilient. When you are older you are less resilient and those slams, those radical restarts, are harder to handle. Late-in-life Rebirths can be so difficult that people do not live through them. The pressure is just too much. They cannot make the necessary adjustments and they die under the pressure. Esoterically speaking, the concept of death and rebirth can be a very fine line.

Examples? Although it has never been termed as such, the third Rebirth cycle, which occurs at age 27, is well-known in the rock world. So many major rock stars died when they were 27 that it was considered the curse of the 27th year.

rebirth years

283

newmerology

The Following Musicians Died in Rebirths

> JANIS JOPLIN: Born 1-19-1943. Birth Path Number = 37/1.
> Died 10-4-1970, nine months after third Rebirth Year began.

> MARVIN GAYE: Born 4-2-1939. Birth Path Number = 28/1.
> Died 4-1-1984. He had one day to go in his Rebirth cycle.
> He had one more Rebirth waiting in 1993.

> JIM MORRISON: Born 12-8-1943. Birth Path Number = 37/1.
> Died 7-3-1971, seven months into his third Rebirth.

> FREDDIE MERCURY: Born 9-5-1946. Birth Path Number = 34/7.
> Died 11-24-1991, ten months after his third Rebirth.

> STEVIE RAY VAUGHN: Born 10-3-1954. Birth Path Number = 32/5.
> Died 8-27-1990, died with one month left in his fourth Rebirth.

> KURT COBAIN: Born 2-20-1967. Birth Path Number = 45/9.
> Died 4-5-1994, six weeks into his third Rebirth.

other notable deaths in a rebirth year

> MARILYN MONROE and JOHN F. KENNEDY.
> Kennedy would have experienced a lot of Rebirths.

Fortunately, someone dying in a late-in-life Rebirth Year is the exception, not the rule. A lot depends on how people handle change in their lives, how much they need to adjust in a Rebirth Year, and what the Birth Path Number is. A happy 3 or a free and easy 5 might have an easier time of it than an 8, who would experience big money issues with every Rebirth.

Your last Rebirth Cycle is your last opportunity to make the corrections you need to get on your path. You don't get another chance. It is the last time that the universe will grab your attention and say, "You need to look at this. This isn't going to happen again." By the time you have your final Rebirth, you are either going to get on your path or not.

Always try to go with the energy and direction of your Rebirth Year. Do not fight it. If you are in an 8 Rebirth Year, it means you want to develop wise money management. If you are foolish and blow your money in an 8 year, then you are working against the theme of your Rebirth Year.

Whatever you do or don't do in a Rebirth Year is magnified. If you do not learn the lesson of your Rebirth Year, you won't learn it for another nine years. If you don't get it in your last Rebirth, you don't get it at all. One thing a Rebirth Year demands is that you *pay attention*.

business rebirths

Because of our limited lifespan, human beings only experience a limited number of Rebirths. But a long-standing entity, country, or institution, like the New York Stock Exchange, can stop Rebirthing, and then begin again in a different century. The New York Stock Exchange's Birth Date is May 17, 1792 (a 41/5). It has Rebirthed 19 times. Its last Rebirth was in 1990, and it won't do it again for a long, long, long, long time. A business in a Rebirth Year could experience a major reorganization. If it is weak, it could collapse under the pressure of a Rebirth Year. Whether a business or an individual, it is a time to reinvent oneself.

chapter 12

Intersecting Numbers

I ntersecting Number Years occur when your Personal Year matches a number in your Newmerological Realm other than the Birth Path. So if you are in a **26/8** Personal Year and your Environmental Number is a **26/8**, you are in an Intersecting Number Year. If you are in a **20/2** Personal Year and your Subconscious Motivation Number is a **20/2**, you are in an Intersecting Number Year. Remember, your Newmerological Realm includes the Environmental Influence, Conscious Desire, Subconscious Motivation, and Dharma Number.

Depending on which number it matches, an Intersecting Number will boost and accentuate the themes in your Newmerological Realm. If, however, your Personal Year Cycle does not match any of the numbers in your Newmerological Realm, it does not inhibit any of them from coming to fruition anyway. Your Subconscious Motivation Number can still manifest your dream; You can still take advantage of your strengths as indicated by your Dharma Number; Your childhood desire can still materialize as indicated in your Conscious Desire. When an Intersecting Number does occur, however, it can accelerate your progress toward fulfilling an aspect of yourself.

newmerology

meanings of the intersecting aspects

When Your Personal Year Matches Your Environmental Influence Number

This is a time of visibility, recognition, and appreciation. It is a time when how people see you matches who you are. Take advantage of this time. You may need to do things or meet expectations you don't like, but it would be wise to do them anyway. Goodies like this one happen a few times in a life. People are going to have a strong awareness of you. This is a good time to make amends, adjust, or correct your reputation if it needs it. If you do not take advantage of this time, the universe will exercise no penalty, (unlike a Personal year.) However, *do not* be reclusive or pull back from society during this time. If you do, you could erase yourself from people's memories for a long time.

When Your Personal Year Matches Your Conscious Desire

This is a time when you can accomplish something you have wanted to do since you were young. You realize your youthful desires. This aspect happens rarely. So if it does, you really need to take advantage of this. The universe is handing you a very special gift. What should you do during this time? Think back to when you were young and involve yourself in whatever it is you wanted then. Did you always want to be an actor? Go back to school? Make a lot of money? Help the needy? Travel to Thailand? Go after something you have wanted for a long time. Take steps to bring it to fruition. It could happen much more quickly than you think.

Example
Gary Coleman

In **2005**, his Personal Year is going to match his Conscious Desire Number, **17/8**. Look for him to have a career resurgence that year.

When Your Personal Year Matches Your Subconscious Motivation

Because of the millennium change, your Personal Year Cycle is far more likely to match your

Subconscious Motivation Number, or your Dream Number. The Subconscious Motivation Number tends to be a low number and because we had high Universal

Numbers in the latter part of the twentieth century, it was unusual to see a Personal Year equal the Subconscious Motivation. In the new millennium, the Universal Year will be low for years to come (2003 is a 5 year). This means that Personal Year Numbers will be low as well, creating a time when more people will benefit from an Intersecting Personal Year and Subconscious Motivation Number. Why is this so fortunate? This is a year when a dream could come true. You could realize something that has been buried in the back of your mind and motivating your behavior in ways you were unaware. At this time, you will recognize it and feel motivated, even compelled, to turn your dream into reality. If this Intersecting aspect happens at a young age, you could have an opportunity for success early in life or your dream could come true at a much younger age. This is a good aspect for parents to note for their children.

Example

Pro tennis player Anna Kournikova is an example of an upcoming Personal Year Cycle matching a Personal Year Cycle Subconscious Motivation Number. Kournikova's birthday is 6-7-1981. Her Subconscious Motivation Number is 23/5. In 2008, her Personal Year Cycle will be 6 + 7 + 2008 (10) = 23/5. At that point a window of opportunity will present itself for her "dream" to come true. At this point she has not won a major singles title since turning pro in 1995. Will it take that long for her to hit it big? She turns 27 in 2008; she is still young enough to be competitive in professional tennis. Maybe then she will realize what she deeply yearns for. A 23/5 is a precursor to meeting the right mate. We will have to wait to find out; so will she.

When Your Personal Year Matches Your Dharma Number

This year, you can come into your power. Your strengths get even stronger and are recognized by others.

chapter 13

Compatibility

Why relationships succeed or fail, create great happiness or misery, sustain for years or last the length of a batting eyelash has eluded poets, psychologists, and metaphysicians for centuries. There is always a bit of magic in the chemistry between people that eludes all predictions.

Newmerology determines the potential between two individuals by looking at aspects that we will examine in the following chapters, including communication issues (Mirroring), temporary attractions (Crossed Paths), and closeness due to common traits (Bonding).

At the essential level, Newmerology determines compatibility through a two-step process. First, it looks at each person's Birth Path Number to see how the basic personality traits relate to each other. Then, it adds up the individual Birth Path Numbers, and arrives at a number that describes the relationship. The relationship, then, has its own identity number, created from the two individuals.

Example

You are a 4, solid and dependable. Your partner is a 9, compassionate and service oriented. Would these be compatible traits? 4 + 9 = 13 = 4. The nature and character of a four is security and foundation. So, yes, they would be compatible. Adding you numbers together, see what you find in the numbers following.

When it comes to relationships, the numbers themselves do not distinguish among romantic partners, business partners, or friends. The numbers simply assess the numerological dynamic between two people. However, some compatibility numbers may be better for businesses or friendships rather than marriages.

the 1 in relationships

1 with a 1 creates a 2

This creates a partnership. Here you have two strong energies coming together that respect each other.

1 with a 2 creates a 3

An aggressive individual gets together with a passive individual. The classic scene between a 1 and a 2 is where the 2 says: "I love you" and the 1 responds, "I love me too." They add up to a 3, which is friendship and this is where it is best left. Not an especially good combination for romance.

1 with a 3 creates a 4

The independent individual meets up with the outgoing, verbal, and vocal person. It creates a 4, which is a very solid relationship in business or romance. These two need to be sure that they

don't over analyze whether they should be together or not. This is a good relationship.

1 with a 4 creates a 5

Very independent, egocentric person gets together with someone who is conservative. They will not get in each other's way, but there's not much of a commitment either. The 4 wants to stay home, the 1 wants to go out, and they will agree upon that arrangement. They may not fight or argue, but by the same token this is not a cohesive relationship.

1 with a 5 creates a 6

Very good for marriage. Here we have an independent person with someone who likes to come and go. Together, they are a 6, the happy home. They will respect each other. The 1 says "don't tell me what to do," and the 5 won't let anyone tell them what to do. Because they don't step on each other's toes, they can coexist. Together, they learn responsibility and trust. These are two potent personalities and together can create a lot of sexual heat.

1 with a 6 creates a 7

This is the individualist with the person who likes to nest; the go-getter with the homebody. They make a 7, which means they will grow spiritually, but it means they will spend a lot of time alone. It takes two very aware people to make this relationship work. It could become a very intellectual relationship.

1 with a 7 creates an 8

These two people like their own space and will stay out of each other's way. Together, they have a lot of power. One is about action and the other is about planning. These two people can make a

compatibility

lot of money together. But they can't let the relationship be just about money. It could easily become overly materialistic.

1 with an 8 creates a 9

There's a lot of power here. These two personalities know how to complete each other. Because the 1 and the 8 are both about being a leader, not a follower, they learn how to give in to the other. They learn compassion.

1 with a 9 creates a 1

The 1 dominates here. The 9 waits for everything and the 1 waits for nothing.

the 2 in relationships

2 with a 2 creates a 4

All things are created equal in this relationship. There's a sharing of emotions that create a good foundation. By the same token, they have to make sure that they *can* leave each other's side. They may tend to be joined at the hip.

2 with a 3 creates a 5

Better left as friends. This is the quintessential partner (2) with the good time gal or guy (3). This creates a lot of freedom, but the 2 doesn't want freedom The 2 wants someone who is around.

2 with a 4 creates a 6

This is the partner with someone who is sound and reliable creating a family scenario. Both people are willing to take on responsibility. It is a very good match.

2 with a 5 creates a 7

Here, you have the emotional person (2) getting together with a noncommittal one (5). This creates a 7, which means somebody is left alone. The 5s are very sensitive although they don't always show it. The 2 may create too much sensitivity in the relationship and that may make the 5 look for space. This is not a good match.

2 with a 6 creates an 8

The partner gets together with a family-oriented person. It's good as long as they remember why they got into it. The relationship is an 8, which means they are powerful together. They both like nice things or things that have an intrinsic value to it.

2 with a 7 creates a 9

The partner with the loner. Doesn't sound good? It's not.

2 with an 8 creates a 1

The 8 personality will take the 2 under its wing. The 8 is the leader. The 2 is the apprentice. The 8 teaches the 2 how to stand on their own. The 2 teaches the 8 how to feel more. The 1 partnership they create means unity. This is a good match.

2 with a 9 creates an 11

This is a situation where the people could worry themselves and the relationship to death. It is a highly emotional relationship. The 2 is the partner, the 9 is the compassion, feeling, and empathy.

the 3 in relationships

3 with a 3 creates a 6

This is a great one. Both people like to go out and enjoy people and then come back and become a family. Two communicators, they have the ability to really hear what the other says and listen to each other. There's not a lot of blame in this relationship. Because the number 3 represents being attractive, these two people will find each other attractive on a physical level. There is lots of sexuality on a physical level. Their talk is foreplay.

3 with a 4 creates a 7

This is an expressive person with a conservative person. A lot of time will be spent in thought. They may not see eye to eye in their approach to life. They can learn from each other. If they learn, they will evolve. The 3 will have a lot of friends. The 4 just wants a few people. This one takes work.

3 with a 5 creates an 8

This relationship can have sparks and be exciting. These two people have similar qualities. As a couple, others will admire them and want to be around them. Early in the relationship, they will be so distracted by how much of a good time they have together, they will lose site of everything else. They can make money, but they can also spend it. Therefore, they need to be careful with what they do with money. As long as these two people are grounded and stay focused on whatever the crux of the relationship actually is, this duo actually works out well.

3 with a 6 creates a 9

These two people will have similar tastes when it comes to decorating and art. But the 3 will want to show off the home, the 6 doesn't want anyone in it. They will have a good understanding of each other. But some of their commonalities will be in conflict. They will balance each other out. The 3 will make the 6 go out and 6 will make the 3 stay home. And they will work it out.

3 with a 7 creates a 1

The 3 gets the 7 to communicate. The 7 gets the 3 to listen and think. The 3 draws the 7 out and says what is on their mind. Together, they create a 1, which is unity.

3 with an 8 creates an 11

This is a very charismatic, potent relationship. They need to be careful that they do not high energy each other to death. They can light up a room, but when they go home they have to turn it off.

3 with a 9 creates a 3

These two are better off as friends. There is good conversation in this relationship.

the 4 in relationships

4 with a 4 creates an 8

This is a great business relationship, but not a great romance. These are two workaholics.

4 with a 5 creates a 9

These two, individually, do not get along. But if they take time to learn from each other, it can be a good relationship. They need each other. The 4 can learn to loosen up from the 5. The 5 can learn structure and focus from the 4.

4 with a 6 creates a 1

Unity is created with the 1. Both are willing to work and take on responsibility, so it is very evenly matched. There are good morals and ethics in this relationship. This is the combination of the all-American family. An excellent match.

4 with a 7 creates an 11

This can be a very high-strung relationship. The 4 is analytical, the 7 is in their head, and both like their space. But communication can be an issue here. They won't step on each other's toes, but there is not a lot of interaction either. This could be a very insightful relationship, with a lot of ideas. This is very good for intellectual relationships, but not very romantic.

309

4 with an 8 creates a 3

They make good friends, but there is also a lot of work going on. This is very good for business relationships, but boring for romance. When the 4 goes out the door to work, the 8 says, "Make lots of money, honey." That's the problem here: Lots of money, not enough honey.

4 with a 9 creates a 4

The 4 will be supportive of the 9. This relationship actually has a foundation to it. It is solid. The 4 personality is one of the few numbers that has the patience for the 9, who has to wait for things to come to them.

the 5 in relationships

5 with a 5 creates a 1

Two individuals, constantly on the go, but when they come together, they appreciate the unity between the two of them. They enjoy their downtime together. They are both on the go and very busy and yet, they actually miss each other when they are apart. They will never try to restrict each other or step on each other's toes. They are very sexually dynamic and enjoy each other's company on all levels. This is a good match.

5 with a 6 creates an 11

Here we have dysfunction. The 5 is on the go, the 6 is always at home. Be careful with this because this could create a family life where one parent is on the go while the other one never gets out of the house. The 5 likes to be out and about and the 6 likes to domesticate. Any pull on the other to do the opposite creates the anxiety of the 11.

compatibility

5 with a 7 creates a 3

Here we have the changeable and charismatic person with the intellectual. They can have communication because the relationship adds up to a 3, but they have different interests. The 5 has lots of energy and seeks a lot of independence while the 7 is sitting there observing, contemplating, and being quite passive. The relationship will result in a lot of people around. The 5 will love it, but the 7 will not. A 5 and 7 combination is better left as friends.

5 with an 8 creates a 4

These two can accomplish a lot. But the 5 eventually will grow bored. Good for business, not romance.

5 with a 9 creates a 5

They have traveling in common. But when they are not traveling, what are they going to do? The 5 is looking for excitement and the 9 is looking for feelings. The 9 stands a chance of getting hurt because the 9 wants commitment and the 5 won't want to give it to the 9. To commit, a 5 needs someone who intrigues them. And 9s are not intriguing enough for a 5. The 9 is patient and tolerant, the 5 is not. They both could learn a lot from each other, but the 5 will rule here.

the 6 in relationships

6 with a 6 creates a 3

These two are similar in their ideals and beliefs. They make good friends. They will be so compatible that they will be more like brother and sister. They could date and get along really well, but wake up one day and feel a fraternal closeness, rather than a romantic or sexual bond. They have a really good connection, but not romantic chemistry. Therefore, they remain friends, perhaps for life.

6 with a 7 creates a 4

They have a good foundation with a lot of ethics and morals here. The 6 gets the 7 to take care of their body. The 7 gets the 6 to take care of heart and soul. A body-mind kind of relationship. This can make for a good solid relationship.

6 with an 8 creates a 5

Family values mix with monetary values, creating a lot of opportunity. This can be a very nebulous relationship, however. People in this relationship have to figure out what the structure and the foundation is in the relationship. Once they figure that out, the relationship has the ability to grow. There is a lot of sexual chemistry.

6 with a 9 creates a 6

Humanitarianism and compassion create a good solid relationship. They will look out for each other. They just have to make sure that they don't kill the relationship with sensitivity. Both will teach and learn a lot from each other. A lot of sharing goes on in this relationship. This works.

the 7 in relationships

7 with a 7 creates a 5

This is a nonrelationship. It's two ghosts. These are two spiritual people, but the relationship never materializes. It's *two* spiritual people that end up being *too* spiritual people. There's nothing grounded in the relationship and there is no sex vibe.

compatibility

311

7 with an 8 creates a 6

This is a good situation because a 7 has to be more grounded in the real world. The 8 needs to be balanced with spirituality, so it is not all about money. Together, they learn how to be responsible. The one will entice the other to go through the changes to make this relationship happen.

7 with a 9 creates a 7

Both of these numbers hint at expectations of perfectionism. This is not good a good situation. At times, the 7 is going to be too cold for the 9. Together, they create a 7, which means being alone. At times, the 7 can be too aloof for the sensitive empathetic 9.

the 8 in relationships

8 with an 8 creates a 7

This is a business relationship, not a marriage. If it was a romance, some bitter lessons would be learned here. This is competitiveness at the highest level. This would be a disaster as a marriage. Both would be out making money. They would never see each other.

8 with a 9 creates an 8

This is rough. The 8 overpowers the 9. The 9 would give into the 8.

9 with a 9 creates a 9

This could be a good relationship as long as one of them is making the first move to get into it. They will respect each other in the relationship, once they are in it. The obstacle is getting into it. The 9 is so nonobtrusive in a relationship that the 9 completes the other individual. The 9 brings the other person into fruition. That's the neat thing about 9s. They help their partner come into who they are. The bad part for a 9 is that the partner takes over the relationship and the 9 gets stuck holding the bag or gets no credit for bringing something to the table.

chapter **14**

Crossed Paths and Mirroring

are you meant for each other, or is it just a passing fancy?

Love at first sight? Magnetic attraction? Can't get enough of a person you have met? Or, on the contrary, is the person you are living with suddenly driving you crazy? These are the signs of a Crossed Path relationship, a time of intensified energies between two or more people. They can be positive energies (*He draws me like a magnet!*), or negative (*Ugh. Go away!*). Either way, you are playing with fire.

A Crossed Path occurs when one person's Compound Personal Year matches another person's Compound Birth Path Number. The aspect causes such a heated attraction that the person with the Personal Year Number seems to cross through the life and being of a person who owns that number natally.

Everyone emanates an energy called the aura. You can get within $7–10$ feet of a person and you can pick it up. Crossed Paths, numerologically speaking, creates an intersection, a space in time where two people's energies intensely connect. This creates an ultra-energy, a desire to be with each other that can be nearly impossible to resist.

Will the attraction last? Usually not with the same intensity and maybe not at all once the Personal Year Cycle (one year from birthday to birthday) ends and the Crossed Path energy is no longer in effect. The problem is that Crossed Paths can create such an intense honeymoon that both people may have the urge to make a snap decision (like a quick trip to Vegas or Reno) before they get to know each other.

In fact, the exact opposite should occur when Crossed Paths are operating. Make no permanent moves with a partner. The relationship may fade. It may sustain. You won't know until this period is over. Crossed Paths kick up so much energy that the dust from the commotion will blind you. The dust storm has got to settle down.

Example
John and Susan

His birthday is 10-20-1955, Birth Path Number 50/5. Her birthday is 10-13-1962, Birth Path Number, 41/5. In September 1999, they met right at the end of her Personal Year Cycle of 50/5. It was instant attraction between the two of them. They dated. They only had one month of Crossed Paths energy. The magic of that aspect was gone after she moved into her new cycle, 51/6. They dated for another year before they got married. The Crossed Path energy brought them together, but they knew not to act on that attraction until time passed and they got past the initial spark. They have now been married for two years.

Crossed Paths do bring people together, inspiring them to overcome emotional blocks to intimacy. That's the good news. If the honeymoon does not end after the Crossed Path period is over, then you know that the relationship is emotionally valid. But let's say that as this cycle begins to wane, problems suddenly arise or one or both of the people begin to get bored. Then you know that you were going through a relationship that was not meant to be long-term.

As a personal advisor, I tell clients: Do not jump into marriage or a legal relationship while this dynamic is in effect. Wait until it is over. Also watch for pregnancy. This is also a time of cross-pollination. This heightened energy between the two people can create circumstances that are irreversible—like a baby.

the crossed path effect on long-term relationships

Crossed Path energy occurs in long-term relationships as well. But here, the energy can reverse to repulsion. After you have been with a person for so long, you get accustomed to a certain exchange, a pattern of being with each other. The Crossed Path aspect sends a lightning bolt through that pattern. Suddenly, the relationship is charged and intensified. In a new relationship, it results in magnetic attraction. In a long-term relationship, it can overload the dynamic between two people.

What happens is that the person with the Birth Path Number feels invaded by the person who is in that cycle. The Birth Path Number represents the true identity, so the personal and private space, in some ways, is violated. You've heard the expression, "He's getting under my skin." That's Crossed Path energy at work in a long-term relationship. In a new relationship that energy is a good thing, more like "I've got you under my skin." In a long-standing relationship, it can be invasive, like a warm knife on hard butter.

The person in the Personal Year Cycle can also antagonize the person with the number natally. Divorce then seems like the only solution, especially if the marriage is already on shaky ground when the aspect begins. Business partnerships have dissolved as well.

Celebrity Example

Tom Cruise was born July 3, 1962, which gives him a Birth Path Number of 28/1. Nicole Kidman was born June 20,1967, which gives her a Birth Path Number of 49/22. They were married on December 24, 1990. They were separated in December 2000, six months after her birthday. She was in a 28/1 year. Nicole crossed into his space. He felt threatened by her power. When she invaded his power base, he fled. FYI: Mimi Rogers, Cruise's first wife, has the same Birth Path Number as Nicole, 49/22.

Penelope Cruz, Tom's current girlfriend, has a Birth Path Number of 53/8 and she is in a 35/8 year. She is Mirroring herself.

Example #2

Ms. RGB has a Birth Path Number of 42/6. She was dating Mr. JTO, who also has a Birth Path Number of 42/6. This number reveals two people that want to control partnerships. His Environmental Influence Number is also a 42/6, which really caused her Birth Path 42/6 to be attracted to him. Because his Birth Path and Environmental Influence Number were identical, I advised her to not read between the lines with regard to his behavior. "What you see is what you get," I said. In December of 2001, while she was in a 30/3 Personal Year, and in a 42/6 month, she chose to confront him about his lack of commitment. Her temporary 42/6 month cycle cut into his 42/6 Birth Path Number like a knife, intensifying the 42/6 energy to an uncomfortable level. Of course, he bolted, never to return.

what you should do during a crossed path aspect

Know that antagonizing energy is at work and back off from the other person as much as possible. The good news is that once the Crossed Path aspect is over, the difficult energy will end. There are also times when a Crossed Path has stimulated a long-term relationship in a positive way. If that happens, take advantage of it, see it as an opportunity to strengthen and reinvigorate the relationship. The cross-pollination effect here can be put to good use.

crossed paths and investing

Crossed Paths also apply to investing in a company. When you buy stock, you are entering into a relationship with the company, or at least the company's stock. Crossed Path energy could prompt some impulsive and/or inappropriate action.

Let's say Intel is a 40/22 and you enter a 40/4 or 40/22 Personal Year Cycle. You will be very attracted to that stock. Before investing, always look to see what Personal Year Cycle the company is in. If it appears favorable, this may well be a good time to invest in that stock, but maybe only for a year.

Whether person or business, a Crossed Path aspect can create your best friend or worst enemy. That's how extreme this is.

mirroring: he said, she said

Like Crossed Paths, Mirroring is a Newmerological aspect between individuals. Mirroring, however, can be even more of a trickster. What happens, literally, when you look in the mirror? Your right eye looks like your left eye, and your left eye looks like your right eye. Everything is flipped. The same thing happens between people when their Base Birth Path Numbers match, but their top two numbers are reversed. Example: One person is a **32/5**, the other, a **23/5**. This numerological Mirroring causes a lot of miscommunication. It's like a perennial Mercury Retrograde between people. One is thinking left and one is thinking right. They get their wires crossed.

The problem here is that the people involved may not recognize the miscommunication. If two people have the same Base Birth Path Number, they think they see things the same way. They experience a synchronicity and similarity that keeps them together. They could feel that there's enough connection between them to make the relationship work. But if their two top numbers are reversed, they are only fooling themselves. They see things as opposite, like a mirrored image. Each person is seeing the reverse of themselves in the other. These two people will engage in a lot of conversations that begin with the words, "I thought you said." One person mishears the other. This creates a push-pull dynamic, a lot of antagonism, and ultimately a love-hate relationship. In the day-to-day of life, the continuous stream of mixed signals results in a lot of anger and frustration because each is constantly being misunderstood by the other.

Example

A wife is a **32/5** and her husband, a **23/5**. They have Mirrored numbers. The have been married **47** years plus, but exist in a relationship that is not cohesive. They constantly bicker due to improper communication. "I thought . . .," "You said that . . ." The Mirroring creates bickering. The key here is that what is mirrored is the number **3** and **2**, communication with the partner. The **2** makes them feel like they belong in a partnership. The **3** keeps them talking. But the Mirroring creates confusion.

When two people have mirrored Birth Path Numbers, the flip-flopped influence is not enough to break them up. Instead, it creates an aspect to throw a wrench into communication, which is so vital to any relationship. This is not a good scenario and for the most part, I don't condone people staying together when Mirroring between Birth Path Numbers occurs, either in marriage or business partnerships. It creates too much miscommunication or insufficient communication. This makes life and love very difficult. Deep down inside these two people may like each other, but the relationship should remain casual.

mirroring between the personal year number and the birth path number

Mirroring is at its worst when it occurs between Birth Path Numbers. It is a permanent condition. But Mirroring also happens for a one-year period when one person's Personal Year number mirrors another. The good news: The aspect stops after twelve months. The bad news: While it is going on, it can be hell, especially when it occurs within families. Communication is often an issue in families. But when Mirroring is in effect, the dynamics between parents and children or among siblings can take torturous turns. There may be love there, but also a lot of manipulation and an on going battle of wits.

Example

With her last birthday, Lynn entered a 25/7 Personal Year Cycle. Her daughter, Sarah, has a Birth Path Number of 52/7. For the duration of Lynn's Personal Year Cycle, Lynn and Sarah have a mirrored relationship. Shortly after Lynn's Personal Year began, communication between the two of them started to break down. Suddenly, Lynn could hear herself repeating phrases to Sarah like: "How many times do I have to tell you? Why do I have to tell you three times to do this?" In response, Sarah would say things like: "I thought you said . . ." Lynn and Sarah's wires were crossed. They misconstrued what the other meant and the dynamic created this love-hate relationship. In one respect, Lynn and Sarah connected like never before because they both shared the same Base Number. On the other hand, they simply were not hearing what the other really said or meant. And so it went, for months, until they recognized the situation for what it was and got clear on their communication with the other.

what should you do when faced with a mirrored relationship?

When you have a Mirroring relationship you cannot avoid, either permanent, as with a child or family member, or temporary, like at work, good communication skills are critical. *Always verify that the other understands any communication.* Confirm that messages have been received. Do not assume anything because you will assume the wrong thing. You will assume what's in your mind, not what the other person is trying to convey. Repeat what the other person says, if necessary. Learn Reflective Response techniques used in therapy: "What I hear you saying is . . ." With Mirroring, communication must become very literal.

chapter 15

Overlapping Aspects and Bonding Numbers

what attracts you, what holds you: overlapping numbers

"**S**he's my dream girl." "We seem so much alike." "He's the man I always wanted from the time I can remember." "Will I ever meet my soul mate?" What's going on when you think or hear these sentiments? Overlapping numbers. Overlapping Aspects occur when one individual's Birth Path or Personal Year Cycle matches one of another person's numbers from the Newmerological Realm—Environmental Influence, Conscious Desire, or Subconscious Motivation. These aspects stoke the furnace of the relationship and turn up the heat between the two people. Sometimes it really lights a flame. Sometimes, it just burns.

when the birth path matches another's environmental influence

This one is tricky. The person is projecting your birthday number through their name or Environmental Influence Number. But remember, the Environmental Influence is only the image.

When someone's Environmental Influence matches your Birth Path, that person may appear to be like you. But it is only that person's image that is like you. The real character is found in the Birth Path Number. This is a classic case of misidentity.

Example

Alex was a **32/5** Birth Path who met Andrea, whose Environmental Influence Number was **32/5**. He thought that he and Andrea were a lot alike. She seemed to be easy-going, freedom loving, and fun. But, in fact, her Birth Path, her real identity, was a **42/6**, a homebody who needed a lot of structure and control. She was really very different than Alex first thought. Alex projected a part of himself onto Andrea because his Birth Path Number matched her Environmental Influence Number. But it was a misidentity. And they stopped dating.

when the birth path matches conscious desire

The emphasis here is on desire. This combination can create a lot of sexual tension. It can draw two people together.

when the birth path matches subconscious motivation

This could be the person of your dreams. This really could be Mr. or Ms. Right. However, if it is the Personal Year Cycle matching the Subconscious Motivation, be careful. Mr. or Ms. Right could turn out to be Mr. or Ms. Right Now.

bonding numbers

Whenever two people have a Bonding number, the issue represented by that number is the lynch pin of the relationship, the part of the relationship that cannot be desecrated. Bonding Numbers occur when one individual's Base Birth Path or Base Personal Year Number matches one of the Compound Numbers in another person's Birth Path.

Example

A wife is a 41/5 and her husband is 57/3. The Bonding Number between them is 5, meaning freedom. Yes, they are married, but because their Bonding Number is a 5, each must have change and freedom in the relationship. They cannot try to possess each other. As they give each other that freedom, their bond actually grows.

$$41/5 \longrightarrow 57/3$$
$$\frac{41}{(5)7}$$
$$3$$

When the Bonding Number occurs between two people's Personal Year Numbers, that number represents the dominant issue between the two individuals for a year.

newmerology

If one person is in a Personal Cycle of **28/1** and the other person's Personal Year Number is a **35/8**, the **8** is the Bonding Number, meaning that these two people should pay attention to money issues this year.

meanings of bonding numbers

1

The unity of the relationship is the issue at hand.
Allow your individuality to strengthen the unity of the relationship.

2

Managing emotions is essential.
It is a time to pay attention to the partnership.

3

The bond is communication, communication, and communication.
Communication is the key to survival. You also should have a good time together.

4

A time to restructure and organize.
Sometimes the bond to the relationship is work.

5

The key to the relationship is adaptability and change.
Respecting the freedom of the respective partner.

6

Family matters, children, home and shared responsibilities dominate.

7

Creates a spiritual bond.
Also a bond around learning.

8

Money, power, and money-management rule this relationship.
Good for business.

9

There is compassion towards each other.
Respect for each other is important.

327

chapter 16

Winning Names and Numbers for People and Business

I t may be a warhorse cliché by now, but, truthfully, Shakespeare had no idea of the power of his statement: "What's in a name?" As far as Newmerology is concerned—plenty. Your address, phone number, Post Office box, business start date, or any other significant number in your life also can hold a surprisingly amount of influence in your life. With these numbers, however, you can make a conscious choice on what numerological vibration they contain and communicate to most benefit you and those around you.

Here's how:

naming a child

As you've read earlier in this book, your name is the handle, the label that your parents gave you. It is a reflection of their hopes, wishes, and image of what you might be like. Or sometimes, a name is a family tradition. Your name also creates your identity to the outside world. It is the first

thing people ask about you. Very often, it is the first piece of information you give out about your-self, at least verbally.

But as we know, numerologically speaking, your identity, your true self, is found in the Birth Path Number. And the difference between someone's image (the name) and their true identity, (the Birth Path Number) can lead to a lot of confusion as a child or young adult. Or, it can lead to a mid-life crisis later in life.

So how do you create a name that reflects your child's true identity? Have the name (the Environmental Influence Number) match the Birth Path Number. Parents, keep your egos out of naming your child. The child is not an extension of you on this level. If you match your child's Birth Path Number with the Environmental Influence Number, you will be doing them a *big* favor. You will give them a label that matches their identity. You will be giving the book a matching cover.

The best way to create a full name number that matches the Birth Path is to adjust the middle name to the day the child is born. Once the general due date is known, decide on the first and last name and then have several different middle names ready, so the Environmental Influence Number will match the Birth Path.

Example

It was my intention to help eliminate the possibility of an identity crisis for my daughter, Serena. Months before she was born, she told me her first name in a dream, which, by the way, was verified by the way she looked. I told my wife that she would arrive with a full head of black hair and surely enough she did. Her middle name is Auriel, a variation of the female form of the Archangel Ariel. Her Birth Date is 11-30-2000, giving her a Birth Path Number of 43/7. Her name is Serena Auriel Newmont. Her Conscious Desire is 31/4. Her Subconscious Motivation is a 12. This makes her Environmental Influence a 43/7.

Her Birth Path and Environmental Influence, real identity and image, match. Her Dharma Number is 86/5. Her only Karmic Lesson is 9, meaning she has to finish what she starts. The point of naming a child in which the Environmental Influence Number matches the Birth Path Number is so

people will project upon her who she actually is. To this point people say that she is wise and evolved. These people don't know her numbers!

If you want to accomplish this for your child, you must have several names available or several variations of the name available to match the Birth Path Number.

the power of your address, post office box, and phone number

Ever live in a house where you immediately felt at home? Or, miserable from the start? Ever live in a house that seemed to eat your checkbook for lunch with repair and remodel bills? Or have a Post Office box that always seemed to be filled with checks and good news? The number of your home, business, or the place that where you receive your mail can affect your life experiences. The same is true for your business or personal phone number.

For places of residence, an address that adds up to a 6 is the number of the family and home. The 4 enhances stability in the home. The 3 house is friendly and attracts friends. The 2 house is good for a couple, but may end up too small if children come into the picture. If you are single, an address that amounts to a 1 might be good because it indicates self-empowerment and independence. The 7 address is good if you want to be left alone. If you work out of your house, an 8 address can draw money. However, if you do not work out of your house, an 8 address can cost you money with repairs and such. Usually, a 5 address (5 representing change) is too disruptive for most people. However, if you are a 5 Birth Path, you may like the excitement this address brings.

Whenever you pick a new address or a Post Office box, think of the numerological energy it is emitting.

newmerology

how to find the numerological value of your address, post office box, and phone number

Address

➤ Calculate the street name by itself first. See if it is compatible with your numbers.

➤ Then add the address. In general, the address is more important than the street.

➤ Then add both the street number and the address to obtain the number of the house.

Example
2343 Jones St.

The street Jones is a **24/6**.
The address **2343** is a **12/3**.
Then add together.
Add the **12** + **24** (top numbers) = **36/9**
The address is **36/9**

SPECIAL NOTE #1: If you live in an apartment, add and evaluate the number separately from the full address number. The apartment number is very important and can actually override the number value of the full address. The apartment is the actual space where you live.

SPECIAL NOTE #2: The zip code is too random to include in your address calculations. However, your zip code can tell what your mail delivery is like in the area. You don't want the zip code total to be a 7. The mail will have a hard time finding you. The 7 is the number of the loner.

SPECIAL NOTE #3: You may want to check the Birth Path Number for the city your live in (found in the city incorporation date.) If the Birth Path Number of the city you live in matches any one of your numbers in the Newmerological Realm, the city could have special significance and energy for you. You can find the Birth Path Number for major cities in the appendix of this book.

Post Office Box Number

This one is simple. Add the numbers across. Just don't underestimate the power of your Post Office box. It can make a huge difference in the kind of mail you get and the kind of life circumstances that your mail reflects.

Example

Matt and Mary lived in such a remote location that they could not receive mail at home. They had to have a Post Office box. The postmistress assigned them a Post Office box at random. They appreciated that the box was at chest level and easy to reach into. Not being aware of numerology at the time, they paid no attention to the Post Office box numerological value.

From the first day of getting this new postal box, Matt and Mary received a lot of good news in the mail. Not all of it was positive, of course, but the vast majority was. They received money month after month as their work increased. Life went remarkably and surprisingly well. So much, that at one point Matt and Mary felt they needed a bigger mailbox. The bigger mailbox, however, had a number they never really liked. They never really "bonded" with the number. Shortly after the change, their luck shifted dramatically. Instead of checks, the new Post Office box held medical bills from a sudden burst appendix Matt experienced. Their expenses went up and their income went down.

Years later, Matt and Mary found out their original P.O. box was #62. An 8. A good number for them and the number of money. Their bigger P.O. box was a #169 or a 16/7, or the explosion in the tower. The number signified an explosion in the house, which happened to Matt. The doctor said his appendix did not really burst, it "exploded." The couple went back to the Post Office and requested their old number, which was still available. Immediately, their life changed for the better. Good health and good fortune returned.

Phone Number

The numerological vibration of your phone number will determine how and what type of calls you may get into your home or business. If you have a 3 number, you will receive a lot of phone calls because the 3 is all about communication. If you want to be left alone, get a phone number that adds up to a 7, the loner. The 8 will bring money in and take money out. A 2 might be good for relationships, especially long distance ones where you talk on the phone a lot. The phone number takes on the characteristic of numerological sum and applies it to the communication.

Finding Your Phone Number Numerological Sum
Telephone number: 310-446-4433 = 5

Find the area code, then come up with a sum: $3 + 1 + 0 = 4$
Then do the prefix, and come up with a sum for that: $4 + 4 + 6 = 14$
Then, do the suffix and come up with a sum for that: $4 + 4 + 3 + 3 = 14$
Add all the sums together: $4 + 14 + 14 = 32/5$
The numerological value of the phone number is $32/5$

naming, starting, and investing in a business

The most important thing to remember in naming a business is to have the number of its name (Environmental Influence) reflect what the business is intended to do, its true identity. That means that, like naming a child, *you will want the Environmental Influence Number to match the business Birth Path Number,* derived from the day the business officially started, either its incorporation date or the date of the business license. Make sure you carefully choose the business' start date so you end up with a fortunate Birth Path Number.

For both the Birth Path Number and the name, try to have a number that reflects what the business is supposed to do. One thing that virtually every business is supposed to do is make money and put out a vibration that attracts people. If possible, have an **8** in the Base Number, the Major Influence, or Minor Influence position. At the same time, you will want a number that reflects what the business actually does.

If you are investing in a business, apply the same criteria as if you were naming or starting the business. Look at the company's Birth Path Number (either IPO date or business incorporation date). Also look at the Environmental Influence Number. These numbers will tell you if the business has money-drawing qualities and if it seems like a good bet for the long or short haul. Also, don't forget, *always* check to see what Personal Year Cycle the business is in.

To get the full description of a business's Compound Number, see the Compound Number definitions listed earlier in the book. In general, the numbers for business have the following meanings:

1

This business will reinvest in itself and not have a big pay off for investors.
It may not be a good place to work as an employee.
You will need to adjust to the will of management and ownership.

2

A passive company.
May be more open to direction and aggressive style from employees.
A **2** stock may not grow much.

3

Good company to work for. Social and friendly.
A 3 company will attract people and investors. It is a people-oriented company.
Good for film or entertainment industries, publishing, and Internet companies.

4

Hardworking and Conservative.
Good for accounting, insurance companies, computer hardware industry and consultants.

5

A company based on growth, but it can be reckless.
A company that is a 5 has to make sure it manages its business.
Good for travel or internet companies.

6

A responsible company. Looks out for people. Very humanitarian.
Great if you opened a medical center on a 6 day.
Good for any health-related business, biotechnology, corporate training, and design.

7

Good for a metaphysical or spiritual business or organization.
Also good for a company that does a lot of
research, educational institutions, or technological invention.

8

Geared toward making money. Best company to invest in.
Eight is power, money, and the corporate structure.
Management could be cold and indifferent toward employees.
Do not allow your business to be a **44/8** Birth Path or Environmental Influence Number.
The number creates too much pressure.

9

Good for educational or helpful businesses,
travel and transportation, or corporate training.

11

Technological invention.
Good for film, television, and media.

22

Big companies with grand plans or history of accomplishment.
If you are in a start-up business, do not allow your business name to amount to a **22**.
You're creating a much higher expectation than what you can probably live up to.

chapter 17

Predictions for World Events, Leaders, and Newsmakers

The day was May 7, 1997. I was doing my Public Access television show with a special guest on the subject, "Untimely Deaths." Included in my prepared list of notables, that crossed over seemingly before their time, were the likes of John F. Kennedy, Marilyn Monroe, Elvis, John Lennon, and others. I also had worked the numbers of Princess Diana, who was alive at the time. In near shock and dismay, my guest said, "Why are you bringing her up? She is not dead." I profoundly replied, "She has to be careful of the media. She's in a dangerous cycle. She must be careful." Three months later, Princess Diana was gone.

The incident was an unsettling testament to the accuracy and predictive power of Newmerology. The power of the system has reinforced itself to me time and again and in public places. I was attending a conference with 25 business people in Los Angeles in February 1997. After a speech by a stockbroker who predicted that the Dow Jones index would eclipse 8,000 that May, someone who knew I was a numerologist, turned to me and asked if I agreed. I did some calculations and announced, "The Dow will hit and close above 8,000 on July 16th of this year." On the afternoon of July 16, 1997, the Dow Jones Index did just that. It rose to 8,000 for the first time in its history.

Less popular but still accurate was my prediction that the stock market would change course in 2000. The NYSE went from a 50/5, a time of great growth, to a 24/6, a far more conservative approach. I knew it would pull back.

One event that I was able to predict with Newmerology was the unprecedented 2000 Presidential election. As early as 1997, I was telling friends and clients that George W. Bush would be our 43rd president. How did I know this? I looked at his numbers and saw that George W. Bush had a clear numerological advantage of the likely Democratic candidate, Al Gore. Gore is a 56/2, someone who prefers to be a No. 2 man. Plus, in 2000, he was in a 36/9 year, which indicates endings on the home front. This was not the Personal Year of someone who was about to be elected president.

Bush, on the other hand, is a 33/6, someone who can be loved and hated simultaneously. His Dharma Number (strength) is a 66/3, which means he does not get pushed around. Moreover, on his birthday, July 3, 2000, he went into a 15/6 year, putting him in position to cause change on the home front. I also predicted that within a year and a half after Bush's birthday in 2001, we would be in a war. Why? Because on his birthday, Bush went into a 16/7, the number of sudden, radical turns of events, symbolized in the tarot as the explosion in the tower. And indeed, the country experienced an explosion in the tower on September 11, 2001.

I bring up these past predictions to show how and why Newmerology can foresee future trends in the world, in the stock market, and in our world leaders.

Numerologically speaking, large-scale events usually occur due to a combination of factors, including the Personal Year numbers of countries, their leaders' numbers, and the significant organizations or entities. Often the numbers are interconnected and have an impact on each other.

Here is what we can expect in the years to come.

future predictions

World Events

I feel that many world leaders are on their last legs in power. The tension with Iraq will continue, but I do see the end of the Saddam Hussein regime. Numerologically, he is coming to an end. If opposing forces don't get him, his own people will. I don't see a long drawn out war with Iraq on the ground. I feel there will be air strikes, but not the kind of war that people fear could happen. In 2003 the aggressive leader will be Tony Blair of England. In May of 2003 he goes into the explosive 16/7 cycle. England could see strife on their turf.

United States of America

The United States was born on July 4, 1776, making its Birth Path Number a 32/5, indicating a character and identity that values freedom. With the new millennium, the U.S. entered unprecedented numerological territory. Because the universal years are such low numbers for the next two decades, the U.S.'s Personal Year Cycles are now the lowest they have ever been in the history of the country. This is quite literally a new energetic landscape for the U.S. The country went from a 39/3 year in 1999 (the end of good relations) to a 13/4 year (a time when the country would establish a new foundation). For several years to come, the Major Influence number of the U.S. will be a 1, meaning we will be on our own far more than in the past. In 2007, the country begins three years where the Major Influence is a 2, indicating that our partners will have an influence on us. The year 2009, a 22/4 for the U.S., will see a huge focus on global affairs. But in 2010, the U.S. goes into 14/5, so we will be back to fending for ourselves again.

On July 4, 2003, the country enters a volatile one-year period, a 16/7, in which the U.S. may actually experience an uprising. The 16/7 is the number of the explosion in the tower and can signal a time of great upheaval, unrest, and great differences on the home front. There may be protests as people feel our security is threatened. Congress will be rife with disagreement and debate. The anger and frustration will be realized on paper as laws will be changed and policies rewritten. This period will last one year.

newmerology

On its next birthday, the U.S. enters a strong economic and political period. The country will feel quite powerful. It will be in a $17/8$ year, the number of the star, from July $4, 2004$ through July $4, 2005$. Whoever wins the presidential election in 2004, will be heralded as a "messiah" of sorts. This person will be someone admired, even beloved, on a larger scale than what we have seen in recent years. This person will be seen as someone who truly unifies. This person will be well-known, but not necessarily as a longtime politician. He or she will be noted and trusted in another field, as Ronald Reagan was. This person will take power easily and calm tensions.

George W. Bush

As president of the U.S., George W. Bush has an important impact on the destiny of the country. Between his birthday on July $6, 2002$ and July $6, 2003$, Bush will experience tremendous popularity. He will be in a $17/8$ year, the year of the star, one of the best years anyone can experience. He will have a lot of power and influence during this period.

On July $6, 2003$, Bush will enter an $18/9$ period. Between his birthdays in 2003-2004, an incident or action in Bush's past may catch up with him. In the latter half of 2003 and going into 2004, we will see events and public sentiment backfire on Bush. He may not finish his term. The reason I say that is because he has a year of high popularity, $17/8$, followed by an $18/9$, a period of completion.

While he is experiencing this immense popularity and the polls are high on him during his $17/8$ year, Bush may do something along the way that fills his pockets. He may do something with money or something financial that will be improper. As he gets closer to his $18/9$ year, he will get found out. Why? Because he will be in the $18/9$ year as the country is in the $16/7$. His past is going to catch up with him. Whatever he is doing now, it is going to show up later. On Bush's birthday in 2004, he is in an $18/9$ year, a year of endings. His actions will affect his power, which comes to an end. His power ends as the country is in the period of a healing that causes a change.

Politics

In 2004 the Democrats will be back in office. I see Senators Tom Daschle and Hillary Clinton as front-runners for the Democrats. Al Gore will try to run again but will not be their candidate. At the time of the election, Daschle will be in a 26/8 year, giving him strength with a partner. Clinton will be in a 42/6, which will support a partner's responsibilities. Also, Daschle is a 42/6 Birth Path Number, creating Crossed Paths with Hillary. If she is patient, eventually she will be the first woman president.

I have felt for years that Arnold Schwarzenegger would cross from entertainment to politics. He is a 58/22 Birth Path Number that makes him globally and economically aware. In 2004 he goes in to a 44/8 year, a huge responsibility. Look for him to hold office in 2005.

Look for Bill Clinton to reemerge in the political arena in 2004 as he will be in a 33/6 year. At that time, he will be part of a group that exposes serious problems in the Bush administration.

The U.S. Economy

The Enron scandal of 2002 is only the tip of the iceberg in the U.S. stock market fiasco. In 2003 when the U.S. goes into a 16/7 year, the people will demand justice. In 2004, a 17/8 year, the people will demand money. It will become so undeniably clear that the financial markets were manipulated by executives filling their pockets. I see the government being forced to give tax rebates to individuals who were invested in certain stocks, especially funds that affected retirement money. I also feel that some government officials are going to have a hard time explaining their financial gains, which will leave Washington with egg on its face. The Dow Jones Index will rebound in the first five months of 2003, and then pull back. Do not look for a true upward swing until spring of 2004 when the market goes into a 28/1 year.

The Stock Market: NYSE

The NYSE was established May 17, 1792, making its Birth Path Number, 41/5. From January 1, 2003 to May 16, 2003, the NYSE should experience gains. It is in a 26/8 year, which means that people will accept the prospect of steady, but slow growth. (The number 6 has to do with unearned money. The number 2 is slow, conservative, and passive.) This period will be a good year for the housing market. Between 2003-2004, the NYSE goes into a $27/9$ year, which is a retiring, low-key number. The market will pull back during that time. Here is an example of Crossed Paths at work. Interestingly enough, guess who's Birth Path Number is a $27/9$? Alan Greenspan (March 6, 1926). Greenspan-led policies are going to mess with the market.

The Greenspan-NYSE connection is also an example of Mirroring. In 2003, Greenspan will enter a Personal Year Cycle of $14/5$, which means he will misread the NYSE, which is a $41/5$ Birth Path Number. In 2004, the NYSE takes off again because it goes into a $28/1$. But slow growth will be the general trend for most of this decade.

The Stock Market: Nasdaq

The Nasdaq was established on February 8, 1971. Its Birth Path Number is a $28/1$. The Nasdaq will not be strong again until 2005, when it goes into a $17/8$ year. In between—and you don't have to be a psychic to predict this—you will see a lot of companies on the Nasdaq go out of business. The Nasdaq will be much more tailored. The year 2004 will be especially difficult for the Nasdaq. It is in a $16/7$ year, the explosion in the tower.

Predictions for Newsmakers

➤ DICK CHENEY: January 30, 1941. In 2003, he goes into a $36/9$, which means he will really need to watch his health.

➤ THE AL QAEDA: The Environmental Influence Number for Al Qaeda, as we normally see it spelled, is $16/7$. This means that people see Al Qaeda as a disruptive force. Notice that when Al Qaeda tangled with President Bush, he was in a $16/7$ year. His Personal Year Cycle intersected with what the Al Qaeda projects. After Bush's birthday in 2002, Bush will gain the upper hand on Al Qaeda. From July 2002 to July 2003 it will be quiet between the Al Qaeda and the U.S. However, after the U.S.'s birthday in 2003, the U.S. will enter another battle with Al Qaeda. At that point in time, look for the U.S. to take up an even bigger offensive that disperses Al Qaeda.

➢ RUDOLPH GIULIANI: May 28, 1944. He was in a 36/9 year on September 11, 2001 and he was in a 56/11 day. In 2004, he goes into a 48/3. Look for him back in office in 2004.

➢ TONY BLAIR: May 6, 1953. Birth Path 29/2. In 2003, he goes into a 16/7 year, meaning the explosion in the tower. Not a good year for him.

➢ YASSER ARAFAT: August 27, 1929. He is a 56/2, which is all about dysfunction. He went into a 39/3 year on his birthday in 2002, which means that people are going to bring him to an end. People will ask him to step down. Public opinion might be against him.

➢ SADDAM HUSSEIN: April 28, 1937. He is a 52/7, which makes him moody as hell. His leadership is going to get shaky. He is in a 36/9 year. He is heading toward the end of his regime.

➢ ARIEL SHARON: February 27, 1928. He is a 49/22. He is in a 33/6 year. Another world leader who is on his way out.

➢ ISRAEL: May 14, 1948. Its Birth Path is 41/5. On its birthday in 2002, Israel entered a 23/5, which has made them more lenient. But at the same time, both its Birth Path and Personal Year at this time is a 5. Israel still has strength. I wouldn't turn my back on them.

➢ INDIA: August 15, 1947. Its Birth Path is 44/8. They are always in a struggle. They are going into a 27/9 in 2002. India will back off from Pakistan, but it should be careful not to be conned by Pakistan.

newmerology

- **JAPAN:** April 28, 1952. Japan is a 49/22. Japan is in a 36/9, so they are on a downslide. They will go back up in 2003.

- **CHINA:** October 1, 1949. Its Birth Path is 34/7. A 14/5 headed into a 15/6, it looks like they have a bigger population explosion coming. China is going to be dealing with more equality for women. This will happen over the next couple of years.

- **IRAN:** October 7, 1906. Its Birth Path is 33/6. Iran just went into a 20/2 year. There will be a long-time feminist movement in the country. Women in Iran will be gaining equality.

- **IRAQ:** July 14,1958. Its Birth Path is 44/8. They are like India. Countries like this will always have economic problems. They went into a 25/7 year in 2002. The country will be Mirroring whatever their leader, Saddam Hussein does. There is going to be a lot of miscommunication.

- **PHIL JACKSON:** September 17, 1945. His Birth Path is 45/9. He waits for experiences to come to him. He knows how to play that energy. He doesn't push too much. However, in 2003, he becomes more vocal. Look for him over the next few years to become more media-oriented. He will be doing more television appearances, and also look for him to write a book within three years.

- **KOBE BRYANT:** August 23, 1978. His Birth Path is 56/11. He is going to have a career year in 2002-03. He is in a 35/8 year.

- **TIGER WOODS:** December 30, 1975. His Birth Path is 64/1. In most of 2001, he was in a 44/8 year. This was an off year for him. Look for him to be even more successful in 2003.

- **MARTHA STEWART:** August 3, 1941. Her Birth Path is 26/8. Her given name is Martha Kostyra. Her Conscious Desire is a 7. Her Subconscious Motivation is a 10. Her Environmental Influence is a 17/8. As Martha Stewart: Her Conscious Desire is

an 8. Subconscious Motivation is a 6. And Environmental Influence is a $14/5$. In 2002, when the scandal over her ImClone stock sale was brewing, Stewart was in a $14/5$ year until August. Her Personal Year Cycle was overlapping her public name, meaning that she had to be careful of her reputation. That is why she was being exposed. At her birthday in 2004, she will be in a $17/8$ year, which overlaps her real name Environmental Influence Number. The outcome will either be a tremendous comeback or a disaster. My feeling is in 2004 she will reinvent herself, due to her involvements with her stock. Also note her Birth Path Number $26/8$. She *is* all about the money.

Sports

The 2002-2003 season will be Michael Jordan's last. After February 2003, he goes into a 6 year bringing up nagging injuries. His body will tell him it's time to quit. The Los Angeles Lakers will have a strong regular season until May and then stumble into the 2003 playoffs. Kobe Bryant will be the leader most of the season as he will be in a $35/8$ year. While they are stumbling, Shaquille O'Neal will upright them enough to win their fourth straight championship. The Sacramento Kings will look like the favorite, but in June they go into a $20/2$ month. Not a good time to be #2.

Entertainment

➤ JENNIFER LOPEZ will be in a $35/8$ year in 2003, which is abundance, and part of that abundance is pregnancy.

➤ DAVID LETTERMAN is in a $20/2$ year until April 2003. Look for significant romance to enter his life in 2003 . . . and that's no joke.

Appendix

companies

company name	stock symbol	birth date	birth path number
Nasdaq Index		2-08-1971	28/1
NYSE		5-17-1792	41/5
S&P		4-21-1982	45/9
Adelphia Communications	ADLAC	8-12-1986	44/8
AdobeSystems	ADBE	8-13-1986	45/9
Advent Software	ADVS1	1-16-1995	51/6
Amazon.com	AMZN	5-15-1997	46/1
American Airlines	AMR	2-16-1982	38/2
American Express	AXP	6-10-1965	37/1
Amgen	AMGN	6-17-1983	44/8
Apple Computer	AAPL	12-12-1980	42/6
Applied Materials	AMAT	10-12-1972	41/5

newmerology

company name	stock symbol	birth date	birth path number
BancFirst Corporation	BANF	4-01-1993	27/9
BankFirst Corporation	BKFR	8-27-1998	62/8
Barnes and Noble.com	BNBN	5-25-1999	58/4
Bed Bath and Beyond	BBBY	6-05-1992	32/5
Broadcom	BRCM	4-17-1998	48/3
Caterpillar	CAT	12-31-1929	64/1
Cheesecake Factory	CAKE	9-18-1992	48/3
Cisco Systems	CSCO	2-16-1990	37/1
Coca Cola Bottling	COKE	5-17-1972	41/5
Dell Computer	DELL	6-22-1988	54/9
Delta Airlines	DAL	3-16-1967	42/6
Disney	DIS	4-02-1940	20/2
DuPont	DD	9-04-1915	29/2
Eastman Kodak	EK	10-25-1901	46/1
Ebay	EBAY	9-24-1998	60/6
Echo Star Communications	DISH	6-21-1995	51/6
Fannie Mae	FNM	9-01-1968	34/7
Fed Ex	FDX	4-12-1978	41/5
Ford	F	3-29-1956	53/8
Fox Entertainment Group	FOX	11-11-1998	49/4
Gap	GPS	5-11-1988	35/8
General Electric	GE	4-15-1892	39/3
Home Depot	HD	9-22-1981	50/5
IBM	IBM	6-15-1911	33/6
IDEC Pharmaceutical	IDPH	9-17-1991	46/1
Intel Corp	INTC	8-07-1981	34/7
International Paper	IP	6-23-1941	44/8

company name	stock symbol	birth date	birth path number
JDS Uniphase Corp.	JDSU	11-17-1993	50/5
Johnson and Johnson	JNJ	9-30-1944	57/3
JP Morgan	JPM	4-01-1969	30/3
Merck	MRK	12-27-1934	56/2
Microsoft	MSFT	3-13-1986	40/4
Motorola	MOT	5-04-1973	29/2
Nextel Communications	NXTL	1-28-1992	50/5
Oracle Corp.	ORCL	3-12-1986	39/3
QLogic Corporation	QLGC	2-28-1994	53/8
Qualcomm	QCOM	12-13-1991	45/9
Pfizer	PFE	1-31-1944	50/5
Phillip Morris	PM	2-21-1919	43/7
Proctor and Gamble	PG	8-30-1929	59/5
Southwest Airlines	LUV	3-09-1967	35/8
Starbucks Corp.	SBUX	6-26-1992	53/8
Sun Microsystems	SUNW	3-04-1986	31/22
United Airlines	UAL	12-30-1968	66/3
United Technologies	UTX	5-31-1929	57/3
US Air	UAWGO	2-01-1983	24/6
Veritas Software	VRTS	12-09-1993	43/7
Viacom	VIA	6-04-1971	28/1
Virgin Express	VIRGY	11-13-1997	50/5
Vodafone	VOD	10-25-1988	61/7
Wal Mart	WMT	11-20-1972	50/5

newmerology

world leaders and politicians

name	birth date	birth path number
Arafat, Yasser	8-27-1929	56/2
Ashcroft, John	5-09-1942	30/3
Biden, Joe	11-20-1942	47/2
Blair, Tony	5-06-1953	29/2
Bloomberg, Mike	2-14-1942	32/5
Bradley, Bill	7-28-1943	52/7
Bush, George	6-12-1924	34/7
Bush, George W.	7-06-1946	33/6
Bush, Jeb	2-11-1953	1/22
Bush, Laura	11-4-1946	35/8
Castro, Fidel	8-13-1926	39/3
Cheney, Dick	1-30-1941	46/1
Clinton, Bill	8-19-1946	47/2
Clinton, Hillary	10-26-1947	57/3
Daschle, Tom	12-09-1947	42/6
Dole, Bob	7-22-1923	44/8
Gore, Al	3-31-1948	56/2
Giuliani, Rudolph	5-28-1944	51/6
Hatch, Orrin	3-22-1934	42/6
Helms, Jesse	10-21-1921	44/8
Hussein, Saddam	4-28-1937	52/7
Jackson, Jesse	10-08-1941	33/6
Kemp, Jack	7-13-1935	38/2
Kennedy, Edward	2-22-1932	39/3

352

name	birth date	birth path number
Lieberman, Joseph	2-24-1942	42/6
Lott, Trent	10-09-1941	34/7
Mandela, Nelson	7-18-1918	44/8
McCain, John	8-29-1936	56/2
Milosevic, Slobodan	8-20-1941	43/7
Nader, Ralph	2-27-1934	46/1
O'Connor, John Cardinal	1-15-1920	28/1
Pataki, George	6-24-1945	49/22
Pope John Paul	5-18-1920	35/8
Powell, Colin	4-05-1937	29/2
Prince Charles	11-14-1948	47/2
Prince Harry	9-15-1984	46/1
Prince William	6-21-1982	47/11
Putin, Vladimir	10-7-1952	34/7
Ridge, Tom	8-26-1945	53/8
Rockefeller, Jay	6-18-1937	44/8
Rumsfeld, Donald	7-09-1932	31/22
Sharon, Ariel	2-27-1928	49/22
Taft, Bob	1-08-1942	25/7
The Dalai Lama	7-06-1935	31/4
Thurmond, Strom	12-05-1902	29/2
Torricelli, Robert	8-26-1951	50/5
Tripp, Linda	11-24-1949	58/22
Windsor, Queen Elizabeth II	4-21-1926	43/7

newmerology

business leaders

name	birth date	birth path number
Allen, Paul	1-21-1953	40/22
Buffet, Warren	8-30-1930	51/6
Case, Steve	8-21-1955	49/22
Eisner, Michael	3-07-1942	26/8
Forbes, Steve	7-18-1947	46/1
Gates, Bill	10-28-1955	58/22
Geffen, David	2-21-1943	40/22
Greenspan, Alan	3-06-1926	27/9
Iacocca, Lee	10-15-1924	41/5
Jobs, Steve	8-21-1955	49/22
Lay, Kenneth	4-15-1942	35/8
Perot, H. Ross	6-27-1930	46/1
Steinbrenner, George	7-04-1930	24/6
Stewart, Martha	8-03-1941	26/8
Trump, Donald	6-14-1946	40/22
Turner, Ted	11-19-1938	51/6
Welch, Jack	11-19-1935	48/3

countries

name	birth date	birth path number
Canada	7-01-1867	30/3
China	10-01-1949	34/7
India	8-15-1947	44/8

362

name	birth date	birth path number
Iran	10-07-1906	33/6
Iraq	7-14-1958	44/8
Israel, State of	5-14-1948	41/5
Mexico	1-31-1917	50/5
Saudi Arabia	9-23-1932	47/2
United Kingdom	1-01-1801	12/3
USA	7-04-1776	32/5

entertainment and journalism

name	birth date	birth path number
Affleck, Ben	8-15-1972	42/6
Aniston, Jennifer	2-11-1969	38/2
Bowie, David	1-08-1947	30/3
Bullock, Sandra	7-26-1964	53/8
Cage, Nicolas	1-07-1964	28/1
Cher	5-20-1946	45/9
Connery, Sean	8-25-1930	46/1
Cosby, Bill	7-12-1937	39/3
Couric, Katy	1-07-1957	30/3
Crichton, Michael	10-23-1942	49/22
Cronkite, Walter	11-04-1916	32/5
Cruise, Tom	7-03-1962	28/1
De Niro, Robert	8-17-1943	42/6
Dion, Celine	3-30-1968	57/3

newmerology

name	birth date	birth path number
Douglas, Michael	9-25-1944	52/7
Fox, Michael J.	6-09-1961	32/5
Gibbons, Leeza	3-26-1957	51/6
Grisham, John	2-08-1955	30/3
Hewitt, Jennifer Love	2-21-1979	49/4
Hill, Faith	9-21-1967	53/8
Hopkins, Anthony	12-31-1937	63/9
Howard, Ron	3-01-1954	23/5
Jackson, Samuel L.	12-21-1948	54/9
Jagger, Mick	7-26-1943	50/5
John, Elton	3-25-1947	49/22
Jolie, Angelina	6-04-1975	532/5
Kidman, Nicole	6-20-1967	49/22
Lauer, Matt	12-30-1957	64/1
Leno, Jay	4-28-1950	47/2
Letterman, David	4-12-1947	37/1
Lopez, Jennifer	7-24-1970	48/3
Lucas, George	5-14-1944	37/1
Madonna	8-16-1958	47/2
McCartney, Paul	6-18-1942	40/22
McEntire, Reba	3-28-1955	51/6
McGregor, Ewan	3-31-1974	45/9
Nicholson, Jack	4-22-1937	46/1
O'Brien Conan	4-18-1963	41/5
O'Donnell, Rosie	3-21-1962	43/7
Osbourne, Ozzy	12-03-1948	37/1

name	birth date	birth path number
Osmont, Haley Joel	4-10-1988	40/4
Pacino, Al	4-25-1940	43/7
Paltrow, Gwyneth	9-28-1972	6/11
Philbin, Regis	8-25-1933	49/22
Pitt, Brad	12-18-1963	49/22
Reeve, Christopher	9-25-1952	51/6
Rice, Anne	10-4-1957	36/9
Rimes, LeAnn	8-28-1982	56/11
Ripa, Kelly	10-02-1970	29/2
Roberts, Julia	10-28-1967	61/7
Rowling, J.K.	7-31-1965	59/5
Ryder, Winona	10-29-1971	57/3
Sarandon, Susan	10-04-1946	34/7
Sawyer, Diane	12-22-1945	53/8
Schwarzenegger, Arnold	7-30-1947	58/22
Seinfeld, Jerry	4-29-1954	52/7
Shriver, Maria	11-06-1955	37/1
Shyamalan, M. Night	8-06-1970	31/22
Smith, Anna Nicole	11-28-1967	62/8
Spielberg, Steven	12-18-1946	50/5
Spears, Britney	12-02-1981	33/6
Springsteen, Bruce	9-23-1949	55/1
Travolta, John	2-18-1954	39/3
Williams, Robin	7-21-1952	45/9
Winfrey, Oprah	1-29-1954	49/22
Witherspoon, Reese	3-22-1976	48/3
Zeta-Jones, Catherine	9-25-1969	59/5

appendix

newmerology

athletics

name	birth date	birth path number
Agassi, Andre	4-29-1970	50/5
Bonds, Barry	7-24-1964	51/6
Bryant, Kobe	8-23-1978	56/11
Faulk, Marshall	2-06-1973	28/1
Garnett, Kevin	5-19-1976	47/2
Green Bay Packers	8-21-1921	42/6
Gruden, Jon	8-17-1963	44/8
Hill, Grant	10-05-1972	34/7
Jackson, Phil	9-17-1945	47/2
Jeter, Derek	6-26-1974	53/8
Jones, Chipper	4-26-1972	49/4
Jordan, Michael	2-17-1963	38/2
Kournikova, Anna	6-07-1981	32/5
Kwan, Michelle	7-07-1980	32/5
Los Angeles Lakers	4-27-1960	47/2
New England Patriots	11-16-1959	51/6
O'Neal, Shaquille	3-06-1972	28/1
Pettitte, Andy	6-15-1972	40/22
Piazza, Mike	9-04-1968	37/1
Piniella, Lou	8-28-1943	53/8
Rice, Jerry	10-13-1962	41/5
Riley, Pat	3-20-1945	42/6
Rodriguez, Alex	7-27-1975	56/11
Sacramento Kings	5-16-1985	44/8

358

name	birth date	birth path number
Sampras, Pete	8-12-1971	38/2
Schilling, Curt	11-14-1966	47/2
Selig, Bud	7-30-1934	54/9
Smith, Emmitt	5-15-1969	45/9
Sosa, Sammy	11-12-1968	47/2
Torre, Joe	7-18-1940	39/3
Vinatieri, Adam	12-28-1972	59/5
Webber, Chris	3-01-1973	24/6
Williams, Serena	9-26-1981	54/9
Williams, Venus	6-17-1980	41/5
Woods, Tiger	12-30-1975	64/1

Glossary

BASE NUMBER: The bottom number that sits under the line of the two Influence Numbers. This is also the simple definition used in basic or elementary numerology.

BIRTH PATH NUMBER: This is true character and personality of the individual as obtained from the full Birth Date.

BONDING NUMBERS: These numbers tie two individuals together to create compatibility. The Main or Minor Influence Number of one person's aspect will match the Base Number of another person's, creating a common bond. This can occur also in Personal Year Cycles.

COMPATIBILITY: As defined in numerology, numbers that work in harmony with each other.

COMPOUND NUMBER: The double-digit number that sits above the Base Number. The Compound Number influences and expands the meaning of the Base Number. It creates the appearance of an inverted fraction.

CONSCIOUS DESIRE: The sum of the value of the vowels that illustrates what we desire early in life.

newmerology

CROSSED PATHS: A temporary period when the Personal Cycle (year, month, day) of one individual matches the Compound Birth Path Number of another individual.

DHARMA NUMBER: This is the strength number. It is found by adding the Birth Path Number with the Environmental Influence Number.

ENVIRONMENTAL INFLUENCE NUMBER: The sum of the Conscious Desire and Subconscious Motivation Numbers creating the full value of the name. The aspect that is our label or how we are perceived.

INTERSECTING ASPECTS: The occurrence when the Personal Year Cycle matches an aspect in the Numerological Realm other than the Birth Path Number.

KABBALAH: The ancient Judaic teachings of mysticism and wisdom. In Judaic, the term literally means "what has been handed down."

KARMIC NUMBERS: Numbers that are missing from the personal Numerological Realm, creating aspects that to be worked on. The word karma is from the Sanskrit language meaning act, work, or deed.

MAIN INFLUENCE: The number that sits to the top left in the Compound Number. It is the major defining factor of the Base Numbers of all aspects.

MASTER CHALLENGE: Any number that is a factor of 11 (i.e., 11, 22, 33, etc.), causing more of a challenge in the particular area where it appears.

META LANGUAGE: *Meta* literally means "greater than." This refers to communication that is beyond the norm.

METAPHYSICAL CLOCK: The innate sense of timing. It is reflected back to us by the predictive sciences allowing for a greater probability of making wise choices in a particular area of life.

MINOR INFLUENCE: The number that sits to the top left of the Compound Number. It is more of a subconscious influence on the Base Number.

MIRRORING: The reversal of the Compound Numbers in comparison between two or more people or companies (e.g., 41/5 vs. 14/5). It often causes communication problems, or love-hate relationships.

MISSING NUMBERS: Any of the numbers from 1-9 that do not appear in the personal Numerological Realm. If any are missing, they constitute the karmic lessons.

NEWANCES: A twist on "nuance," new theories that are revealed in Newmerology, previously not seen in past books.

NEWMEROLOGICAL REALM: The main aspects of personal numerology: Birth Path, Conscious Desire, Subconscious Motivation, Environmental Influence, and Dharma.

NEWMEROLOGY: The title chosen for this book based on the newly discovered proven theories.

NUMEROLOGICAL SUM: The adjusted manner of adding the Birth Date to create the Compound Birth Path Number.

NUMEROLOGY: The study of numbers and how they influence life and the future.

OVERLAPPING NUMBERS: This occurs when the Birth Path Number of one individual matches either the Environmental Influence, Conscious Desire, or the Subconscious Motivation of another individual.

PERSONAL MONTH: The personal cycle in broken into monthly increments for predictive use.

PERSONAL YEAR CYCLE: The calendar year added to your Birth Date, creating a temporary vibration that changes every year.

REBIRTH YEAR: The Personal Year Cycle when the Compound Birth Path Number recurs mathematically. A numerological pivot point in life that causes change or a feeling of starting life over.

SUBCONSCIOUS MOTIVATION NUMBER: The sum of the value of the consonants of the full name. The realizations of maturity.

TRIAD OF NUMBERS: The three-digit Compound Number.

UNIVERSAL YEAR: The calendar year.

glossary

About Nick Newmont

NICK "THE NUMBERS GUY" NEWMONT first realized his talent and fascination with numbers as a child growing up in Pittsburgh, Pennsylvania. Unusually quick and accurate, when discussing the statistics of his favorite athletes and their teams, it wasn't long before Nick started delving into the real meaning behind these numbers. Soon Nick was using the language of numbers to predict the outcomes of not only his favorite sporting events, but also world events, and the stock market.

Ultimately, his interest and instinct has led to a successful practice in Los Angeles where Nick helps his clients predict opportune times for financial gain and investment, marriage, and other important life choices and challenges. Numbers speak a clear language to Nick Newmont, making his fascinating new book *Newmerology* a natural extension of who he is and the gift he possesses.

Nick lives in Los Angeles with his wife and two young daughters. He has appeared on NBC's *The Other Side, Mike & Maty—Los Angeles, KABC Talk Radio—Los Angeles,* and recently has produced a half hour public access show in Los Angeles. Many celebrities and business-oriented clients have utilized Nick's form of numerology to advance their careers and/or companies.

We hope this JODERE GROUP book has benefited you
in your quest for personal, intellectual, and spiritual growth.
JODERE GROUP is passionate about bringing new and
exciting books, such as *Newmerology,* to readers worldwide.
Our company was created as a unique publishing and multimedia avenue
for individuals whose mission it is to positively impact the lives of others.
We recognize the strength of an original thought, a kind word and a selfless act—
and the power of the individuals who possess them.
We are committed to providing the support, passion, and creativity
necessary for these individuals to achieve their goals and dreams.

JODERE GROUP is comprised of a dedicated and creative group of
people who strive to provide the highest quality of
books, audio programs, online services, and live events
to people who pursue life-long learning.
It is our personal and professional commitment to
embrace our authors, speakers, and readers
with helpfulness, respect, and enthusiasm.

For more information about
our products, authors, or live events,
please call **800.569.1002**
or visit us on the Web at
www.jodere.com

JODERE
GROUP